THE DO-IT-YOURSELF GUIDE TO:
CUSTOM PAINTING

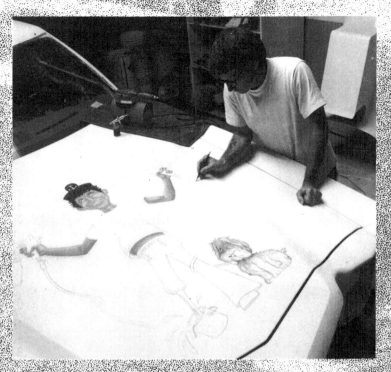

The information contained in this publication is intended as general guidelines for the use and application of equipment or materials discussed. In all cases, manufacturer recommendations, procedures and instructions supersede and take precedence over descriptions contained here. Specific component designs and procedures or qualifications of individual readers are beyond the control of the publisher. Therefore, the publisher disclaims all liability incurred in connection with the use and application of information or illustrations contained in this publication.

THE DO-IT-YOURSELF GUIDE TO:
CUSTOM PAINTING

S-A DESIGN BOOKS
515 WEST LAMBERT, UNIT E
BREA, CA 92621

EDITED BY LARRY SCHREIB
PRODUCTION BY LARRY ATHERTON

ISBN 0-931472-10-5

TABLE OF CONTENTS

The publishers and the author would like to thank the following companies and individuals for providing valuable assistance during the preparation of this book: Badger Airbrush Company, Binks Manufacturing, The Metalflake Paint Corporation, SEM Products, Inc., Sperex Corporation, Thayer and Chandler and especially, Mr. Gary Glenn of Signs & Designs.

INTRODUCTION

In a world of mass-produced "sameness" many people see their automobile as more than just a means of getting from point A to point B. A car can easily be an expression of personal taste, a sign of what you are and how you view life! And today it is easy to gain a small bit of individuality by adding mag wheels, but to really set yourself and your car apart from the crowd, nothing measures up to custom bodywork or a fantastic custom paint job.

Custom bodywork will definitely give you a distinctive car, truck, or van but the cost can often be more than the initial price of the vehicle. And, after all that expensive bodywork is done, it still has to be painted. If you opt for custom painting in the first place, your costs will be much lower and the finished result will still be very distinctive. Custom painting has several advantages over custom bodywork: painting is less expensive, a beginner can master basic custom painting (while it takes years of practice to perform complicated bodywork) and if trends change it is much easier to re-do a paint job.

Beginners really can master custom painting at home with a minimum of equipment. You need to be realistic enough to realize that your first attempts will seem crude, compared to the work of a professional, but as you continue to paint, your work will get better and better. Professional painters weren't born with silver sprayguns in their hands; they made a lot of mistakes during the time it took to master their craft. The good thing about learning custom painting is that you can start with simple, yet effective, paint tricks and progress as your skill and confidence allows. Many of the most basic custom painting tricks only require the use of an airbrush and a stencil. You can buy premixed custom paint from companies like Metalflake, and you don't even need a compressor, if you use a beginner's airbrush that operates on cans of aerosol propellant. Due to the light weight and fine mist of paint, an airbrush is much easier to master than a production spray gun and is an excellent and inexpensive way to develop basic painting skills.

A lot of trick painting is also done with a touch-up gun, which is about half the size of a regular spray gun. *These touch-up guns have all the quality*

You're not going to miss this Plymouth in a crowded parking lot. Candy ribbons, faded stripes, airbrush artwork, and mylar lettering all contribute to the wild effect. You can easily use similar custom effects with your stock paint job.

Deep, shimmering candy apple red lacquer and ghosted pearl flames transform this basically stock Shelby Mustang into a one-of-a-kind custom.

characteristics of full-size spray guns, but they are much easier to manipulate. Also, they spray a smaller amount of paint at a time, so there is less chance of runs and sags. Professionals can do amazingly intricate tricks with bulky, full-size spray guns, but beginners will be much happier working with airbrushes and touch-up guns until such time as they feel confident to handle the larger guns.

The best advice for any aspiring custom painter is to practice, practice, practice. Paint anything you can get your hands on. Trunk lids, doors, or hoods from "junk cars" (when you are practicing, a Rambler hood is just as good as a Rolls Royce hood) can usually be picked up at wrecking yards for $10 to $20. And, an old hood can be repainted over and over, as you learn and practice different techniques. *For practice paint, use whatever inexpensive paint you can find.* There is no need to shell out for premium lacquer and pearl pigment when you are practicing. Solid colors are fine for practice. Ask your paint store for the cheapest paint in stock or if you live near a body shop, you might ask them if they will sell you a few old partially used cans of paint they no longer need.

The equipment you purchase depends on your financial means. *Expensive equipment doesn't guarantee professional results, although the best advice is to buy the best equipment you can afford.* Top notch equipment will last you 10 to 20 years or more, and it is much easier to concentrate on painting when you don't have to worry about equipment failure. Big compressors are a necessity in professional shops that run equipment hour after hour, day after day, but most custom paint tricks can be handled with relatively inexpensive one- or two-horsepower compressors. There are examples of prize-winning amateur painters who turned out show quality work with just a one-horsepower home compressor in a single-stall garage.

If you are unsure of what kind of equipment to get at first, you can usually rent different types and kinds of equipment from a tool rental store or sign up for a painting course at your local vocational school or junior college. A course in general painting probably won't touch on custom painting, but it will give you very valuable knowledge about painting in general. Such a course should teach you how to handle a regular spray gun and what paints to use for most general conditions and requirements.

Besides being a personally satisfying craft, custom painting can be a financially lucrative skill. Top-notch custom painters are always in demand by fine body shops. Some painters have such a devoted following that customers will wait months to have their cars painted. *Salaries comparable to those earned by doctors and lawyers are obtainable by well-established custom painters. But, even if you* *have no aspirations to become a full time painter, you can save a great deal of money by painting your own cars.* Or, you can often exchange paint work for another specialized skill (e.g., a brake job, a rebuilt transmission, rebuilt engine, etc.) If you like to travel during the summer, skill with an airbrush or as a pinstriper can provide a means of seeing the country's finest automotive events. Pinstripers and airbrush artists are in high demand at rod runs, car shows, and car-club conventions and when you are good (and fast) this can be a surprisingly lucrative "vacation."

The benefits of custom painting are many, both personal and financial, but probably the best part is the satisfaction of driving a sharp car and being able to say, "I did it myself."

Custom painting techniques can be used for a variety of effects—from subtle to wild or just plain fun, such as the multiple images on this Ford truck.

A wide variety of custom paint tricks can be used effectively on early cars. This '47 Ford coupe has multi-colored candy panels over a silver base.

FREE TECH SERVICE
FOR PARTICIPANTS

CHAPTER 1
TYPES OF PAINTS AND THINNERS

- LACQUERS AND ACRYLIC LACQUERS
- ENAMELS AND ACRYLIC ENAMELS
- PUTTIES, SEALERS, AND FILLERS
- THINNERS AND SOLVENTS
- SPECIAL CUSTOM PAINTS
- TWO-PART PAINTS

UNDERSTANDING PAINT AND RELATED PRODUCTS

A car or truck without a protective and attractive coat of paint would be downright ugly. If cars weren't covered with paint you could see all the rough seams and welds. An unpainted vehicle would soon get even uglier thanks to a massive covering of rust. This ever-increasing layer of rust would eventually destroy the car far before its time. For these reasons and many more, paint is a vital part of cars and trucks. Paint protects the vehicle from the elements, makes it last longer, and greatly improves the aesthetic value of what would otherwise be lumps of rusted steel.

The variety of paints and related products is almost endless. There are reams of scientific literature detailing the chemical makeup of paint. There is also the whole area of how the eye interprets colors and the psychological effects of color. If you are interested in knowing all there is to know about the makeup and science of paint

Custom painting doesn't have to be flashy and gaudy. The hand-rubbed black lacquer on this Camaro is subtle but striking. Painstaking preparation and attention to details make it a quality custom paint job.

and colors, large libraries should have many books to satisfy your curiosity. For the sake of brevity, though, this chapter will just give an overview of paint and related products.

LACQUERS AND ACRYLIC LACQUERS

In broad terms, paint falls into two main categories: lacquer and enamel. This is far from the whole story, but for the purposes of the average painter, lacquer and enamel paints are the two main types most often encountered. Acrylic lacquer is a much more recent development than traditional nitro-cellulose lacquer. Many people refer to any type of lacquer paint job simply as "lacquer," but today, chances are that the paint is actually an acrylic lacquer.

The technical differences between modern lacquers lie largely in the binder material. Acrylic lacquer paints use a liquid plastic as the binder (or base) part of the paint while traditional nitrocellulose lacquer uses natural substances (cellulose and resins) for the binder.

Automotive paint, as it comes in the can from the factory, consists of just the binder and pigment. Before it is applied, it must be thinned with a solvent.

Lacquer type paints dry by evaporation of the solvents. They dry from the inside out, at a rate that is much faster than that of enamels. Because lacquer paints dry so quickly, they are the best choice for custom painting. You can add multiple coats or colors at a much quicker rate than if you were using enamel type paints. The fact that lacquer dries so quickly also makes it much easier to correct mistakes. This is especially important to beginning painters.

Lacquer type paints need to be rubbed out to achieve maximum gloss. Lacquer paint jobs are often color sanded with very fine sand paper and water as a means of obtaining a deep shine. Color sanding and rubbing out take time and the work is rather tedious, but the results are unlike anything you can get from an enamel paint job.

ENAMELS AND ACRYLIC ENAMELS

Just like lacquer type paints, enamel paint comes in traditional enamel and acrylic enamel. And, just like lacquer paints, acrylic enamel is the most common and most often used type of enamel. Enamel paints are based on varnish binders and dry in a

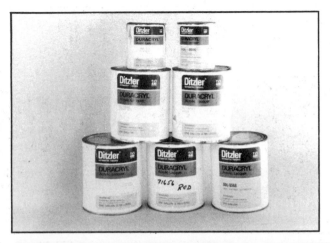

Modern acrylic lacquers, like Ditzler Duracryl, are the best choice for beginning painters. They can be mixed to get "custom" colors, can be painted effectively without a spray booth, dry quickly (so you can readily correct mistakes), and rub out to a beautiful mirror-smooth finish.

Enamel paints, like Ditzler Delstar acrylic, are used primarily for "production" paint jobs because they are durable, they can be applied in one coat, and they dry to a glossy shine that doesn't have to be rubbed out.

Straight enamel paints are usually used to reproduce factory-type finishes. They go on smooth and glossy, and are more durable than lacquers. Quality preparation makes the difference in a custom enamel job, as on this fine early Corvette.

of rubbing out the paint.

Professional collision repair shops with spray booths and heat lamps like using enamel because for them it is quick and easy to apply. However, home painters spraying enamel without a spray booth must contend with dust and other debris which can mar the finish.

Enamel paint has another advantage that appeals to production shops: it can be sprayed over lacquer without any problems. On the other hand, lacquer sprayed over enamel won't adhere properly and will often craze or wrinkle the underlying surface. If you wish to apply lacquer over an old enamel paint job, it is best either to remove all traces of the enamel paint or cover the old paint with a sealer or primer-sealer.

Another advantage of enamel that

two-step process. First the solvent evaporates and then contact with the air causes oxidation of the binder. Enamel paints take quite a while to dry properly, which is why they aren't a very good choice for custom paint tricks that require many different applications of paint. Enamel does have the advantage of being quite tough, and it does not require the extra work

Certain types of enamels are good for specific jobs. This Ditzco alkyd enamel is a "non-smudge aluminum" used for GM rally wheels.

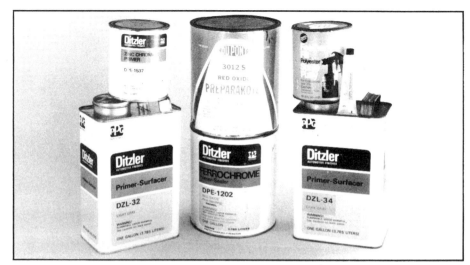

Primer paints are available in several different types and colors to suit specific situations or needs. Primer-surfacer is the most commonly used type because it fills sanding scratches and very minor surface imperfections; primer-sealers are used over old paint that might "bleed" or "lift."

the national budget paint shops like is that two coats of enamel will give the same coverage as 5 or 6 coats of lacquer. For the custom painter, enamels work well for chassis parts and engine painting, although there are special paints that are even better than enamel for frames and engine parts.

UNDERCOATS AND PRIMERS

Lacquers and enamels are considered top coats while primers and similar products are known as undercoats. It is a rare paint job that doesn't require some type of undercoat. If paint were applied to bare metal it wouldn't stick very well or last very long. Topcoat paint needs a surface with some "bite" as a base so they will adhere properly. Undercoats provide a coarse base surface and as such they provide the adhesion needed by smooth lacquers or enamel topcoats. Undercoats also serve to help prevent rust.

There are many different types of primers, but as a general rule they are broken into two main categories: straight primers and primer-surfacers. The main difference between the two is the amount of solids in the product. Primer-surfacers contain more solids than straight primers and therefore can be used to fill minor imperfections.

Primers come in several colors with the most common being light gray, dark gray and red oxide. A painter will usually select a primer color that is closest to the shade of the topcoat. And, at times two different shades of

primer are sprayed, one over the other, to aid in verifying smooth body panels. After the second color has dried, the body is block sanded. Wherever the second primer remains, low spots or scratches exist.

Besides the more common types of primers, there are special-purpose primers. When painting over aluminum, you should use zinc-chromate primer which is usually a yellowish color, although it is also available in black. The Metalflake Corporation even makes colored primers to match their custom topcoat finishes. Metalflake primer-surfacer is available in 22 different colors.

Primers are available in both lacquer and enamel bases. The lacquer-based primers dry faster, but many painters feel that the enamel-

Some painters like to use the same brand of materials for all steps of a paint job. This usually insures compatibility between the various products and is a good idea whenever possible. Metalflake, like most companies, makes all-purpose primer-sealer in red, black, and both light and dark gray.

Especially with custom lacquers, the color of the primer can affect the shade or tone of the topcoat. Therefore, it is best to match the color and tone of the primer as closely as possible to that of the topcoat. Metalflake makes primer-surfacers in 22 different shades to make matching possible.

Sealers come in a variety of brands and types, usually in primer colors and already reduced for spraying. Always use a sealer whenever there is reason to doubt the stability of underlying paint. It's good insurance.

Spot putty, or glazing putty, is really condensed primer in a tube. Use it sparingly to fill pinholes or small scratches, applying it with a small plastic squeegee.

based primers have more bite. Either lacquer or enamel topcoats can be sprayed over enamel-based primers.

SEALERS

Sealers are another type of undercoat. The purpose of a sealer is to isolate the original paint from the new paint, in case they are not chemically compatible. Sealers are especially important when painting over colors that have a tendency to "bleed," like maroon and red. The bleeding of maroons is very likely when the new paint is white or a similar light color. Ditzler makes a special Bleeder Sealer (DX-1075) especially for use over red and maroon paint.

There are some special sealers on the market. Ditzler makes a Primer-Sealer that serves the dual function of priming and sealing. SEM Products

There are catalyzed filler putties that can be sprayed with a gun...but let's hope your car doesn't need this much filler.

makes Aero-Lac Clear Flexible Sealer for use when repainting the bumpers and flexible parts found on many newer cars like the Corvette.

PUTTIES AND BODY FILLERS

Putties and body fillers are another part of the substrata that make up the undercoat. Putties are closely related to primer-surfacers; body putty is actually highly concentrated primer. Putties come in various colors but the two most common are gray and red oxide, like the primers they are derived from. The 3M Company makes putties in red, green and blue. It is an advantage to use a putty that is different in color from the primer; you can locate

Plastic body filler (actually a blend of resin and magnesium silicate) has been improved considerably in recent years and today "Bondo" (a trademarked brandname that has become popular as a general term for any type of plastic body filler) is used widely by the pros. Top quality fillers are available from several manufacturers and they make minor body repairs relatively easy, even for the beginner.

high spots during block sanding of the primer coat (the putty will show through).

Putties should only be used for minor, shallow scratches and pin holes. The pin holes usually show up in areas that have been repaired with body filler. Sometimes the curing of the body filler leaves tiny holes where air bubbles have burst. Body putties should be applied in very thin coats with a rubber squeegee.

Body filler is used to repair dents that can't be removed with the traditional hammer and dolly. Body filler is also used over the top of a hammered dent to fill any imperfections. Body filler "bondo" or "plastic lead," as it is often known, requires a catalyst to harden the resin-base material. The amount of working time before the filler hardens depends on the amount of catalyst used and the ambient temperature. The hotter it is, the less hardener needed to cure the filler.

SOLVENTS

As mentioned in the discussion about lacquers and enamels, paints are a three-part substance consisting of the color pigment, the binder or base, which is the vehicle of suspension for the pigment, and the solvent which is added to the raw paint to achieve a sprayable consistency. Solvents make it possible to get the paint on the vehicle, after which they evaporate and leave the paint adhered to the surface.

There are two main types of solvent: lacquer thinner and enamel reducer. Many people call all solvents thinner, but thinner can only be used with lacquer and acrylic lacquer paints.

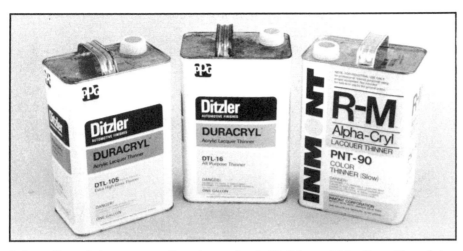

Automotive paints are generally not pre-mixed with thinner. This allows the painter to select a specific thinner that is best suited to the weather conditions and the type of finish desired. Slow thinners, like Ditzler DTL-105 or R-M PNT-90, produce a high gloss in lacquer finish coats.

Enamel solvents are properly referred to as reducers.

There are a wide variety of thinners and reducers but the main difference is their temperature range. Most conditions are suitable for all-purpose solvents. In hot weather a slow solvent or "retarder" is needed so that the paint doesn't dry too quickly. In cold weather, fast solvents are needed, otherwise it would take forever for the paint to dry. There are also special high-gloss solvents and other special solvents designed specifically for spot repair painting. For a good idea of the variety of solvents and their capabilities, check the various manufacturers' catalogs or consult your local paint retailer.

There are many different grades of solvents, and some are considerably cheaper than others. However, it is false economy to skimp on thinners and reducers. Cheap solvents may not spray smoothly and they often don't give as glossy a finish as top quality solvents. Nonetheless, less expensive solvents are generally suitable for clean-up operations. DuPont makes a special Gun and Equipment Cleaner 3924 S that is less expensive than top coat solvents.

Some special types of solvents are known as wax and grease removers. (These solvents eliminate silicones left from wax and other contaminants that can harm a paint job.) They are available under various brandnames, such as DuPont 3919 S Prep-Sol, Ditzler DX-330 Acryli-Clean and Ditzler DX-440 Ditz-O.

METAL CONDITIONERS

There are a variety of products that should be used when the vehicle has been stripped down to bare metal. The use of metal conditioners is especially important in areas where rust has formed. After all the visible rust has been sanded or ground away, the metal conditioner etches the area and retards the reappearance of rust. Besides the standard metal conditioners which are used on steel parts, there are conditioners for use on aluminum parts, where paint adhesion can be a problem. There are also special metal conditioners for galvanized surfaces.

PAINT REMOVERS

If you feel that you need a completely clean surface to paint, then some method of paint stripping is necessary. You can have the car professionally stripped by a chemical stripper or a sandblaster, but if you want to do the work at home you will need to use chemical paint removers. Paint removers are highly caustic products and rather unpleasant to use. The fumes are both harmful and annoying, and it is important to wear a respirator. Heavy rubber gloves are also necessary as the caustic chemicals will attack the skin. Even the best paint removers usually require some sanding, so unless you delight in tedious work, stay away from paint removers.

CUSTOM PAINTS

Early customizers and painters had

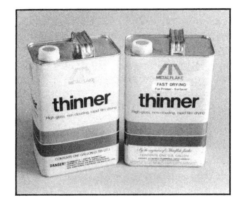

It is a good idea to match thinner and paint brands to insure complete compatibility. Nearly every company that makes paints also makes appropriate thinners to use with them.

When you're buying materials for a paint job, remember that you will need two to three times more thinner than paint, including some for cleanup. Therefore, it's best to buy one- or five-gallon containers. Only special reducers are available in quarts; an example is this catalyzed, high-gloss, T-3200 thinner from Aero-lac.

Solvents for enamels are called "reducers." Like lacquer thinners, reducers are rated according to how quickly they evaporate and produce a dry paint finish. If you are using a synthetic paint, such as alkyd enamel, be sure to use a matching reducer, like the Ditzco DTE-202 (left).

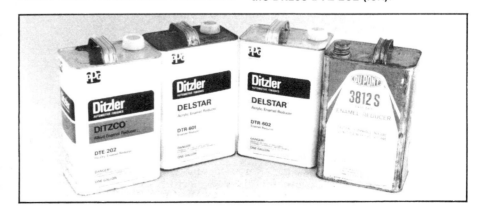

Urethane and two-part acrylic enamels require special reducers. For example, Metalflake PAE reducer is made specifically for their PAE clear.

Wax and grease removers are mild solvents that are specially formulated for cleaning surfaces immediately prior to painting. For a trouble-free paint job, the surface must be treated with such a cleanser, applied with a clean, oil-free rag.

to rely on their own skill and imagination for custom finishes. Early experimentation by painters like George Barris, Joe Bailon, and Larry Watson lead to discoveries like candy paints and pearl paints. At first each painter had his own closely guarded "secret" formulas compounded from available paints and toners. Eventually, several major paint companies began formulating similar custom paints and currently a tremendous variety of preformulated specialty paints is available for the do-it-yourself custom painter.

Modern custom paints are virtually foolproof. They are formulated to the same exacting specifications as original equipment manufacturer (OEM) paints. You can even buy pre-thinned specialty paints, so all you have to do is load your spray gun and start to work.

Today the selection of custom paints is virtually limitless. Although certain types of paints (e.g., candies) are basically the same among the different manufacturers, each name-

brand strives to promote special features and unique selections. By looking at the color charts for the different manufacturers, you can increase the number of colors available for your painting.

Often custom paints are best known by a general name that is actually a brandname, even though it is used in a generic sense. Candy Apple is a good example. Many people think all candy or translucent paints are "Candy Apple," but this name is actually a trade name of Metalflake, Inc., of Haverhill, Maine. SEM Products, Inc., of Belmont, California, calls its translucent paints Aero-Lac Candy Colors and Ditzler Automotive Finishers of Detroit, Michigan, calls its version Star-Apple. This same generic generalization exists for "Metalflake." Metalflake, as you might have

guessed, is the trade name of Metalflake, Inc. Other brandnames for flake paints include Aero-Flake, Sun-Gleam and Radiance.

It would be impossible to detail all of the custom paints available, so we will just familiarize you with some of the more common and more popular paints. For a complete overview of colors and product availability, contact your local paint store or write directly to the various manufacturers listed in the appendix.

CANDY PAINTS

Translucent candy paints are one of the mainstays of custom painting. They provide brilliant colors and a mile-deep shine that has terrific eye appeal. It is the unique translucent nature of candy paints that gives them

Metal conditioners clean rust from bare metal and etch the surface for proper paint adhesion. Dilute them with water for application. Dupont 225S and 226D is a two-part system for preparing aluminum.

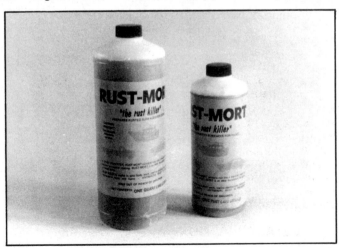

If you paint over rust, it will continue to "grow" under the surface. However, Sem Products offers a metal conditioner that "deadens" rust so that it need not be completely removed.

"Pearls" or pearlescent paints were originally created by mixing fish scales (that had been ground into tiny flakes) to ordinary paints. This gave the finish a unique, iridescent, mother-of-pearl glow. Modern versions, like Star Pearl from Metalflake, are generally available in pastel tones of pink, light blue and soft green.

Although many companies offer pearl and candy finishes, Metalflake is certainly one of the oldest and most respected names in the field. They have a wide selection of custom finishes, and most are available in quarts or gallons (for large jobs) or smaller containers (for multi-hued detail work).

Since candy paints are transparent, they must be applied over a special base coat, usually a bright metallic-like silver or gold. Aero-lac also offers white and black candy bases. Selecting a lighter or darker base coat will affect the hue and tone of the final finish.

the illusion of great surface depth.

Candy colors must be sprayed over a base coat. These base coats are usually of a metallic nature (like silver, gold, or bronze) although there are also plain white and black base coats. Candy paints can also be sprayed over a pearl base. To insure consistent results, you should use the same brandname base coat as the candy top coat.

There are many colors available in candy paints. Metalflake offers 15 different Candy Apple colors and SEM Products makes 12 shades of their Aero-Lac Candy Color paints. When you consider that these candy top-coats can be sprayed over any of 5 or 6 different base coats, the number of possible combinations increases considerably. Add to this the fact that you can mix topcoat colors to get your own "custom" tints and that the intensity of any candy color is affected by the number of coats, and you end up with a tremendous number of possibilities.

The fact that candy colors require

Purportedly invented by customizer Joe Bailon in the 1950's, "candy" finishes are currently produced by many paint manufacturers and are generally available in a wide spectrum of transparent, popsicle-like colors.

many coats is one of the major drawbacks to this type of custom paint. Candy paints are not at all forgiving when it comes to spraying mistakes. Any runs or dirt in the paint will be readily apparent and these mistakes can't be repaired without starting all over. The translucent nature of candy paints also makes it extremely difficult to match panels. The larger the area, the more difficult it is to paint with candy paints. Beginners would be advised to use candies on small design panels or in flame patterns where it is difficult to check for color continuity between areas. Leave the 20-coat candy paint jobs on 18-wheel trucks to the pros.

PEARL PAINTS

Pearls are a type of iridescent paint that gives a surface appearance similar to its namesake. Pearl paints are fascinating to look at because they shimmer and reflect different colors when viewed in different lights and from different angles. Of the big three in custom paint (candies, pearls, and flakes) pearl paints were developed after candies and before flakes. The original pearl paints used fragments of fish scales to gain their unusual radiance. The ground up fish scales weren't very practical because they were expensive and not very durable. Modern pearl paints use mineral products (like crushed mica) for their brilliance.

Pearl paints are usually sprayed over a base coat of white or black, although they can be mixed with other types of paint for distinctive effects. Pearls can be mixed with candy colors for a "softer" candy effect or added to a clear topcoat for extra brilliance.

Pearl tones are most effective with light, thin topcoats and they must, therefore, be applied evenly, over a very uniform base coat, to insure consistent hue and tone. Metalflake makes specific base colors for this purpose.

Several companies, such as Aero-lac, now offer pearl paints in a variety of colors, bases, and unique two-tone effects.

Pearl concentrate can be used with almost any type of paint, such as candies or straight colors, to give it a pearlescent glow. A small amount of the additive is simply mixed into the base paint. The pearl should be added sparingly, however, because it is quite strong. Start with a tiny amount and add more until you get the effect desired.

Metalflake calls their pearl paint line Star-Pearl which comes in nine colors and is also available in premixed, ready to spray cans. Aero-Lac calls their pearl paints Candy Pearls and they are available in quarts, gallons and aerosol spray cans.

Both Metalflake and Aero-Lac offer jars of pearl pigment. These concentrated pearl pigments can be mixed with other paints for unique special effects. Except for the platinum color, all the Aero-Lac pearls are two-tone; the primary color has a secondary reflective color. Gold has a bluish reflection; red has a green reflection; blue has a gold reflection; and green has a red reflection.

Metalflake also makes a pearl paint which is two-toned. It is called Flip-

Two-tone pearls, like Metalflake "Flip Flop," contain diffraction particles that appear to change colors as light hits the surface from various angles. This produces a unique shimmering color effect.

Flop Pearl and comes in five main colors: aqua, blue, green, yellow and red. When viewed from different angles Flip-Flop Pearl changes colors. It comes in ready-to-spray quart and 4-ounce cans. Many of the Metalflake products come in the handy 4-ounce cans, which are ideal for mural work. The small cans make it possible for you to have a wide variety of colors without spending too much money or having a lot of leftover paint.

Aero-Lac makes a unique type of pearl called Design Colors. Design Colors are a pearl pigment suspended in a mineral spirit medium. This causes slow drying, so you have plenty of time to make designs in the paint with brushes, sponges, plastic wrap, or whatever else you care to use. Design Colors are available in platinum, gold, red, blue and green. They work best over a dark base. Design Colors can be applied either over or under acrylic

Aero-lac "Design Colors" are special pearls that are premixed with mineral spirits to lengthen drying time. This allows special surface effects to be created with brushes, foil, or plastic wrap (see chapter 9). They are also available in aerosol cans, making them convenient for special effects work in small areas.

Metalflake "Eerie Dess" is another brand of slow-drying pearl. It is intended for techniques that "work" the still-moist paint after it has been applied to the surface.

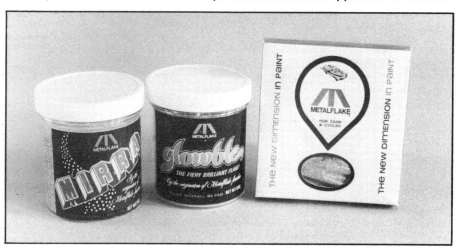

The first "metalflakes" were simply finely chopped squares of tinfoil that were added to candy paint. Today the Metalflake Corporation offers dozens of colors and several sizes of glittery reflective particles. They can be added to clear, candies, and to other paints for a variety of appealing effects.

lacquer. The unusual patterns that can be made with Design Colors are especially suited to custom lettering.

Metalflake also has a pearl design paint known as Eerie-Dess. It comes in the same five colors as Aero-Lac's Design Colors and also works best over a dark base color, and Metalflake suggests that a slightly wrinkled piece of aluminum foil is great for making interesting patterns with Eerie-Dess.

Pearl paints have a great variety of uses. At one time it was popular to paint entire vehicles in pearl colors but today pearls are used mostly for accent work. Besides being used in clear topcoats, pearls are very useful in mural painting, flames, and lettering. Subtle use of pearl highlights can give custom painting that special touch that is the mark of a creative painter.

FLAKE PAINTS

Flake paints are just that, flakes of color suspended in a clear or candy medium. The name most closely associated with flake paint is Metalflake, the trademark and company name of the Metalflake Company. Even though the word "metal" is part of the name, the actual flakes are tiny pieces of Mylar. The bigger the size of the particles, the more brilliant the paint will be. However, the bigger the flake, the tougher it is to spray because extra care is necessary to keep the flakes in constant suspension to insure an even application.

Silver is the main color of flake particles although the Mylar particles can be dyed any color. Standard Metalflake comes in 36 colors and two particle sizes.

In addition, another Metalflake product, Glowble, is a more brilliant

Aero-lac offers dry flake particles, as well as pre-mixed flake paints, available in 13 colors. The pre-mixed colored flake paints should be sprayed over a silver base.

Clear topcoats are a perfect medium for special effects, like Metalflake "Mirra." The particles are added to the thinned clear and can be sprayed over the entire car or just in specific areas or panels. The surface will look like it has been dusted with diamonds.

To create unique candy colors, it is possible to blend concentrated candy toners, such as these from Aero-lac (in quart cans), into clear paint. Just be certain to blend enough paint to do the entire job. It may be difficult to recreate the exact same shade if you run short!

Catalyzed enamel and urethane clears require special care during application, but they can provide an amazingly glossy and tough protective coating for virtually any type of custom finish. They can be applied over lacquers or enamels.

flake that comes in 12 colors. And, Metalflake's Mirra is a combination of several colors of flake, producing a sparkling rainbow effect.

Aero-Lac calls its flake paint Aero-Flake. It comes as a ready-mixed blend of acrylic lacquer colors and flake particles and is available in 12 colors, in either large- or small-size flakes. (The small flake is available in aerosol cans.) Aero-Lac also markets dry, silver, polyester, flake particles, in large or small sizes, for mixing with Candy Colors or clear.

Bare flake paints have a rather rough surface due to the random landing of the reflective particles. For this reason, flake paint jobs are generally finished with several coats of clear to gain a smooth surface sheen.

CLEAR TOPCOATS

Most custom paints benefit from a topcoat of clear lacquer or clear enamel. With some paints, like Metalflakes, clear topcoats are mandatory. And, clear is very important in mural painting because the variety of colors used are very thin. They would scratch and fade very easily if not protected by coats of clear. Besides its protective properties, clear is also an excellent mixing medium for flakes, pearls and toners. By using clear with a variety of toners, you can make your own special colors (a toner is a full strength translucent color). For example, Aero-Lac suggests mixing their Toners with

In past years clear lacquers were notorious for yellowing and cracking, but modern clear acrylic lacquers are a versatile and durable topcoat for custom finishes.

three parts clear acrylic lacquer.

There are two basic types of clear available: those that are lacquer based and thinned with lacquer thinner, and those that are enamel based and require the use of a catalyst. Many painters prefer the newer two-part clears because of their plastic-like toughness. The two-part clears are especially good for race cars where fuel spillage can be a problem. The lacquer based clears should be lightly color sanded, but the two-part enamel clears don't require any rubbing out.

Urethane two-part clears, like Metalflake "Poly Gloss," dry to a wet-look finish, plus they can be color sanded and rubbed out like lacquers to gain a mirror smoothness. When using such paints, precisely follow all manufacturer's instructions to avoid problems.

TWO-PART PAINTS

Like the two-part clears, there are also colors that use a catalyst for a super-tough finish. Two-part paints are known by a variety of names like polyurethane, epoxy, urethane and Imron. Imron is the trademarked name of a DuPont two-part enamel. These rugged finishes were originally developed for commercial vehicles like trucks and airplanes. At first, the choice of two-part paints was limited, but now several custom paint

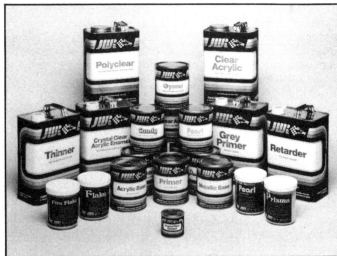

SEM Products, among others, offers a complete line of fabric dyes, vinyl sprays, top coatings, and other special finishes to make the interior of your vehicle look as good as the custom finish you apply to the outside.

Painting has long been a popular "custom touch" in England where John Woolfe Racing Ltd. is the major supplier of high-quality candy, pearl, metallic, clear acrylic and other custom finishes.

manufacturers make two-part paints in a wide variety of popular colors. Metalflake calls their two-part paint Cryst-Cryl and it comes in fifteen metallic and six solid colors.

Two-part paints have their own special reducers. Metalflake calls their polyurethane reducer P.A.E. (for Polyurethane Acrylic Enamel) Reducer. Ditzler has a special Durethane DTU-502 reducer for use with Ditzler Durethane paints. Ditzler even has a primer (DPU-35) just for Durethane finishes.

Two-part paints have always been a good choice for chassis work because

of their durability and resistance to corrosion, and many painters use a clear urethane final coat to protect a custom lacquer or mural paint job. Although they can be tricky to apply, the catalyst makes them harden quickly, so mistakes can be sanded out and resprayed, as with lacquers. Catalyzed enamels can also be color-sanded and rubbed out like lacquers; consequently you can spray them in your garage without fear of dust or airborne debris ruining the finish. If applied properly, however, two-part enamels will dry to a glossy, smooth finish that requires no buffing.

VINYL AND FABRIC PAINTS

Custom painting doesn't have to end with the exterior of your car. There are a whole range of products for changing or renewing the materials used inside your car or truck. These paints can also be used if you have a vinyl roof. A truly professional job of vinyl or fabric painting involves several steps and products.

The surface must be very clean before the new color can be applied. There are special cleaners for both leather and vinyl. SEM Products markets a complete line of vinyl and

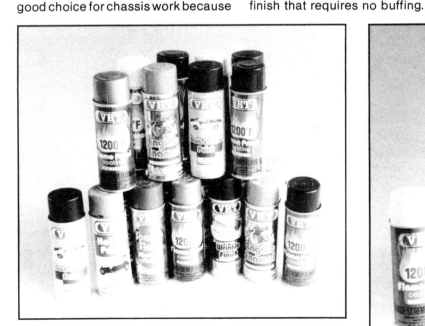

Good quality aerosol paint has a definite place in any custom painter's cupboard. They are perfect and practical for small jobs that require a special color, e.g, chassis parts, engine parts, interior trim. VHT also offer special-effects spray paints like wrinkle finish, hammertone, or matte black for distinctive and professional-looking detailing of the engine or interior.

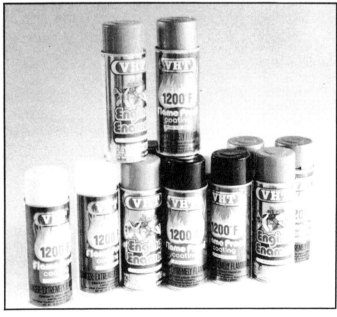

VHT is best known for the special high-temperature finishes that are very handy and popular for painting engines and headers. These spray paints provide a handsome and durable protective coating but the directions on the can must be followed closely for proper results.

leather cleaners, color coats and protective clear coats. SEM also makes a carpet and woven-fabric dye.

Besides complete color changes, vinyl colors are useful for touching up door panels and other interior areas that occasionally receive overspray.

AEROSOL SPRAY PAINTS

While many purists will say that there is no place for aerosol cans in custom painting, they do have some very good uses. The primary benefit of spray cans is their convenience. There is no mixing and no clean up. You pay for this convenience in that the average spray can contains far more propellant than actual paint (but then, air compressors and spray guns aren't exactly cheap either).

Aerosol paints aren't suitable for any large areas but they can be effectively used in small design patterns. They are also handy for spraying small chassis parts or engine pieces. Companies like Sperex make engine enamels in exact factory colors, plus a number of custom colors. Their engine enamel is known as VHT Engine Enamel, and their ever-popular Flame Proof Coating is also available in aerosol containers for painting exhaust manifolds.

The key to using aerosol paints is to use top quality products. You get what you pay for and the bargain paints are best left for painting wheelbarrows and garbage cans. Quality paints usually have better paint nozzles, an important key to smooth application. The nozzle must also be kept clean, otherwise you'll get a spattered paint job.

It is even possible to get custom finishes in aerosol cans. Aero-Lac markets their Candy Colors, Aero-Flake, Design Colors, Acrylic Lacquer Bases, Clear Acrylic Lacquer and Pearl Candies in aerosol cans. VHT makes Sparkle Flake in eight colors and they also offer several special paints, like primers, vinyl sprays, epoxy enamels, wrinkle finishes, hood and deck paint, and metal tint, in aerosol cans.

Aerosol paints aren't for every occasion, but they are a handy supplement to other custom finishes.

SPECIAL PAINTS

In addition to all the paints already described there are dozens of other special paints. If it is anything you have ever seen on a new car, some paint manufacturer makes it. There are special "flat" paints for flat-black, non-

Some companies also package their special paints in aerosol cans. If you have very little equipment and a tight budget, you can still apply creative designs in small areas. Aerosol cans are also handy when you need just a touch of color to match a factory-type paint.

Shown here are two types of low-gloss black lacquer: the one on the left for "black look" trim, the one on the right for anti-glare hood panels.

gloss hood treatments. There are special paints for duplicating the colors on factory Rally wheels. You may think that all Rally wheels are just painted silver, but there are many different shades and types of paint depending on the year and make of the wheels. There is a special paint for blacking out chrome trim, special chassis paints, special engine paints, paints that resemble chrome plating, paints for lawn equipment, motorcycles and farm implements, and special heat-resistant paint.

The special engine enamels and heat resistant paints will make the engine compartment of a modified vehicle look as trick as the exterior. The best known type of high-temperature paint is VHT Coating from Sperex Corporation. It was originally developed for the space program. VHT products are available in either bulk cans or aerosol spray cans.

To really appreciate the huge variety of paint products manufactured, flip through a few catalogs the next time you visit your local paint store. There truly is a paint for every need.

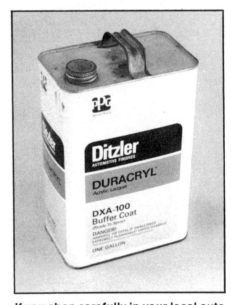

If you shop carefully in your local automotive paint store (and check the catalogs) you will find an amazing array of paint products. There is something available for nearly anything you can imagine. For instance, this Ditzler DXA-100 is a special buffer coat for blending touchup or spot-painted panels to existing paint.

17

CHAPTER

SELECTING PAINT AND BODY EQUIPMENT

- BODY AND SURFACE PREP TOOLS
- COMPRESSORS AND ACCESSORIES
- SPRAY AND TOUCH-UP GUNS
- AIRBRUSHES

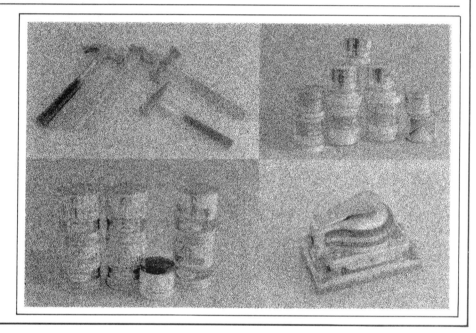

THE TOOLS OF THE TRADE

The tools of custom painting are many and varied. They can range from a piece of sandpaper and a single aerosol can of paint to an exotic spraybooth with thermostatically controlled drying lamps. The level of equipment that you will need probably falls somewhere between these two extremes, and it is heartening to know that a resourceful amateur can gain excellent results with relatively modest equipment.

The amount and types of tools you will need depends on the extent of custom painting and bodywork you wish to attempt. If you are only interested in simple design panels or small murals, you should be able to get by with a minimum of equipment. If, on the other hand, you want to try a

The range and array of painting equipment may seem complicated or confusing but some simple guidelines will help you select useful and durable tools that will last a lifetime.

complete repaint including minor bodywork, a bigger investment in tools will be necessary.

Painting and bodywork tools are available in a wide range of quality and price. As with most products, you usually get what you pay for, so our advice is to buy the best quality tools you can afford. You will be happier with a few good tools that will last decades than a lot of cheap tools that fail when you need them most. You can do a lot of custom painting with a basic tool selection and add to it later as finances permit. Remember, you can also rent special tools you don't use often.

We suggested buying quality tools, but this doesn't always mean the tool that is most expensive. Compare products and compare stores. Most specialized painting equipment isn't sold in ordinary automotive stores, but the large general retail chains like

Professional-type tools, such as these air-driven sanders, may seem extravagant for the novice driveway painter, but they save an incredible amount of time and allow you to concentrate on doing a top notch job, rather than wearing yourself out with the inevitable drudgery of prep work. You can justify the cost by the money you save, compared to the cost of a professional paint job, and you'll be able to use these tools for many, many years.

Of course, there are limits to the equipment you can justify for home painting. A professional spray booth like this Binks unit provides ventilation, proper lighting, and the virtually dust-free enclosure required to produce a top-notch enamel paint job. You probably can't afford one, but if you want the perfect spray environment, don't overlook the possibility of renting "booth time" from a nearby paint shop or trade school.

Sears, J.C. Penney and Montgomery Ward carry basic painting equipment like compressors, sprayguns, airbrushes and some air tools. These stores are also likely to have painting equipment on sale occasionally. And, there are mail-order tool firms that feature very attractive prices on air tools and some spray equipment. These companies usually advertise in the major car magazines.

Another thing about the most expensive tools is that very often they aren't matched to the rest of your equipment. The top-of-the-line professional model tools are meant to be used in shops with commercial air compressors. These compressors usually have electric motors with a minimum of 5 horsepower and are capable of putting out a continuous 15 to 25cfm (cubic feet per minute) of air, whereas most home compressors put out between 5 and 10cfm. Check the air requirements of any air-powered tool you buy to be sure it will work with your compressor. Poorly matched tools and compressors mean that the compressor will be heavily taxed and that the air tool won't work as well as it was designed to work. Remember that delivery volume (cfm) is rated at a given air pressure and at higher pressure settings the delivery volume will decrease. This volume may be less than you will need for some painting applications.

One way to determine if you can afford a certain tool is to get an estimate from a professional shop for the job you are considering. Very often the cost of the tools will be the same or less than what it would cost to have the job done by someone else. Using this

The most basic body prep tool is the sanding block. They are cheap, so buy a few, or you will be stopping constantly to change from coarse to fine or from wet to dry paper. Not only do they produce a smoother finish, but also they save your hands from sandpaper abrasion.

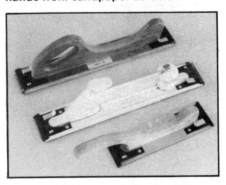

Sanding boards, or "bondo boards" as they are often called, hold a long strip of sandpaper and are particularly good for smoothing and leveling large, flat areas that have been repaired with body filler.

rationalization, you can figure that the next time you use the tool it isn't costing you anything.

The main thing to keep in mind when purchasing tools is to make an honest appraisal of your needs. Buy the quality necessary for a good job, but don't waste money on frivolous gadgets.

A "Jitterbug" is an air-powered sanding block. It can be used for a variety of jobs from working body filler to sanding paint. If you are going to invest in air tools, this is probably the one to buy first.

BODY AND SURFACE PREP TOOLS

Even if you can't apply the final finish or if you lack the confidence to try, the area of custom painting that you can most easily accomplish yourself and where you can save the most money is surface preparation. Most surface prep can be accomplished with very few tools and a lot of labor. The amount of tools you buy in this category depends on how much muscle power you want to expend and how much time you have. The faster and easier you want the surface work to go, the more tools you will need.

On the most basic level, a selection of sandpaper and a sanding block will handle most surface prep. You can even substitute a block of wood for a sanding block. At the other extreme, you can purchase a wide range of air- or electricity-powered surface prep tools.

Sanding blocks and sanding boards come in a variety of sizes. There are long, short, and medium lengths in various widths, constructed of wood, plastic, or rubber. There are sanding boards that require the use of both hands and there are single-hand models. Most sanding blocks and boards are designed to take pre-cut pieces of sandpaper, although you can cut larger pieces of sandpaper to fit sanding blocks. A standard sheet of sandpaper is just right to make four strips for a normal hand-held rubber sanding block.

If you are just starting, the two sanding aids you should buy are a standard hand-held rubber sanding block and a long, two-hand sanding board. The rubber block is good for wet or dry sanding, especially in small panels. The long sanding board is good for large areas where you want to avoid waves and ripples. The long board is also good for sanding body filler.

Sanding is tedious work and air tools can greatly reduce the time and effort needed to prep a car. Assuming you have a suitable air compressor and your budget permits, the hot tip for fast preparation work is an air sander. There are three main types of air sanders: an air file, which works the same as a hand-held long sanding board, a jitterbug, which approximates a hand-held rubber sanding block, and a circular dual-action sander. Circular sanders are also known as D-A sanders and are good for feather-edging around repair areas. All three types vibrate or oscillate with air pressure to cause sanding action.

Which air sander to choose is a matter of personal preference and depends somewhat on the type of vehicle you are prepping. For example, an air file would probably be best for a van where there are lots of large panels. However, each type does certain jobs better than others and pro shops often have all three. But for the beginner, the jitterbug is usually the best all-around tool.

Another type of power sander is the air or electric grinder. Grinders are used with very coarse sanding discs. These tools are used to remove paint, grind down welds, and clean corroded areas. Grinders need to be used with care because they are powerful and can cut deep gouges in the metal. There are also many small grinders, including right-angle models, that are perfect for those little nooks and crannies that are impossible to reach with any other tool. These small grinders are very good for detailing engine compartments.

There are several basic body tools that anyone can master and use to remove basic dents. The removal of several small dents, dings, and scratches can cost several hundred dollars at a professional body shop, yet you can do the same work at home with about $100 of equipment and a little work. What you need is a selection of common body hammers and dollies, a grinder, and a dent puller.

Body hammers are made in a variety of sizes and with different head shapes. They are designed exclusively for bodywork and are intended to work in conjunction with a hand-held body dolly that supports the metal from the back. Don't try to substitute a carpenter's hammer or a ballpeen hammer. By using the right combination of a hammer and dolly (dollies are also made in different sizes and shapes) you can slowly reshape virtually any contour or dent.

Metal files are also known as vixen files. Good file holders can be adjusted for either flat, concave or convex

Air-powered grinders are also available. They are designed to operate in various speed ranges (depending on the number of reduction gears used in the air motor). This one has had the disc cut in a star pattern for cleaning a curved surface.

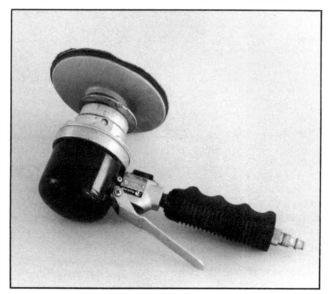

Commonly called a "D-A," this dual-action sander produces an orbital pattern. It is usually used with finer grit sandpaper (which attaches to the head with adhesive) for featheredging or spot-paint sanding.

Before buying air tools, invest in a good electric grinder. Anyone doing bodywork needs one, especially for cleaning the surface to bare metal. A two-speed model, such as this Craftsman, can also be used on low speed with a buffing pad for rubbing out paint.

An air file is similar to a bondo board, and is therefore designed to smooth large areas of body filler. If you've ever done the job by hand, you'll wish you had one. But they are expensive and require a compressor with a relatively large air-delivery capacity.

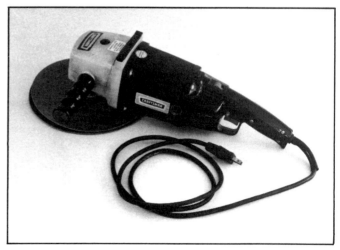

surfaces. For flat surfaces, you can use just the file without the holder.

Dent pullers are also known as slide hammers. They work by drilling a series of small holes in the dent, screwing the tip of the dent puller into the holes, and using the sliding weight to knock out the dent. Dent pullers are especially good for use when there is no access to support a hammer dolly behind the dent.

After a dent has been roughed out you will need some type of filler for the remaining imperfections. A variety of plastic spreaders are useful for apply-

Grinders will accept a variety of sanding discs, usually in very coarse grits, plus buffing pads. Lamb's wool and foam rubber buffers are shown on left.

ing body filler. There are also easy-to-clean plastic pallets for mixing filler, though many painters just use a piece of cardboard and discard it or else they use a piece of sheet metal and clean it with a grinder. Besides the plastic-filler spreaders, there are also special rubber squeegees that are used with spot putty.

A very handy and inexpensive tool for use with body filler is a cheese grater file. These files are known by various brand names, e.g., Stanley's Sur-Form files. These files come in a wide variety of shapes and sizes. They will save you a lot of time if you use them to remove the excess filler when it has hardened just enough to come through the file in thin stringy pieces.

COMPRESSORS

Compressed air is vital to custom painting. Even if you are only using aerosols, the cans are a source of compressed air. Small murals and design panels can be handled with the little hobby compressors, but for any complete vehicle painting you should have a one-horsepower or larger com-

pressor. A good compressor is the type of tool investment that will last for many years and once you have one, you will wonder how you ever got along without it.

Our advice on compressor selection is to buy an electric model, preferably one that runs on 220 voltage. Buy the compressor that has the most air capacity you can afford. As you become better at painting and as you acquire better equipment you will need a substantially larger air volume. Larger compressors also have larger air-storage tanks which will ease the strain on the compressor. A small compressor with a small storage tank will be in almost constant operation during a paint job, whereas a larger compressor with a larger reservoir will only have to operate for short periods to keep the tank sufficiently charged with air.

We suggest 220, rather than standard household 110-volt current, because it will increase efficiency and reliability. If your compressor is on the same line as your house, a fuse may blow if the kitchen stove is turned on when you are in the middle of a paint

Body hammers, shown on the right, are lightweight with wide striking heads to minimize metal stretching. The body hammer at lower right also has a sharp "pick" end for working out very small dings. Never use a carpenter or ballpeen hammer (left) for auto body work.

It takes a deft hand to apply body filler smoothly, but a good spreader helps. Use wide plastic ones for large flat areas, smaller ones for narrow spaces or for applying spot putty. A large rubber spreader is good for applying filler on a curved surface, since you can bend it between your fingers to match the contour. Always clean spreaders thoroughly (in acetone or lacquer thinner) after each use.

This Craftsman professional body tool kit is probably more than you need for home repairs, but it shows a sampling of the wide variety of hammers and dollies that are available for working out dents of all shapes and sizes.

If you can't get a hammer behind a body panel to knock out a dent, there are other ways to attack it. A large suction cup, like this, can quickly pop out a large, simple indentation.

Sears makes an inexpensive "starter kit" for home body repair. It includes a grater, hammer, dolly, dent puller, and sanding block. This is a good basic selection for a beginner (though your assortment of "special" tools will grow as you gain experience).

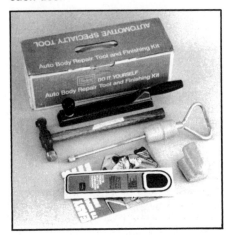

"Cheese grater" files are excellent for shaping body filler before it fully hardens. One flat and one curved blade are usually adequate. Most bodymen use them without any handles (because the detachable handles inevitably become lost in the normal shop litter).

Pro paint shops use stationary industrial compressors like this 15 horsepower Binks. These large compressors can simultaneously power several industrial-grade spray guns or air tools, but the average home workshop generally requires something more modest!

Most preparation and painting can be accomplished very nicely with a compressor that is rated between one and three horsepower, like this excellent Craftsman 3hp model. Opt for a 220-volt model (3-phase, if at all possible), as they have more efficient motors. Run the compressor from a dedicated line (or make certain there are no other major appliances hooked to the same line) to reduce the possibility of a fuse failure in the middle of your "ultimate" paint job.

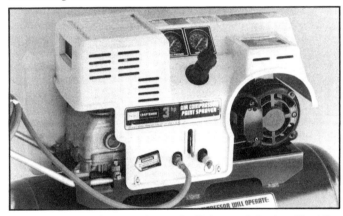
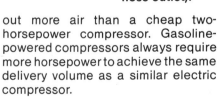

Many home compressors have a built-in regulator to adjust the line pressure. This Sears model also has a circuit-breaker switch and an air-pressure safety valve (just to the right of the hose outlet).

job. The power company will have to be consulted if you want commercial 220-volt power available in your house, but 220 current will also allow the compressor to be fitted with a more efficient, heavy-duty motor. It is usually the larger compressors that run on 220 power, but there are also one-horsepower compressors that will run on either 110 or 220.

Compressors are often rated in terms of horsepower, but as mentioned earlier what really counts is the cfm rating. All compressors with similar horsepower motors don't have the same cfm ratings. A top-quality one-horsepower compressor will often put

out more air than a cheap two-horsepower compressor. Gasoline-powered compressors always require more horsepower to achieve the same delivery volume as a similar electric compressor.

For most home-painting tasks you should consider a compressor that delivers a minimum of 3cfm (standard cubic feet of air per minute) at 35 psi (pounds per square inch). For heavy usage and use with larger air-powered tools, you might want to consider a model that delivers up to 9cfm at 50psi. All good quality spray guns and air tools generally specify in the instructions the minimum air requirements (in

volume and pressure) needed for satisfactory operation. Check these instructions carefully before buying a new tool. And, if you already have certain tools in mind that you want to use, check the air requirements before you buy a compressor. Hopefully, this will prevent you from buying a compressor that is either too large or too small. Generally, the home custom painter will find that a compressor fitted with a 1-2 hp motor should be suitable.

COMPRESSOR ACCESSORIES

There are a variety of tools that are

If you plan to use only an airbrush or a small touch up gun (and you won't be spraying an entire car), you could get by with a small diaphragm compressor like this one from Thayer and Chandler.

If your compressor doesn't have a regulator, you should add one (preferably one with a gauge), to set output pressure to the range specified by the equipment you are using. You should also add a water trap (right) at the compressor, and possibly a second one nearer the spray gun.

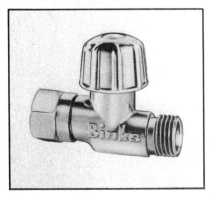

It is often necessary to make small pressure adjustments during the job. It is very handy to attach a small, inline air valve directly to the gun, so you don't have to keep running over to the compressor. A model with a built-in gauge also eliminates the problem of computing air pressure drop per length of hose. The gauge will indicate the exact pressure at the gun. (Some experienced painters, however, simply adjust their gun by "feel.")

either mandatory or highly recommended for use with a compressor. Some form of pressure regulation is mandatory. Some compressors have regulators built in, but most use add-on regulators. There are even small regulators that attach to the base of a spray gun so you know exactly how much air pressure is available to the gun.

Some regulators are mounted in conjunction with an air filter. An air

This Binks industrial unit combines a high-volume filter with a regulator and gauge. Always use a good, clean filter or airborn dirt particles will be sprayed on the surface along with the paint. Always drain the water trap at the end of each day.

filter, or moisture trap, is a good idea to keep the air that flows through your spray gun as clean and dry as possible. Some air filters have a second part that serves as an oil fog lubricator. The purpose of an oil fogger is to lubricate air-powered tools; it must not be used with spray guns since you do not want oil to contaminate a painting surface.

You will need 25 to 50 feet of air hose to get the air from the compressor to the spray gun. Hoses come in different diameters. The larger diameter hoses are best, but remember that the effective size of the hose is dependent on the diameter of the smallest restriction in the line. It is better to use a larger line, rather than use an extension cord to move the compressor closer to the job. But keep in mind that delivery pressure decreases when a longer hose is used (see chart on page 33).

Air hoses are made with various wall thickness and covering material. The heavy ones will last longer but the light ones are easier to move around. There are also special coiled air hoses that are handy for use with air tools.

A very useful air hose accessory is the quick connect. These connectors make it possible for you to quickly and easily change spray guns or air tools without using a wrench. Quick connectors are inexpensive and very handy.

Dusting or blow gun attachments are another handy compressor ac-

cessory. They are inexpensive and will save you a lot of time during sanding. By blowing away sanding debris you will make sanding quicker and more efficient. Blow guns are vital for removing moisture from tiny crevices after wet sanding. Trapped moisture may be blown onto the paint surface by the spray gun and ruin a portion of the paint.

SPRAY GUNS

The spray gun is the custom painter's paint brush. Strictly speaking, a spray gun is a mechanical device for combining paint and air in an atomized state that can be easily controlled for

23

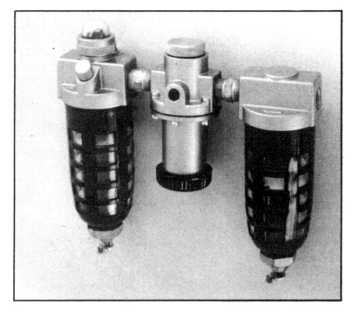

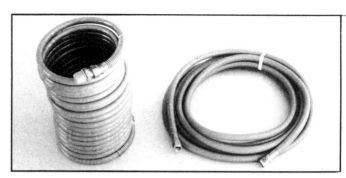

The air hose is not an exotic item, but it is important to have a good, strong hose that is long enough to allow easy access all the way around the vehicle. The coiled hose at left is strictly for air tools, the rubber hose at right for painting.

This setup, designed strictly for use with air tools, combines a water trap (right) with an inline oil fogger (left) to lubricate the tools. *Never use an oil fogger in a painting system and never use a hose that has ever had oil in it.* If you use air tools with your compressor, lubricate them by occasionally adding a few drops of oil into the air fitting on the tool.

applying the paint to a variety of surfaces. In order to provide just the right mixtures of paint and air, a spray gun must be a precision instrument. The small passages inside the spray gun are designed and manufactured to precise standards. Since a spray gun is a precision instrument it must be treated with care (see the chapter 3) in order to provide good service. With proper care, a spray gun will last for many, many years.

Air and paint are combined in the spray gun in a beautifully simple process. The paint is syphoned up from the paint cup as air moves through the gun from the air source. The outermost tip of the spray gun is known as the air nozzle. It has two horns or wings that are 180 degrees apart and there are tiny orifices in the ends of these horns. The air comes out here and mixes with the paint which comes out of the fluid nozzle. The fluid nozzle is inside the air cap and the tip of it protrudes through the center of the air nozzle. The trigger controls both the flow of air and fluid paint. As

the trigger is pulled back, it retracts the needle valve which allows the paint to flow through the fluid nozzle. The trigger also controls the air valve, which turns the air that reaches the air nozzle "on" or "off." The proportions of air and paint are controlled by two adjustment knobs at the back of the spray gun handle. The top knob controls airflow that "shapes" the fan pattern (air volume is controlled by the pressure regulator), the lower knob is the fluid control knob, which controls the flow of paint into the pattern.

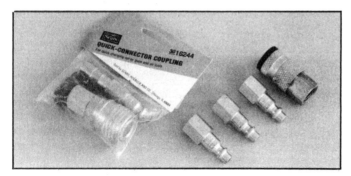

Quick-connect couplers are so handy they should be considered a mandatory part of nearly any system. Get several of the same kind, since different brands won't mix (and always keep a few spares on hand).

Of course there are many other handy air accessories. An air gun is very useful to blow dust or water from the surface during preparation and immediately prior to painting.

Although spray guns vary in size, type, and intended use, most are similar in general design. For automotive painting the "standard" spray gun is an external-mix, siphon-feed type. If you can possibly afford two guns, get a top-quality unit like the Binks Model 7 (right) for finish coats, treat it with special care and keep it spotlessly clean. Use a less expensive gun, like the Craftsman at left (fitted with a Sharpe dripless cup), for primering and undercoats.

Spray gun air caps come in different sizes for use with different types of paints or materials. There are also variations in air jet designs for different fan patterns.

Spray gun adjustments are standardized. The top knob at the back of the handle (1) is the air adjustment and controls the width of the fan pattern. The lower knob (2) is the material adjustment and controls the ratio of paint to air.

There are several different spray gun designs: internal- or external-mix nozzles, syphon- or pressure-feed nozzles, and those with attached or remote paint cups. The spray gun that is almost universal with the custom painting trade is a syphon-feed gun with an external-mix nozzle. This gun is best suited for automotive finishes and instances where many color changes are encountered.

The external-mix nozzle combines air and paint outside of the air nozzle. The action in an internal-mix nozzle is virtually the same except that the mixing is done inside the nozzle. Internal mix nozzles can be identified by their lack of air horns or wing ports. Also, the tip of the needle valve doesn't protrude through the fluid nozzle as it does with an external-mix nozzle.

Syphon-feed spray guns use atmospheric pressure to force the paint from the paint cup. This is why it is so important to keep the air hole free of obstructions. When the gun trigger is pulled it sends air through the gun. This stream of air creates a low pressure in the paint syphon tube, which allows the atmospheric pressure to force the paint from the cup. Air only flows through a syphon-feed spray gun when the trigger is pulled.

In pressure-feed spray guns air from the compressor is used to pressurize the cup. When the trigger is pulled, the paint is forced out of the cup or remote container. The most common use of pressure-feed systems in automotive painting is for a remote paint container. Since the remote container holds more paint than the standard one-quart cup used on most syphon-feed spray guns, this system is useful for spraying large quantities of a single color. And the remote container means that the painter only has to handle the spray head, reducing fatigue in high-volume production shops.

You can use either external- or internal-mix nozzles with pressure-feed guns. Internal-mix nozzles can only be used with pressure-feed systems. Internal-mix, pressure-feed systems don't require as much air as external-mix, syphon-feed systems. This is why most small, hobby setups usually use internal-mix, pressure-feed systems. There is less overspray with these systems, but the quality of the finish usually isn't as smooth as with external-mix, syphon-feed spray guns.

For the purpose of custom painting, stick with the standard, external-mix, syphon-feed spray guns. There are different air caps and fluid nozzles for varying situations. Consult your paint

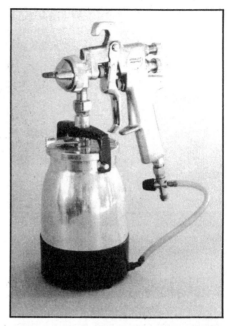

There are many specialty spray guns and paint cups. This Stewart-Warner gun features a special agitator cup. It is ideal for paints with a high metallic content (metalflakes and pearls).

equipment store for special application parts.

Most spray guns are suitable for automotive painting just the way they come out of the box. Certain guns are recommended for lacquers and others are best for heavy paints like primer-surfacers. If you can afford it, it is a good idea to have two or three spray guns. Use the best gun only for lacquer top coats. Use the next best gun for only enamels and designate one gun for primer use. This method will make your guns last longer with less maintenance. Also, you won't have to spend as much time adjusting the gun for the different types of paint.

There are some special paint cups that you may have occasion to use. The most common one that should almost

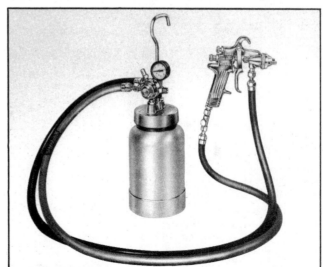

A remote gun system, sometimes known as a "pressure pot," is excellent for production automotive painting. The cup holds two quarts of material, so you don't have to stop to reload, and the gun can be turned any direction, even upside down, without dripping paint.

Since siphon-feed cups must be vented to the atmosphere, they can drip through the air vent if turned sidways or upside down. To remedy the problem, manufacturers have come up with different varieties of "dripless cups." Binks simply uses a small length of plastic tube on the vent. The vent must be thoroughly cleaned after painting; otherwise the paint will not siphon properly.

be considered mandatory is a dripless cup. Dripless cups can be adapted to the spray heads of almost any brand gun. There are agitator paint cups that are a big help when spraying paints with a heavy metallic content. There are even hot cups that heat the paint to about 160° F, but hot cups are seldom, if ever, used for ordinary automotive painting.

Besides the different types of paint cups, there is more than one way of attaching the cup to the spray gun. The less expensive guns are threaded like a glass jar. The better guns use a quick release system that only requires a quick turn of a lever to release the paint cup. Paint refills and color changes are much easier with quick-release paint cups.

TOUCH-UP GUNS

One of the most useful pieces of equipment for custom painting is the touch-up gun. A touch-up gun is basically a scaled down production spray gun. Most touch-up guns are external-mix, syphon-feed, precision guns that are just easier to handle and better adapted to painting small areas. Some professional painters can handle a full-sized gun with uncanny precision, but for ordinary painters, the touch-up gun is a great tool.

Just the fact that the touch-up gun is lighter and smaller makes it ideal for custom paint tricks. You can concentrate on painting rather than the manipulation of a heavy spray gun. The touch-up gun produces a much smaller pattern than a regular spray gun; this fact makes it well suited for murals and design panels where you want a minimum of overspray. Touch-up guns are also good for door jambs and any interior painting.

Another design factor that makes the touch-up gun good for murals and design panels is that the trigger is

There's nothing worse than laying down a smooth, glossy coat of wet paint and then having your gun drip on it. Since nearly all automotive guns use a siphon-feed system, it is wise to invest in a dripless cup. Fortunately, cup attachment systems are fairly standard, and one dripless cup will usually fit several different brandname guns (if you have more than one gun).

The special cup on this Binks gun has a paddle that agitates the paint each time the trigger is pulled. Agitator cups are virtually a necessity with flake paints.

At the lower end of the price and quality scale are dual-purpose spray guns. Each has a knob that changes the gun from siphon to pressure feed. Such guns often come with home compressors and are best relegated to primer work or painting old furniture.

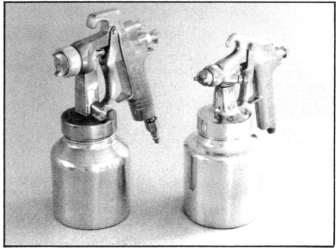

Besides being great for their original purpose—painting small repair areas—touch-up guns are very handy for applying custom paints in small areas or design panels.

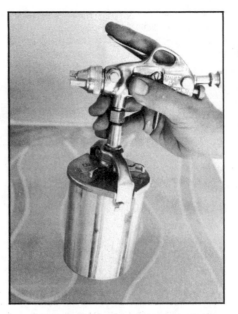

A touch-up gun operates in the same manner, but is about half the size of a regular gun. Note that the trigger is on the top of the gun. The light weight and small size make these guns very easy to handle. A touch-up gun also uses less air volume that a full-size gun.

When car painters discovered the airbrush, a new era in custom painting was born. It takes some skill to master, but in the hands of an expert an airbrush can produce breath-taking effects.

Even if you don't have an air compressor, you can try your hand with an inexpensive airbrush kit powered by aerosol propellant. Such kits are better for fogging and shading than for fine-line work.

mounted on top of the gun and is controlled by the index finger. Many painters feel that this method of control puts you in closer touch with your work, giving you more direct control of the paint. The pattern and fluid controls are the same on a touch-up gun as on a regular spray gun, only the location of the knobs may vary.

The touch-up gun is relatively easy to master and a great confidence builder for beginning painters. It is an excellent compromise between a full-size spray gun and an airbrush. In effect, it allows the precise control of an airbrush with a capacity that allows you to paint at a reasonable rate. Touch-up guns are one of the most versatile tools in custom painting.

AIRBRUSHES

The airbrush is another piece of equipment that helped to revolutionize custom painting. If it weren't for the airbrush, many custom paint tricks and virtually all mural work would simply not exist. The delicate patterns produced by an airbrush have allowed painters to become artists who paint on metal rather than canvas.

Airbrushes have been around since the 1800's but it is only recently that they have been used for automotive purposes. Modelers and other hobbyists have long known the value of airbrushes, as have professional illus-

trators, but it took the mural craze to bring the airbrush to the attention of custom painters. Airbrushes have the capacity to apply patterns ranging from 1/16-inch to 2 or 3 inches wide. This makes the airbrush a very versatile tool for custom painting. Overspray can be kept at a minimum with airbrushes. This is a very good feature for mural painting where sharp definition is desired.

There are basically three types of airbrushes: the mini spray guns, the single-action airbrushes and the dual-action airbrushes. The mini spray gun is the most basic and least expensive airbrush, about $10. They are single-action, external-mix style airbrushes, but whereas external mixing is preferred in full-size spray guns, it is not desirable with airbrushes. The external-mix feature means that there is more overspray and the pattern isn't as easy to control. The mini spray guns

are suitable for painters on a strict budget, but you won't get the precision quality you can expect from an airbrush.

Next in complexity and price is the single-action airbrush. Single-action airbrushes feature internal mixing and a single lever or control button that releases the atomized paint. A needle adjuster at the back of the handle controls the width of the spray pattern. The pattern can be further controlled by switching paint tips. A single-action airbrush is easier to control than a dual-action airbrush, and is a good choice for a beginning painter.

Dual-action airbrushes are the most complex and costly. Finer control is possible with a dual-action airbrush, which is why most professional mural painters use dual-action airbrushes. Dual-action airbrushes also have an internal mixing action, but both air and paint are controlled with a single

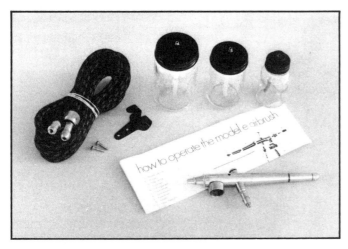

If you are serious about learning airbrush technique, it would be best to start with a good single action, internal mix type like this Thayer and Chandler Model E. It is easy to use, yet versatile and quite precise.

Most professionals use a dual action airbrush since it allows control of both air and paint flow separately or simultaneously. This is a Thayer and Chandler Model C, which comes with three sizes of screw-on paint containers.

trigger lever. Pushing down on the button increases the amount of air flowing through the airbrush while pulling back on the lever increases the amount of paint. This means the user can vary the spray pattern from an ultra-fine mist to a solid spray of color, depending on the manipulation of the control button. Double-action airbrushes also have interchangeable paint tips to control the amount and type of paint that can be sprayed.

There are a variety of paint containers for use with airbrushes. The most common size jars are four-ounce, two-ounce and 3/4-ounce. There are also small metal paint cups known as paint thimbles, although these tiny containers are most often used by graphic illustrators (paint thimbles only hold 1/4-ounce of paint) The easiest paint containers to use are those with slip fittings. A tapered fitting on the paint jar makes it possible to

change between premixed jars of paint easily and quickly. It is also a good idea to have a jar of thinner handy to clean the gun between colors. Airbrushes can clog easily if not kept clean at all times. Never allow paint to dry in the tiny internal passages.

A wide variety of air sources will power an airbrush. A standard compressor is the most common source, but the smaller hobby compressors are fine for airbrushes. These little compressors are light and portable. They usually develop 1/4-1/2 horsepower, which is ample for most airbrushes. Some of the mini spray gun kits come with cans of aerosol propellant. Aerosol propellant will get small jobs done, but cans of propellant cost a couple dollars apiece, which can

Paint containers for airbrushes come in a wide variety of sizes from 1/16-ounce thimbles (far right) to 4-ounce jars. Some attach by slip fit (those on the right), while others screw on. It's best to have several extra containers, with lids, for storing the various colors needed for one job.

The air flow requirements of air brushes are so low that a small hobby-type compressor is often preferable over a full size compressor.

Air brushes do not need high-pressure air hoses, but the braided type (left) is preferable over plastic hose since it won't wear out as quickly.

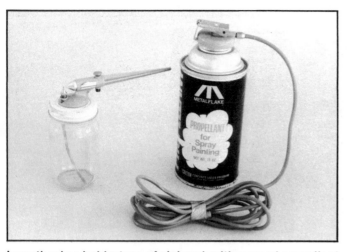

Investing in a hobby type of air brush with canned propellant might be false economy since replacement cannisters are expensive and the capabilities of the airbrush are quite limited.

If you are going to do automotive painting, invest in a good respirator with replaceable filters...and use it. Small throw-away dust masks are O.K. for shooting primers or lacquers, but acrylic enamels or urethanes are quite toxic, so use a good respirator while working around them. If you're in an un-ventilated garage, always wear a good respirator.

quickly equal the price of a small compressor.

Airbrushes are handy tools for custom design tricks, murals, and lettering. A wide variety of intricate designs can be executed with a good airbrush. Every custom painter should have one.

SAFETY EQUIPMENT

Safety equipment is a very important part of custom painting. Paints are comprised of very potent chemicals. It stands to reason that you would never drink paint or thinner, but breathing large quantities of paint fumes can be harmful over a period of time. Certain types of paint, such as urethane enamels, produce very toxic fumes. It is for this reason that a top quality respirator should be considered a mandatory piece of painting equipment.

There are many types of respirators. Some are designed for protection from dust, while others are designed primarily for protection from paint. The paper hospital type masks are of little value. The best type of respirator is the dual-canister type with replaceable filters. Always wear a respirator when painting and change the filters often.

There are several other safety items that you should have for various painting and bodywork functions. Heavy rubber gloves should be worn when using metal etching chemicals and paint removers. Safety glasses or face shields should be used during any grinding operations. Safety glasses are also a good idea when using a hammer and a dolly, as little pieces of metal are often dislodged by the action of the hammer. Hearing protectors should also be used with some body tools, e.g., air chisels. Of course, you should always have at least one or two good fire extinguishers around any painting area.

Pick your tools wisely and take good care of them. They will provide you with years of good service and make custom painting fun. Good tools make it possible to concentrate on your work and thus end up with a better paint job.

Since all automotive paint products, especially reducers, are flammable it should go without saying that at least one, and preferably two, industrial strength fire extinguishers should be located in the working area.

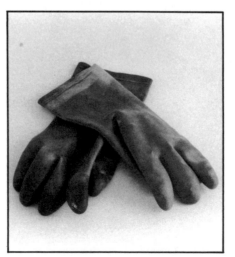

Rubber gloves and protective goggles are always good to have around a painting/bodywork area. Use both when handling acids like paint stripper or metal conditioner. It's wise to wear eye protection when using a grinder. And rubber gloves (even the dishpan type) will keep your hands from wearing out when you are hand sanding a whole car.

EQUIPMENT CARE AND MAINTENANCE

- **SPRAY GUN MAINTENANCE**
- **SPRAY GUN PROBLEMS AND CURES**
- **AIRBRUSH MAINTENANCE**
- **COMPRESSOR CARE**

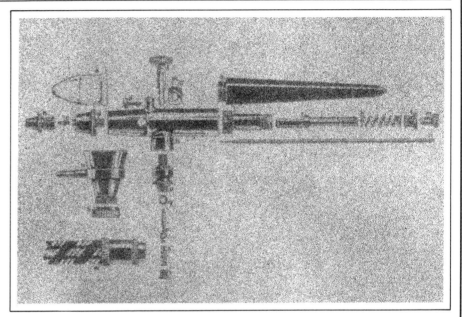

YOU CAN'T EXPECT A GOOD PAINT JOB FROM BAD EQUIPMENT

There is an old saying that states, "A craftsman is only as good as his tools." This is particularly true of a custom painter. Skill and artistic talent play a large part in custom painting, but even the most talented painter is in trouble with a dirty spray gun or a defective air compressor. If your equipment is giving you trouble, it is very difficult to concentrate on the creative aspects of custom painting. Bad equipment maintenance is an inexcusable reason for spoiling a paint job. With simple attention to a few details you should never have to worry about problems caused by defective equipment.

Assuming you purchase your equipment new, you should be able to keep it in top notch shape for many, many years. If you decide to buy any used painting equipment, be careful. Hopefully, the seller has a very good reason for selling the equipment, such as moving up to newer or better equipment. Never buy any expensive

Stan Betz of Betz Speed and Color in Anaheim, California, keeps this paint encrusted gun hanging on the wall to remind customers not to let their equipment get into this condition if they want to spray quality paint jobs.

equipment (e.g., a compressor) without seeing it work. Inspect a spray gun carefully by taking off the fluid nozzle and checking to see if any of the passages look clogged. If it is at all possible, have the seller spray some thinner through the gun so you can check the adjustment controls.

If you are the original owner of your painting equipment there is no excuse for not taking excellent care of it. Any time saved by not cleaning up thoroughly after painting will only be multiplied in the time lost the next time you go to use the equipment. Wet paint is far easier to clean than dried paint. If paint dries inside the passages of the spray gun, it will be virtually impossible to clear them without completely disassembling the gun. It is best for a beginning painter not to totally disassemble a spray gun unless he has complete assembly and disassembly instructions. Properly cleaning a spray gun can use up quite a bit of thinner, but a few ounces of thinner is far cheaper than a new spray gun. Take extra care in cleaning small equipment

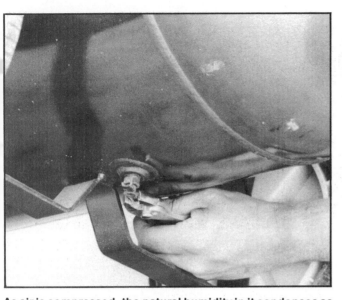

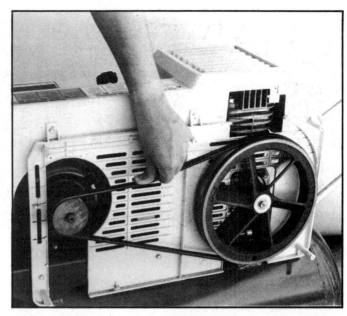

As air is compressed, the natural humidity in it condenses as water, collects in the compressor air tank and is transmitted through the lines. Drain your air tank regularly, especially after heavy compressor use or in humid weather. If the tank has a screw-out plug rather than a petcock (as shown), be sure to bleed all air pressure from the tank before removing it.

A slipping belt also yields inefficient compressor operation; but do not tighten the belt beyond manufacturer's specs or you can wear out the bearings in the motor. As a general rule, half an inch belt deflection is normal.

like airbrushes because the tiny passages are highly prone to clogging. The slightest amount of debris can greatly affect the operation of an airbrush.

COMPRESSOR CARE

Compressed air is vital to custom painting. A steady source of clean, dry air must be available at all times or else you may ruin hours of painstaking

Of all compressor maintenance, especially on portable types, this is the most important: check the air intake filter regularly, and brush it clean or replace it when dirty. Leaving the compressor in the area where you are painting (i.e. the garage) will cause the filter to clog quickly with overspray. A clogged compressor filter, just like a dirty air cleaner on a car's engine, will reduce the unit's pumping efficiency, cause overheating, and ultimately lead to drawing oil from the crankcase into the air stream...which causes severe fisheyes in the paint.

work. Cleanliness and preventative maintenance should keep your compressor in top working condition.

Keep your compressor and the area around it as clean as possible. If the compressor gets dusty, blow it clean occasionally. Locate the compressor where it can receive a good supply of fresh air. It is best if the compressor is near a door and away from the immediate work area. If you do any sandblasting, be sure to isolate the compressor because sand particles can work into the motor and wear out the piston bores.

Every time you use a compressor, drain the moisture from the air holding tank. And, if you have any additional moisture traps in the air line, drain them at the same time. If you use an inline moisture trap, make sure it is always in a vertical position. Otherwise, the moisture won't collect near the drain cock as it should. Too much moisture in a compressor tank can lead to damaging corrosion, which can eventually weaken the walls of the tank.

At least once a week, check the condition of the air intake filter. Blow off the dust periodically and replace the filter at regular intervals. A restricted air filter won't permit the compressor to work at full capacity. This will increase your electrical bill and may even cause the compressor to start pumping lube oil into the air supply.

Replacement air filters are inexpensive and easy to replace. There are usually only a couple of screws holding

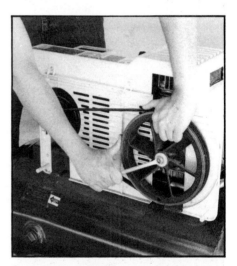

Compressor vibration can lead to loose fasteners, which must be periodically tightened. Be sure to check the flywheel nut; if it gets loose it can ruin the main shaft.

the filter to the top of the compressor cylinder head. It is very important that you don't operate the compressor when the air filter is removed.

If the compressor drive belt is properly adjusted, you should only need to check it once a month. The belt should be just tight enough that it doesn't slip. When checking belt tension, check for wear. A belt that is starting to fray should be replaced. It is a good idea to always have a spare belt on hand. This way a broken belt won't cause a crisis in the middle of a paint job.

Besides checking the tightness of the compressor belt, it is a good idea to check all fasteners on the compressor.

31

Check the set screws on the pulleys and the flywheel. Check the head bolts and the bolts that hold the compressor to the air tank. If the head bolts need tightening, remember that the head is like a cylinder head on a car. It must be tightened evenly and gradually, starting from the center and working out.

Check the oil level in your compressor at least once a week if you use it regularly. Compressors don't have an oil filter so clean oil is very important. Change the oil according to the manufacturer's schedule. The recommendations vary but the oil should be changed at least after every 100 hours of operation. Even if you seldom use your compressor, change the oil at least once a year.

A maintenance item that is not immediately obvious is the condition of the wiring in your garage. Compressors need a lot of electricity to function. It is best if your compressor runs on 220 volts. Most compressors over one horsepower run on 220 power and many smaller compressors can be converted to 220. Besides the greater efficiency of 220-volt motors, there are usually fewer items on the 220 line, and the best situation is to run the compressor on its own circuit.

Compressors are designed to operate on very short power cords. Extensions are not recommended because amperage is lost in every foot of an extension cord. Also each connector in a power line is a source of lost power. It is best to use additional air lines to reach the painting area. Remember, though, that the longer the air line, the greater the pressure drop at the spray gun. This means the regulator setting will have to be greater than the actual pressure needed at the spray gun. Pressure loss can be avoided by using large-diameter permanent pipe to route the air closer to the work area. A quick connector on the end of the pipe will make it fast and easy to connect a short hose when you need to use the air.

Any serious problems with a compressor should be left to a professional repairman. Some common problems are relatively easy to fix, though. If the motor keeps shutting down, there is an electrical problem. The motor overload switch is designed to protect the compressor. The most common electrical problem is voltage drop due to poor wiring in the garage. If the circuit isn't heavy enough to keep the motor working for long periods of time (it takes a long time to repaint a car), consult an electrician about upgrading your garage circuit. A temporary fix is to shut off all appliances in the house that run on the same circuit. It also helps to paint during low load times when your neighbors aren't running a lot of appliances, lights, or air conditioners.

Don't try to circumvent an electrical deficiency by using a fuse rated for higher amperage. This can be very dangerous. Sometimes compressor motors shut off because they are too hot. Check to see that the compressor is receiving plenty of fresh air and let it

Although it's not common, a compressor can blow a head gasket just like a car can. Check cylinder head bolts and tighten evenly from the center of the head working out.

Any air leaks in compressor lines or fittings will cause the unit to work overtime. When tightening brass fittings, use a five-sided flare nut wrench to avoid damaging the couplings.

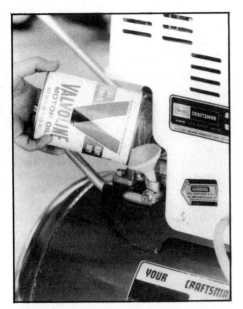

Remember that a compressor is just like a small piston engine. Check the oil regularly, and change it after every 100 hours of operation. Follow manufacturer recommendations for oil type and weight.

AIR PRESSURE DROP CHART

PRESSURE IN PSI AT THE AIR COMPRESSOR		PSI AT THE GUN BASED ON HOSE LENGTH			
		10 Feet	15 Feet	25 Feet	50 Feet
1/4-INCH HOSE	30 PSI	24	23	21	9
	40 PSI	32	31	27	16
	50 PSI	40	38	34	22
	60 PSI	48	46	41	29
	70 PSI	56	53	48	36
	80 PSI	64	61	55	43
	90 PSI	71	68	61	51
5/16-INCH HOSE	30 PSI	29	28	27	23
	40 PSI	37	37	36	32
	50 PSI	48	46	45	40
	60 PSI	56	55	54	49
	70 PSI	65	64	63	57
	80 PSI	74	73	71	66
	90 PSI	83	82	80	74

Air pressure drops proportionately with the length of hose from the setting of the regulator at the compressor. The larger the hose, the less the total air pressure drop between compressor and gun.

To function properly, a compressor needs plenty of clean, cool air to breath and to keep its temperature down. Don't leave your portable compressor in a corner of the garage like this, piled with junk, while you're painting. If possible, move it outside the garage while you're working.

cool off before restarting. Be sure there isn't any junk blocking the compressor air intake or the ventilation holes in the electric motor case. Keep the compressor a foot or two away from walls so that air can circulate completely around the motor.

The tightness of all air fittings is very important. Even a small leak can waste great amounts of air and keep your compressor from delivering all of the air it should to the spray gun.

Problems involving air leaks are easy to fix. Listen for escaping air or run your hand around the area to feel for leaks. If you think you have located a probable leak, you can double check it by covering the area with soapy water and watching for bubbles. If the safety (pop-off) valve is leaking, replace it. Don't try to adjust it. Another item to leave alone is the pressure switch. The pressure switch (which determines when the motor starts and stops) is preset at the factory and should only be handled by trained technicians.

Knocking noises are fairly common with compressors. The two major causes of knocking are a loose flywheel set screw and low oil level. Check the oil level to see that it is level with the top of the fill hole. Wiggle the flywheel to be sure it isn't loose. Tighten the flywheel set screw and also check the set screw on the motor pulley. If knocking still exists, the problem is probably internal, perhaps a bad crank or connecting rod. This means either a trip to the shop or getting a replacement air pump unit.

SPRAY GUN MAINTENANCE

Assuming your compressor is in good working condition, the next most important item is a good spray gun. Your artistic talents will be stifled if you try to paint with a malfunctioning spray gun. Spray guns are precision tools that need to be treated with care. A spray gun is a metering device that mixes paint and air to form a sprayable solution. If any of the gun's internal passages get damaged or clogged, the spray gun won't function as it was intended.

Most problems stem from not cleaning a spray gun immediately after use. As soon as you are through painting, flush the gun with plenty of clean solvent. Don't put the whole gun in a can of solvent because this will ruin the seals and lubricants in the moving parts of the spray gun. Never use any wire or metal objects to clean passages or openings in a spray gun. If this type of cleaning is necessary, use something soft and flexible like a broomstraw. When the spray gun is removed from the paint cup, keep the gun vertical. If the gun is laid down, paint can seep back into air passages.

The process for cleaning a siphon-feed spray gun is as follows. Disconnect the spray gun from the air source. Remove the gun from the paint cup and let the paint drip back down the fluid tube into the paint cup. Pulling the trigger several times will help the

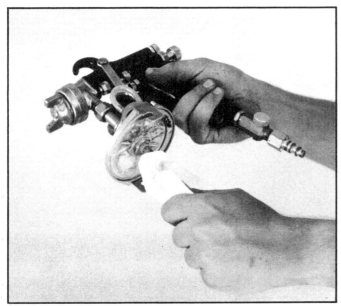

When you're finished painting empty the cup, fill it with a couple of inches of cheap thinner, slosh it around, and spray some through the gun. Then remove the cup, pour out the dirty thinner, and use clean thinner on a towel to wipe down the siphon tube and wash off the spray gun. Be sure to thoroughly clean the air vent before any paint can dry in it.

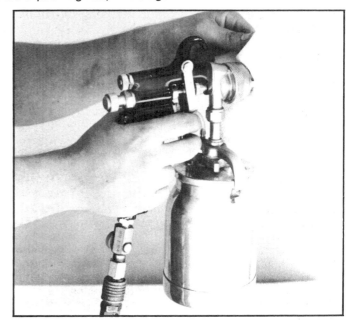

Likewise clean out the paint cup with a towel soaked in clean thinner. Any dried paint that accumulates on the lip will cause the cup to drip paint later.

paint drain out of the gun. Wipe the paint tube with a thinner-soaked cloth or paper towel. Empty the paint from the cup and rinse the cup with clean thinner.

Put some thinner back in the paint cup and attach the gun to the air supply. Spray the thinner through the gun. An old cardboard box makes a good place to spray the thinner. While spraying the thinner, shake the gun. You can also back-flush the gun by covering the nozzle with a cloth and pulling the trigger. This will force air and any excess paint back into the paint cup.

After the gun is clean, wipe the paint cup. Wipe the outside of the spray gun and the paint cup. Be sure that the air vent on the cup is free of paint. Dripless cups with a coiled tube vent require special attention to cleaning. Pour a little clean thinner in the tube and run something like a pipe cleaner through it before the paint has a chance to dry. Store the spray gun in a vertical position.

It is also a good idea to lubricate the spray gun with light machine oil each time you use it. Be sure that any oils you use don't contain silicone. The places to apply lubricant are the trigger pivot, the control knobs, the fluid needle spring, the fluid packing nut, and the air valve packing. All packing nuts should only be finger tightened. Never soak the packings in thinner or any other solvent.

After several paint jobs, you can soak the spray gun air cap in thinner overnight to loosen any dried paint. However, many painters prefer to

While spraying the cleaning thinner through the gun, back-flush it a couple of times by pressing a rag over the nozzle for a second or two as shown (don't use your finger; you can inject yourself with solvent). This will force air and thinner back down the pickup tube. Empty the gun and spray some air through it before storage.

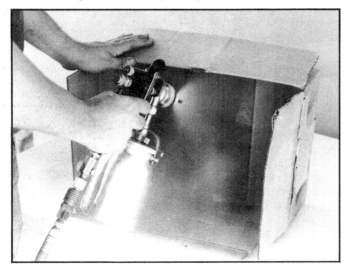

Next fill the cup with clean thinner and spray plenty of it through the gun at a relatively high pressure (60 to 70 pounds). You can spray the thinner into an open cardboard box, as shown, to keep it off other surfaces (like your fresh paint job).

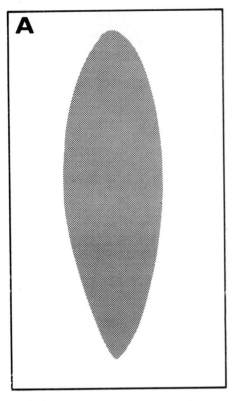

A

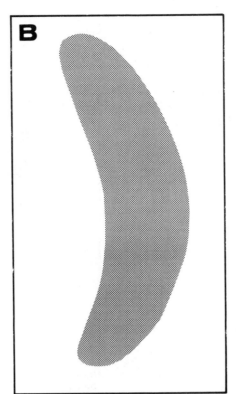

B

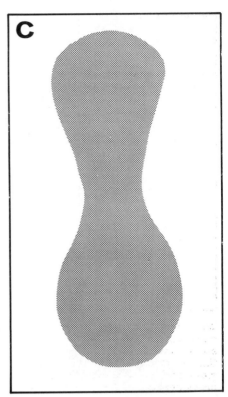

C

A dirty spray gun air cap or fluid nozzle can produce irregularities in the gun's fan pattern. If the gun is clean and adjusted properly, the paint thinned to the right consistency, and the air pressure set correctly, a fan pattern as shown in figure A should result. If the gun sprays a crescent-shaped pattern as shown in figure B, one of the wing ports in the air cap is probably plugged with dried paint or dirt. If the pattern is heavy and wider at either top or bottom, as shown in figure C, the fluid nozzle likely has dried paint around the tip. To clean it, unscrew the air cap, then use a wrench to remove the fluid nozzle. Clean the tip with thinner and a soft instrument like a brush or a Q-tip. Also check and clean the fluid control needle.

briefly soak the air cap after every paint job.

SPRAY GUN PROBLEMS AND CURES

If your spray gun is clean and properly adjusted you shouldn't encounter many, if any, problems. Assuming that problems do occur, here are some of the more common ones and their cures.

Uneven spray patterns are usually due to an improperly adjusted gun or restrictions in the spray gun. If the nozzle is only clogged on one side, a half-moon pattern will result. A partially clogged nozzle yields a heavy-ended pattern. When the orifice is clogged in the center, a bow-tie pattern is the result. Unusual patterns can also be caused by improperly adjusted air and fluid controls.

Spitting or sputtering can be caused by several things. A loose or cracked fluid tube can cause spitting. A clogged vent hole will cause sputtering. If the paint level in the cup is low and you tip the gun, air will get into the fluid line and cause sputtering. Air can also get into the fluid lines through a dried out seal around the fluid needle. When this happens, lubricate the packing or replace it. A defective or loose nut where the gun mates to the paint cup can also cause spitting.

Paint leaks can develop around the packing nut. This is due to either dry packing or loose packing nut. If, after tightening and lubricating, the drip still exists, you need a new packing. If paint leaks from the spray nozzle, the valve needle is either dirty, improperly seated, or the packing nut is too tight.

If paint doesn't appear at all when the trigger is pulled, the paint is probably too thick. Check to see that the manufacturer's thinning directions were correctly followed. Another possibility is a clogged fluid tip. On a siphon feed gun, a blocked air hole can also prevent the paint from leaving the paint cup. In unusual cases, a clogged strainer (if your siphon tube has one) will also prevent spraying, although a clogged strainer usually manifests itself in a sputtering condition.

Air leaks can be caused by a variety of problems. Any debris on the air valve stem or seat will cause a leak. The condition of the air-valve stem is quite important. Besides dirt, a bent air-valve stem can cause an air leak. The air-valve assembly needs to be properly adjusted for tightness to prevent leaks. The gasket around the assembly can deteriorate and leak. If the air-valve packing is too tight, it will promote leaks. A broken air-valve spring is a sure cause of escaping air from the front of the spray gun.

Take care of your spray gun and keep it as clean as possible and you will be able to avoid most problems. Remember to store the gun in a vertical position even when you are in the middle of a paint job. A good idea is to place several hooks around the painting area and under the edge of your work bench. You will then have a place to hang the gun whenever you're not using it.

If you have two or more spray guns you can keep the best one in top condition by only using it for color coats. Designate one spray gun as your primer gun. Primer application isn't as critical as top coats, so this is a good way to keep your best spray gun in tip top shape.

AIRBRUSH MAINTENANCE

Most airbrush problems stem from improper cleaning. Airbrushes are miniature spray guns, so it is even more important to keep the passages and metering devices of an airbrush clean. These tiny fluid and air passages are easily clogged if the airbrush isn't cleaned immediately after use. It is even possible to have an

To clean the air cap, use a stiff bristle brush and lacquer thinner. Never use wire or any other hard object to clean the cap or the wing ports. Many spray guns come with a cleaning brush like the one shown.

Never lay a spray gun on its side when it has paint or solvent in it. Likewise, it is a good idea to store spray-guns upright so that any residual solvent can drain to the cup after cleaning. Binks makes this handy storage rack, but any horizontal bar, or large cuphooks, could be used to store spray-guns when not in use.

airbrush clog in the middle of a job if you let it sit too long while you are masking off an area or mixing add-itional paint. Many painters keep a separate paint jar filled with thinner and periodically clean the airbrush while painting.

Cleaning an airbrush is similar to cleaning a production spray gun. Empty the paint from the paint jar and spray clean thinner through the air-brush. Back flushing is a good idea with airbrushes. Either cover the noz-zle with a cloth or your finger and then depress the control trigger. With the paint jar removed you can clean the color chamber with an artist's paint brush dipped in thinner. Cotton swabs can also be used for this purpose.

A very important element of an airbrush is the needle which controls the spray pattern. If the needle gets dirty or bent it will cause spraying problems. Sometimes the needle gets stuck due to paint buildup. Carefully remove the needle and clean it. When the needle is replaced, don't use excessive force. Make sure it is snug, but don't jam it into the spray tip. If the needle gets bent, it is possible to straighten it on a perfectly flat surface, but it is best to replace damaged needles. Most airbrushes come with a cap for the end of the airbrush. This is to protect the pointed end of the needle. Use it whenever you're not using the airbrush.

Airbrush spitting is usually caused by dirt on the needle or paint that is too thick. Paint that is too thick also manifests itself as a grainy spray pattern. Dried paint on the needle or tip

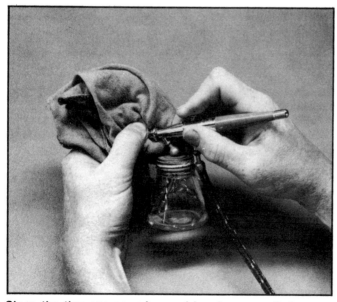

Since the tiny passages in an airbrush can easily become clogged, it is a good idea to spray some clean thinner through them each time you change colors, then back flush by holding a rag over the tip while spraying.

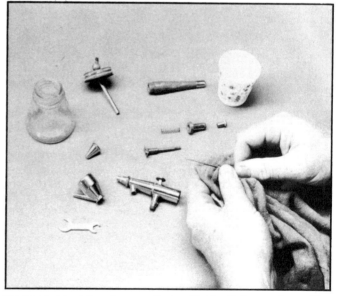

To keep an airbrush operating reliably, it is good practice to disassemble the gun an clean all components in clean thinner after every use (keep a diagram handy to get it reassembled properly).

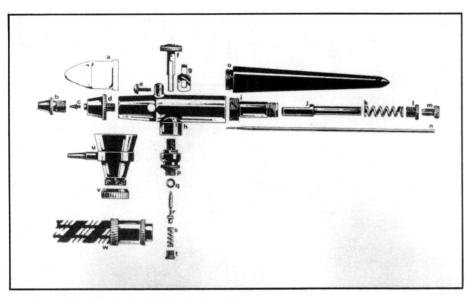

If an airbrush becomes clogged or dirty, it will probably be necessary to disassemble it for cleaning. Since they are delicate and intricate tools, it is a very good idea to have an exploded diagram on hand *before* you take it apart. Such diagrams come with better airbrushes; don't lose them.

can cause splattering. And, if you don't release the fluid control lever gently, splattering may result when the needle snaps back into the nozzle tip.

If you ever need to disassemble an airbrush, it is a good idea to have a copy of the manufacturer's cutaway diagram handy. Be sure to work in an area where the tiny parts can't get lost if they are accidentally dropped or knocked off the work bench. An airbrush is a very delicate instrument, so never use force when working on one.

We've said it before, but it's worth repeating. Cleanliness is critical to the smooth operation and long life of an airbrush!

MISCELLANEOUS EQUIPMENT

The care and maintenance of a touch-up gun is the same as that for a regular production spray gun. The passages are a little smaller, but otherwise a touch-up gun is just a half-scale spray gun. Touch-up guns should be lubricated. Place a drop or two of light machine oil at the following locations: fluid needle packing, air-adjusting valve packing, trigger pivot, and air-valve plunger. Whenever the needle spring needs lubrication, use a coat of light grease.

Air regulators can become clogged with an accumulation of water vapor and small airborne dirt particles. If you suspect a regulator of malfunctioning, bleed off all residual pressure and carefully disassemble it. Corrosion is the biggest enemy of regulators. Sometimes it is possible to clean a regulator, but if the corrosion is too bad the unit will have to be replaced.

Air lines don't need any real maintenance, but inspect them periodically for cuts and leaks. Check the tightness of the fittings. If a hose gets old and brittle, replace it.

Cleanliness is very important to all facets of painting. This is especially true of any items used in the process of mixing paints. Use a new mixing stick for each color you use. Beware of dried paint on a mixing stick, it can dissolve into the new paint. If you use any old kitchen jars or other containers for mixing paint, be sure they are clean and free of any grease or oils.

Safety is an area of painting that is too often overlooked. Paint and thinners are all flammable. Keep your work area free of possible fire hazards, like old rags, open flames, and poor electrical equipment. Don't smoke around paint supplies. Keep at least one good fire extinguisher handy. If possible, keep painting supplies in a locked metal cabinet. It is an even better idea to keep your supplies in a metal storage shed outside of the garage. Try not to keep any more paint and thinner around than you absolutely need. This will reduce possible fire hazards.

Cleanliness and care are the key elements of good equipment maintenance. Take a little extra time to do the job right every time you use your painting equipment and the equipment will last longer, help you paint better, and be easier to use.

Respirators are a vital piece of painting equipment. Try to get a respirator with replaceable filter elements. Replace the filter elements often because your lungs depend on top quality respirators for protection.

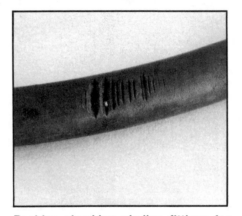

Besides checking air line fittings for leaks, be sure to inspect hoses periodically for wear, cuts, or cracks. This hose got nicked by a grinder and will probably soon leak.

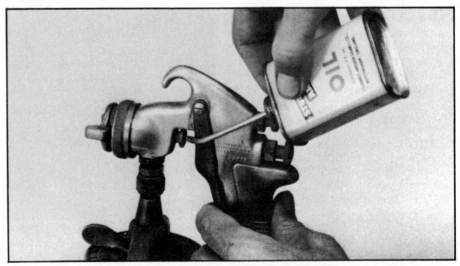

Touch-up guns and full-sized spray guns should be lubricated periodically, especially since repeated cleaning with solvents removes all lubricants from working parts. Be sure to add a drop or two of light machine oil to the needle packing both to lubricate it for smooth operation and to keep it from drying out and cracking, causing an air leak. Do not overtighten the packing nut.

BODYWORK AND SURFACE PREPARATION

- ● BODY AND SURFACE PREP EQUIPMENT
- ● REMOVING DENTS AND DINGS
- ● FIXING MINOR SCRATCHES
- ● PREPARING TO PAINT
- ● MASKING AND PRIMING

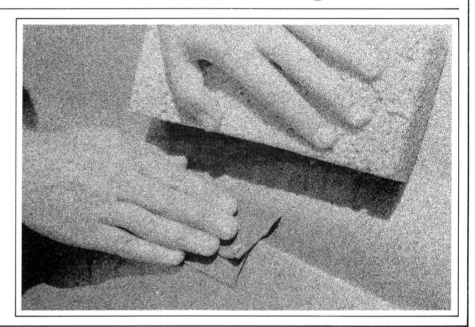

CUSTOM PAINTING DEPENDS ON CAREFUL PREPARATION

The best custom painters are the ones who pay the most attention to small details. A beautifully executed top coat is worthless if the bodywork hidden beneath the surface isn't just as flawless. Paint is like a mirror—it reflects what is under the surface. And, the careful painter spends as much time preparing the sub-surface as he spends on the actual painting. The overall impression of a true custom paint job is perfection.

The amount of surface preparation necessary before the application of a custom paint job depends on the condition of the existing paint on the vehicle. If the original paint is fairly new or in good condition, begin by thoroughly cleaning the surface with a good wax and grease remover, then wet sand all areas to be painted with 360 or 400 grit paper, and you're ready to paint. If the existing paint is crazed, cracked, bubbled, or peeling, however,

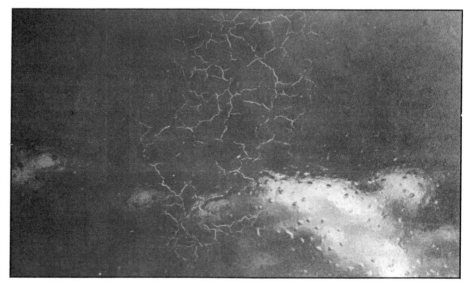

you will have to strip the affected areas down to bare metal or sand them down to a stable layer. Imperfections such as crazing or cracking in the base paint layer, even after sanding and primering, will often "telegraph" through the new paint. If the existing paint is bubbling or peeling, it is not adhering

The most important step in any paint job is proper surface preparation. Paint that is cracked or peeling must be sanded or stripped to bare metal if you want the new paint to be smooth and adhere properly. If you decide to take some shortcuts, you can be certain that the new paint job will quickly show signs of peeling.

Impurities that can ruin a paint job, such as chemicals or oils, can come from many sources. Never wipe down the surface with shop rags, which are usually chemically treated. Clean, detergent-washed towelling is best for cleaning the surface.

to the surface below it. It will continue to bubble or peel even with new paint on top of it. Finally, even a body that looks straight is bound to have some minor ripples, dents, or dings which must be removed before a high-gloss custom paint job will look perfect.

Surface preparation can be rather tedious, but almost anyone can master it. A beginner with the patience to do a really first rate job of preparation can achieve a much better final paint job than some so-called pros who skimp on preparation. Or, if you don't feel confident enough to handle the final painting, you can save money and be sure of a super paint job by doing your own preparation work. Good surface preparation takes more patience than skill.

Use top quality products when doing preparation work. Follow directions carefully. If the directions call for clean, lint-free rags, don't use greasy shop rags (most commercial shop rags are cleaned in solvent-based cleansers, which can leave oily residue on the painting surface). The people who wrote the directions knew what they were doing, so even though it may seem like the long way around a problem, follow the directions. By using top quality materials you will only spend a few dollars more on the total job, but the results will be much better and the work will go faster. Fresh sandpaper cuts much better than worn-out, cheap sandpaper. Likewise, a good tack rag will pick up much

Commonly called "cheese graters," because they look like and cut plastic body filler like an old-fashioned kitchen cheese grater, forming files are a great timesaver for bodywork. They come in curved or flat shapes and can be used with or without various handles to plane down filler just before it fully hardens.

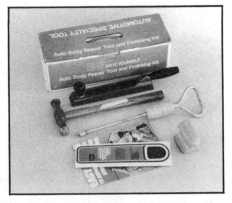

If you are just starting on your first custom paint job, you'll need several special tools for preparing the body. A basic bodyworking kit, such as this one with "cheese grater," body hammer, dolly, dent puller, and sanding block is a good beginner's assortment.

more dust than a cheap one. If you are willing to take the extra effort required for custom preparation, spend the extra money to buy quality materials.

EQUIPMENT FOR BODYWORK AND SURFACE PREPARATION

This is not a book on custom bodywork, but we will cover some minor dent filling, hole filling, and scratch removal in the course of our discussion on surface preparation. With this in mind, we will discuss basic bodywork equipment and equipment you will need for final surface preparation.

If you don't feel confident enough to do your own bodywork, let a professional shop do it. You could ask them to rough out the dent and then do the finish work yourself to save money. Most novices can remove basic dents with a few simple tools, so don't be afraid to try. Leave the major bodywork to the professionals, but give the little stuff a try—you'll be surprised at how easy it is.

For a few hundred dollars or less, you should be able to get enough equipment to efficiently handle most minor dents and all surface preparation work. This might seem like a lot of money, but for comparison, get an estimate from a body shop for the removal of some small dings and scratches. It doesn't take much damage to run up a repair bill of several hundred dollars. You'd be surprised at how minor a "$50 dent" can be until you stop to realize that most body shops are charging $15-$25 an hour for labor and material costs are added on top. A good way to rationalize the cost of the equipment is to remember that quality tools should last several decades or more, so the money will be well spent.

The best bet would be to buy a basic bodywork kit like those sold by Sears. For under $100 you can get a set of the most commonly used hammers and dollies. You can buy them separately, but they are generally a better value when bought together. Inexpensive basic bodywork kits usually include just one hammer and one dolly plus a dent puller, a file, and sanding equip-

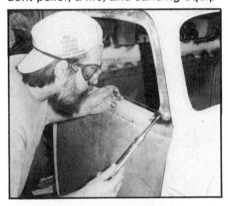

An acetylene welding outfit is not necessary for minor dent repairs, but it is essential for major bodywork or custom alterations like chopping the top on this early pickup.

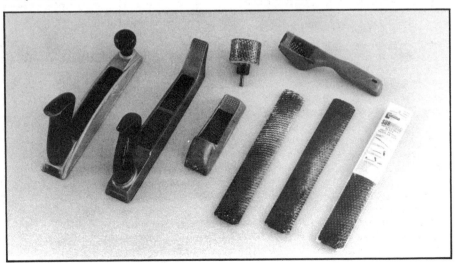

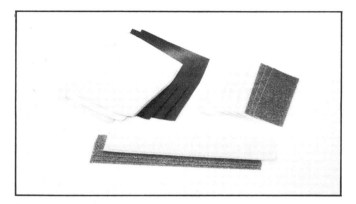

Sandpaper comes in several sizes, types, and grits. Sheets are for hand sanding, small strips fit jitterbugs, long strips are for sanding boards. "Wet or dry" paper is very fine and used primarily for finish sanding with water.

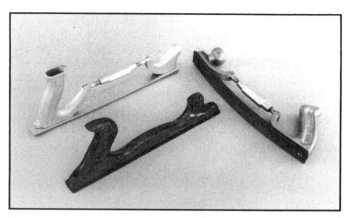

Vixen files aren't used much these days. They are for shaping or smoothing metal surfaces and were a mandatory tool back when all filling was done with hot lead.

ment. These kits are generally priced in the $20-$25 range. They will get the work done, but at those prices, they are not professional quality.

Besides hammers and dollies, there are other tools you may need to remove small dents. Body shops often use a tool called a Porta-Power, a hydraulically operated cylinder that pushes out the dent. A Porta-Power is great for serious bodywork, but it is expensive and more than the average do-it-yourselfer will ever need.

A good alternative is the slide hammer. Slide hammers work well for roughing out dents. You can buy professional models that have interchangeable end pieces for different pulling jobs, or you can get an inexpensive basic model that screws into the dented area. The only disadvantage to these sliding dent pullers is that after the dent has been pulled out, you will still be left with a series of small holes to fill. Also, you need to exercise care when using a slide hammer so that you don't pull the dent out too far and stretch the metal. (Once sheetmetal has been stretched,

it requires the use of a torch and a talented bodyman to shrink the metal back to its original shape.) Another type of dent remover is the suction cup puller—a simple rubber suction cup with a handle. These devices have limited pulling power but they work well for simple pop-in dents where the metal has not been stretched on wrinkled excessively.

Files are a very necessary tool for both bodywork and surface preparation. The two main types are the metal cutting files and the body filler files. The metal files are often called by brandnames, such as "Vixen" or "Kromedge" files. They are used in adjustable holders that bend the file for use on flat, concave, or convex surfaces. The body filler files are known as "cheese grater" files because they look and work very much like cheese graters. The most popular brand of body filler files is the Stanley Surform. They come in a wide variety of shapes and sizes and can be used with or without various handles. A Surform file is a must for working with body filler because it is the quickest way to rough

the filler into shape before the final sanding.

Torches are standard equipment for body shops and they can be very useful for the home bodyman, although they do require some formal training to learn proper usage. A gas torch and an arc welder are both useful for bodywork. Professional welding equipment can get expensive, but a good compromise for the home shop is one of the smaller welders that have recently become available. In most cases, a small oxy-acetylene welding kit would be the best bet for a beginning bodyman. These welders won't handle very big work, but they are fine for small jobs, like filling trim holes.

In the past, air tools were available largely to professional bodymen, but due to improved manufacturing and competitive pricing they are now affordable for even the average do-it-yourselfer. Of course, a good air compressor is necessary to power air tools, but we assume you will either buy or rent a compressor for your paint work. Air tools are the best way to eliminate

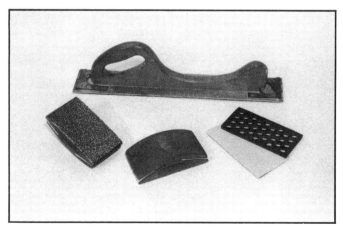

The object of sanding is to make the surface smooth—a sanding block does this much more effectively than your hand. The long sanding board is indispensable for leveling body filler in large areas. Small rubber pad fits inside folded paper to make a smooth hand-sanding block.

A body grinder fitted with a coarse disc is used primarily for cleaning the surface of old paint or rust. It is not designed for sanding down fillers or for smoothing the surface for paint.

the tedium of bodywork and surface preparation because they can supply virtually unlimited "muscle power." Most air tools cost less than $100 and many can be found in the $50 range, especially if you watch for sales or buy from mail-order tool companies.

Big companies like Rodac make a tremendous selection of air-powered tools but those most useful for custom painting are the sanders and grinders. Air chisels, shears, and saws are great for complicated bodywork, but for most people a selection of power sanders will suffice. As mentioned earlier, the sanders come in three basic styles: the dual-action orbital circular sander, the standard orbital-action sander which is also known as a jitterbug sander, the air file or straight line sander. A fourth tool that falls roughly into this category is the air grinder.

Each type of sander is designed to perform a specific job. The dual-action orbital circular sander (known in the trade as a "D-A") is great for feather-edging. Featheredging is the gradual layering of the paint around a ding or damaged area before it is filled with body putty or paint. The "D-A" also works well in relatively tight or curved areas. The jitterbug sander is the one that most closely duplicates the action of a hand-powered sanding block. The jitterbug is good for fine sanding prior to painting. The air file or straight line sander is a long, narrow sanding machine which is especially good for large areas. Its length protects against waves and ripples and it covers a lot of surface at a time.

Air grinders come in a variety of sizes with different angle grinding heads. They are best for removing paint all the way down to the bare metal, such as before filling a dent with body filler. Air grinders are usually used with coarse grit discs, so they shouldn't be used for final sanding before painting. Grinders are very often electrically powered rather than air powered. Electric grinders are much bigger than air grinders and rather heavy, but they can really do the job when the paint needs to be removed from a large area. All grinders rotate the disc head at very high speeds and throw a lot of sparks and debris, so always wear eye protection when using one.

Besides the air-powered machines, there are many "hand-powered" sanding aids. They are usually divided into the two categories, sanding boards and sanding blocks. The boards are longer than the blocks. Sanding boards have handles for single or two-

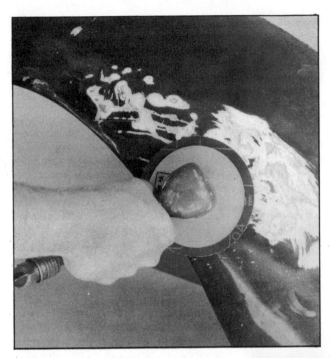

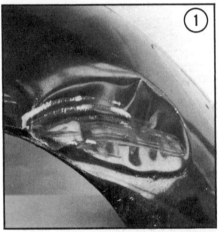

Most disc grinders are electric, but a variety of air-powered styles are now available as well. If you are going to purchase other air tools, you might prefer an air-powered grinder instead of an electric one.

This crunch in a VW fender may not look minor, but it is. The metal isn't severely stretched or folded, and is a good example of the type of dent you can fix at home with basic body tools and plastic filler.

handed operation. They come in various lengths but are usually 2-3/4 inches wide to accommodate standard sandpaper strips. Sanding boards are made of wood, plastic, or fiberglass. The rigid wood ones are best for making large panels ripple-free. The flexible ones work best on curved surfaces. Sanding blocks come in either rubber or plastic, with the rubber ones being preferred by professionals. Sanding blocks should be used to avoid depressions caused by your fingers if you sand without the aid of a sanding block or board. Sanding blocks work well for either wet or dry sanding.

Besides sanding blocks and boards, several other items can be used in conjunction with sanding. For small or awkward areas, a mixing stick can be used as a sanding board. A sponge will work on contoured areas, and 3M makes a special sponge pad for this use. Also, 3M makes tubular-shaped sanding blocks, called Handy Bands, for sanding contoured areas, reverse curves, and tight radius areas. A similar trick is to simply wrap a piece of sandpaper around a section of radiator hose or gas tank filler hose. The gas tank filler hose works quite nicely, if you can find it.

Sandpaper comes in a huge variety of shapes, sizes, and grits. If you have any doubt about the right paper for a specific job, explain your planned job to the counterman at the paint supply store. He will make sure you get the right paper for the job.

Sandpaper is designated by "grit" number. The higher the number, the finer the sandpaper. Grits used most

often for painting and bodywork range from 600-grit fine finishing paper to 16-grit sanding discs for paint removal. Sanding discs come in both open and closed-coat grits. Open-coat discs are best for paint removal because they are less prone to clogging. Closed-coat discs are preferred for metal finishing because the abrasive particles are closer together for a finer finish.

Sandpaper is available in wet or dry types. The dry paper is cheaper, but wet/dry paper (it can be used either way) can be used with water for a better and faster sanding job. Also, since the water carries away the debris, wet/dry paper tends to last longer than plain dry paper. Of course, sanding discs don't come in wet/dry because of the obvious hazard of using an electric grinder with water.

Sandpaper and sanding discs also are available with or without an adhesive backing. The adhesive-backed paper costs more, but it is a handy luxury if you are doing a lot of sanding. The adhesive-backed paper is especially nice for use with air-powered sanders, since they go through paper in a hurry. If you don't mind a little extra bother, 3M disc adhesive will keep your sandpaper firmly in place.

Regardless of what type of sandpaper you use, the most important thing to remember is the importance of changing paper often. If you continue to use paper that is worn, you are only wasting time and effort. Over-using sandpaper is false economy. A few other tips concerning sandpaper and sanding discs are worth mentioning here. Hold grinders close-to-parallel with the work surface (not more than a 10° angle). Use air-powered grinders and sanders only at their recommended air pressures, to insure efficient and safe operation. Be sure that backing pads are properly installed. Keep grinders constantly moving so as not to burn the paint (when polishing) or cut gouges. Don't start or stop a grinder when it is in contact with the surface and don't set a grinder down until it is completely stopped.

The last area of equipment and supplies to discuss are the chemical aids. The main chemical aids are those used for filling small dents, nicks, and scratches. These substances are broken into two groups: body filler and glazing putty. The body fillers are known by many tradenames (like "Bondo") and nicknames such as "mud," but they are all basically the same. Body filler is a two-part product that relies on a catalyst to harden the main resin-based compound. The key to proper use of body filler is to mix it correctly and to apply it smoothly with a minimum of bubbles. The amount of catalyst used during the mix determines how much time you will have to work the filler into place before it sets up. Temperature also affects the drying time, so use less catalyst on hot days. Ideally, you should mix the filler according to the instructions to get the ideal consistency. Filler that doesn't have enough catalyst can remain flexible indefinitely and cause serious problems if you paint over it. Too much catalyst can cause the filler to become brittle and crack or chip. And, to insure proper consistency, the catalyst must be thoroughly and quickly mixed throughout the base compound. If it is not mixed thoroughly, soft spots will be present after the putty hardens.

The smoother the filler is applied, the less time you will spend sanding the area. Carefully work out any air bubbles. Using the right size squeegee to apply the filler will make things

easier. Apply filler only in shallow "coats." Gouges in the metal should be brought out with bodyworking tools. If you must fill a deep depression with filler, do it gradually, so each layer of filler has sufficient time to dry and set.

Glazing putty, or spot putty as it is often called, is just very thick primer-surfacer. Putty should only be used for fine scratches or pin holes left after body filler is used and the area has been primered. Putty is applied in thin coats with a small rubber squeegee or a glazing (putty) knife. It has to be applied in thin coats in order to dry properly. Don't use putty to fill imperfections deeper than 1/16-inch.

Besides fillers, other chemicals you will encounter during surface preparation and bodywork are wax and grease removers, metal-etching and metal-conditioning solutions, primers, thinners, and paint removers. The best advice here is to use top quality, brandname products. For specific applications seek the advice of the counterman at your local paint store.

Whatever products you may use during the preparation of your vehicle for a custom paint job, be sure to use top quality products. Surface preparation is a vital part of custom painting—don't take chances or cut corners.

REMOVING DENTS

The scope of this book doesn't cover body customizing or extensive bodywork, but we will explain how to remove and fill simple dents. These are the annoying parking lot scars that are bound to show up on any car. If you are new at bodywork, limit your first efforts to shallow dents. Avoid the compound dents—those where the metal has been pushed in several directions or dents where the metal has been badly stretched. Leave these to experienced panel beaters.

The first thing to do before attempting to remove any dent is to study the damage. Try to figure how the damage was caused. By determining the sequence of events and the direction of force that caused the damage, it is possible to visualize and apply an opposite force to pull the metal back into original shape. This will make the job easier and eliminate unnecessary strain on the metal. Sometimes an over-zealous wack with a hammer can cause more damage than the original dent.

Although this step is not mandatory, it is nonetheless a good idea to clean the surface before you start to work. Wash the area with soap and

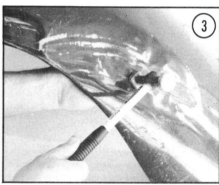

Using a body hammer and an appropriately shaped dolly, "rough out" the dent and shape the metal back to the original contour. At this stage use the dolly directly behind the hammer so that you don't bend the metal beyond the desired shape. Stagger the blows and work in a pattern to uniformly pull out the dent without stretching the metal.

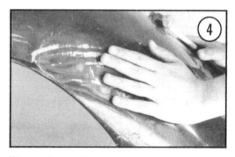

Throughout the process of dent removal, check the progress with the palm of your hand. The sense of feel can detect surface irregularities better than the eye. With experience, the hand quickly becomes very sensitive to even small high and low spots.

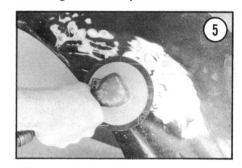

After roughing out the dent, remove the paint from the surface with a body grinder and coarse disc. Clean an area at least six inches larger than the dent itself.

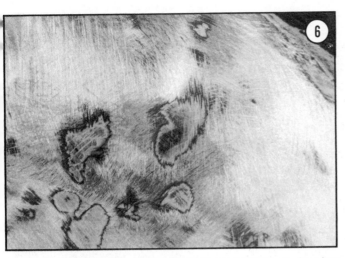

The flat grinding disc will strip paint from high spots, leaving some paint in the low spots.

Next, use a "pick" hammer on the backside of the dent, with a flat dolly on the other, to raise the visible low spots.

water and then wipe it with wax and grease remover. The surface will have to be cleaned eventually, and by cleaning the surface thoroughly you can study the damage closely and remove dirt or miscellaneous debris that may hamper your work.

Using whatever methods you prefer, rough out the dent. Try to form the metal as close as possible to the original shape. When you use a body hammer, tap gently and use a hammer with a head that is compatible with the final shape of the body panel. That is, use a flat head for flat surfaces and a curved head for curved body sections.

Rather than beating away at the panel in a random manner, it is a good idea to use a marking pen to plot the course of your hammer blows. Make X's where you should hit. If you are hitting the surface from behind, tap lightly with the hammer while holding your hand on the other side of the dent to "feel" the blows. Use arrows in your diagram to indicate which way the dent will be removed. Hammer blows should be staggered from top to bot-

tom and from side to side to remove the dent in a gradual manner that won't stretch the metal.

After the surface is roughed into shape, you will want to use a body hammer and dolly to do the final shaping. The basic idea behind hammer-and-dolly bodywork is to use the hammer on one side of the dent and the dolly on the other side to support the hammer blows. The dolly serves as an anvil to keep the hammer blows from stretching the metal in the opposite direction. This method is known as the hammer-on-dolly technique. Neither the hammer nor the dolly should be held very tightly. The idea is to bounce the blows off the surface. Hold the hammer close to the end of the handle, but don't grip it tightly. With a little practice you can feel and hear the hammer taps landing firmly on the part of the surface supported by the dolly.

The second type of hammer and dolly technique is known as the hammer-off-dolly technique. This is where the dolly is placed on a high spot

next to a low spot to be hit by the hammer. The hammer blow causes the dolly to rebound so a single blow will raise a low spot and flatten a high spot adjacent to each other.

With surprising speed you will learn to maneuver the dolly and hammer together to form the metal just as you please. While working out the dent, stop often and feel the area with the palm of your hand. Your hand can feel any high or low spots and guide you to the places that need additional work. Your sense of touch will quickly become one of the most valuable tools you have, and before long you will be able to judge the surface by feel almost better than you can with your eyes.

Dents that can't be reached with a hammer and dolly require the use of a slide hammer. Drill small holes in the panel to accept the screw threads on the end of the slide bar. You may have to pull at several different places to pull a deep dent. Start from the edge and work toward the deepest part of the crease. And, don't get overly enthusiastic with the sliding weight or you may

There will probably be a few high spots as well. Use the pick and dolly to bring them down. Before applying filler, you should get the surface as close to the desired shape as possible. Obviously, any remaining irregularities must be lower than the desired final surface so that the body putty can fill over them.

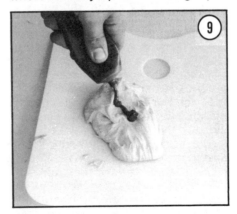

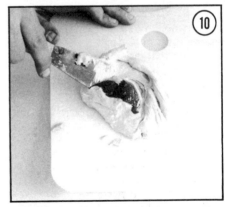

When you're ready to fill the dent, place some filler on a clean mixing surface and add catalyst according to the proportions recommended by the manufacturer. Mix it thoroughly but not so vigorously as to create air bubbles. More catalyst will speed hardening and less will slow the process. Higher temperatures will also speed setup, and vice versa.

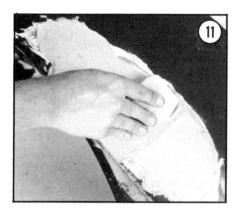

Quickly and methodically spread the filler over the dented area with a rubber or plastic squeegee of appropriate size. Again, it'll take practice to get the right feel for spreading filler smoothly, but the idea is to make long, even passes, pressing the material firmly into all crevices. Follow with succeeding passes to build up a smooth layer. Put on a little more than you need, since you'll be shaving it down to shape.

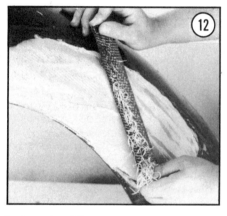

Before the filler has completely hardened, begin to shape it with a "cheese grater" file. The filler should come through the blade in long, rubbery strings. This is the time to remove as much excess filler as possible. If you wait too long, the filler becomes very hard and is much more difficult to file, but don't get carried away—the filler comes off very quickly when it's this consistency.

stretch the metal too much. If you don't have a dent puller or a slide hammer, small dents can be removed with the use of sheetmetal screws and a pair of vise grip pliers.

An expert bodyman can work a dent by alternately pounding with a hammer and heating with a torch until the metal is perfectly shaped to the original contour. As a beginner, you should get to a point where the dent is almost gone, but still is not perfect. This is the time to use the bodyman's best friend—body filler.

Remove all the paint from the dent area including at least an extra inch around the area to be filled. Apply filler only to bare metal, never to painted

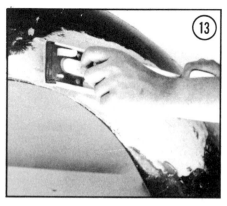

When the filler has hardened completely (at least 2-3 hours), sand it smooth with a bondo board and 40-grit Carborundum (open-coat) paper. Again, work methodically, shaping the surface but not removing so much material that you create low spots. On a curved surface it's best to sand diagonally to the curve, in two directions.

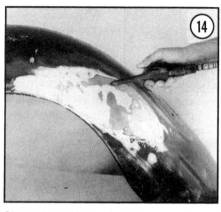

Clean the surface with an air nozzle and run your hand over the repair to check for any irregularities. If any high spots are left (usually showing as bare metal), pick them down with a hammer and repeat the filling and sanding process. When you've got it close to perfect, block-sand with paper of about 80- to 120-grit and blow the surface clean.

surfaces. A coarse, open-coat disc on a grinder is the best way to remove the paint and leave an area with enough "bite" for the filler.

Mix the filler according to the directions and apply with a plastic spreader. Use a large spreader and press the filler into place with one or two strokes. If you "work" the filler as it dries, the surface will become rough and air bubbles will form inside the filler.

The key to smoothly and quickly finishing an area of body filler is to know when it is just right for the cheese-grater file. When the filler first starts to set up, but before it is hard, pull the grater firmly across the filler surface. If the filler will come through the cheese grater in long strings it is time to rough the filler into shape using the grater. At this time you can remove

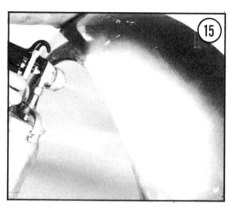

Shoot the repaired area with a liberal coat of primer, let it dry, then sand it down with 180 or 220 dry paper. Check the surface again with your hand. If it's not perfectly smooth, a couple more coats of primer and block sanding may be necessary.

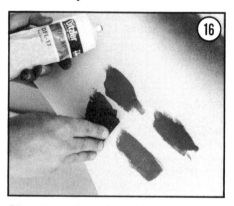

After the primer has dried, pin holes (caused by air bubbles in the filler) or deep sanding scratches can be filled with spot putty applied very sparingly. After this is dry, block-sand with 180 or 220 paper and apply a final coat of primer.

filler quickly and easily. If you wait too long, the filler will harden and it will be much more difficult to work the filler.

After using the cheese-grater file to achieve the basic shape, use an air file or a sanding board to finish smoothing the filler. When you are through sanding, use your hand to feel for any high or low spots. High spots that show up as bare metal protruding through the sanded filler may have to be recessed with a pick hammer. A thin second coat of filler will be needed to bring up low spots. At first you may have to use several applications to get a smooth, evenly-contoured surface, but as you gain experience with fillers, you will find that you can smooth a dent with fewer and fewer applications of body filler.

When the area covered with body filler is sanded and primered, you will probably notice some small pin holes caused by bubbles in the filler. Fill these holes with a thin application of glazing putty. After the putty dries, block sand with fine sandpaper and the area is ready for a final coat of primer. Inspect the area once more after the primer dries as the primer will make small flaws more visible. If there are any bothersome flaws, apply another coat of spot putty, sand until smooth, then apply a final primer coat.

MINOR DINGS AND SCRATCHES

If there is a dent in the sheet metal, the area must be ground down to bare metal and filled with body filler. Apply and work the body filler as discussed in the section on repairing dents. The techniques used to apply body filler to bigger dents will also work well for smaller wounds like parking-lot door dings, rock chips, and scratches.

Areas where the dent is very shallow or where only the paint is damaged can be filled without any hammer-and-dolly work. If only the paint is damaged, the area can be fixed by featheredging the paint. Before featheredging, clean

the surface with soap and water followed by wax and grease remover. The purpose of featheredging is to make such a gradual transition between the damaged area and the rest of the paint that you can't feel any rough edges when you pass your hand over the spot. Featheredging exposes the different layers of paint in a tapered manner.

Wet sanding works best for featheredging. Use a sponge with a lot of water to keep the area wet and free of

HOW TO PULL OUT A BLIND DENT

Often a minor dent will occur in an area where the backside of the metal is not readily accessible, so you can't hammer it out. The quickest way to straighten such a panel is to pull the dent out with a slide hammer or dent puller.

Drill a pattern of small holes through the dented metal. The size of the hole will be determined by threaded head of the puller.

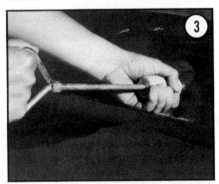

Screw the puller into each hole and slap the weight against the handle to pull the sheetmetal outward. Work from the outer edge toward the center of the dent, pulling the metal out in gradual increments.

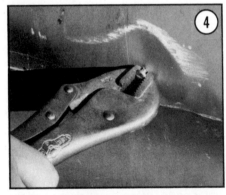

If you don't have a slide hammer, a large sheetmetal screw can be inserted into each hole and Vise Grip pliers can be used to pull the metal outward, but this will only work with small, shallow dents.

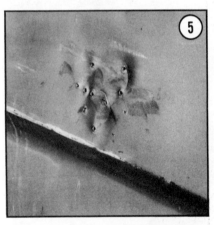

Here is the dent after the first round of pulls. A couple of spots that are still low should be drilled and pulled again.

When the surface is pulled out as smoothly as possible, clean the area with a grinder to remove old paint.

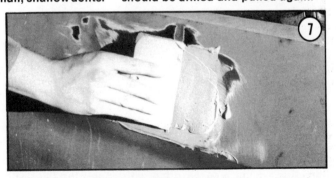

Prepare a batch of filler and cover the wound, letting the filler ooze through the drilled holes. Sand the surface smooth and primer it in the usual manner.

HOW TO FILL A MINOR DING

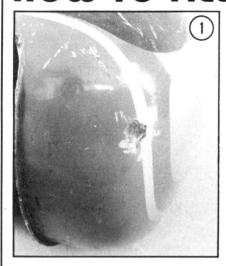

Little dings and dents, such as those caused by pebbles or parking lot dim-wits, can be filled without hammering or straightening the metal. This motor-cycle tank is a perfect example—access with a hammer and dolly is impossible, and drilling for a slide hammer would be foolish.

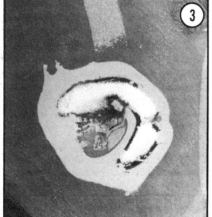

Begin by cleaning the area with a grinder and coarse disc.

Something must also be done with most dents to remove paint residue from deep recesses that a flat disc cannot reach.

A small rotary wire brush powered by a drill or air motor does an excellent job of cleaning hard-to-get residue prior to filling.

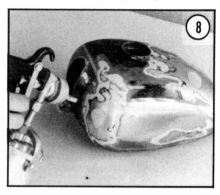

You'll only need a small amount of filler. Here we're mixing up a batch on an old dinner plate, using a popsicle stick to stir in the catalyst. Mix until no streaks are left.

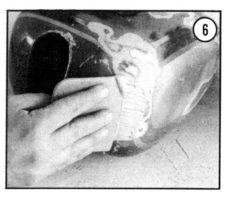

Apply the filler with a small squeegee. On a curved surface like this, bend the squeegee between your fingers to conform to the shape of the metal.

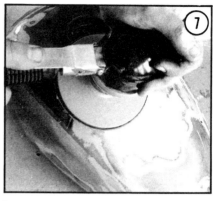

Smooth down the filler after it has dried. A cheese grater isn't necessary on small spots like this; a dual-action sander does the job quickly.

Follow with a coat of primer-surfacer.

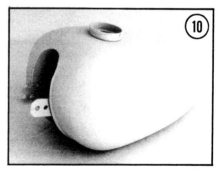

Finish sanding the area with 180 or 220 paper on a sanding block and feel for any further imperfections. If necessary, add a coat of spot putty and sand and primer again.

The finished repair is smooth and invisible.

sanding debris. Use a sanding block or sanding board to keep the sanding media smooth and even. The larger and more gradual the featheredge, the better the repair will be. Primer should be applied to the repaired area. After the primer dries, sand it lightly with fine paper. You shouldn't be able to see where the scratch was. If you can, additional featheredging or an application of spot putty is called for.

The average car or truck body may have dozens of tiny dings and scratches. Carefully locate them and circle them with a marking pen. Every one of these minor flaws needs to worked out if you want a truly fine paint job. It may seem like a tedious task, but the final result will be a smooth surface and a fine custom paint job.

HOLE FILLING

One of the most basic customizing tricks is the removal of trim pieces and subsequent filling of the mounting holes. This is not particularly difficult, so you might want to clean up your car's lines a little before painting by removing some trim pieces.

The small holes are the easiest to fill. Very small holes like those left by a dent puller can be filled with body filler. Trim holes can be filled by this method too, although there is some danger of the filler popping out of the hole at a later date. If you have access to the area behind the holes, try securing a piece of fiberglass cloth or mat behind the holes. This will give the body filler something better to grip.

The best way to fill small trim holes is with a welding torch. Remove the trim piece and then surround the area around the holes with Moist Bestos (a substance available at welding supply stores that helps keep the surface cool to prevent warpage). Weld up the holes with 1/16-inch welding rod and then cover the weld with either Moist Bestos or wet rags to cool the area. After the welds have cooled, grind down any roughness with a grinder or a vixen file. Fill any imperfections with body filler. Sand, prime, and putty the area like any other body repair.

Larger holes like those left by an antenna need a piece of sheetmetal to fill the hole. Use the same gauge sheetmetal as the body to fill the hole. Make the plug and tack-weld a piece of welding rod to it for a handle to position the plug while welding. If you have an arc welder, use it to install the patch piece since electric welding will heat and warp the area much less than gas welding. Finish the patch by grinding, filling, priming, and sanding.

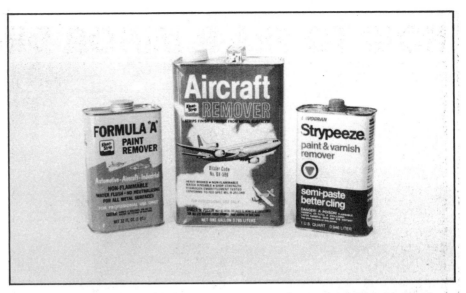

You can use standard furniture stripper (right) to soften and remove old paint from autos, but your automotive paint store should have something stronger to speed the process. Aircraft stripper (center) is best for old cars with several layers of paint.

PAINT STRIPPING

There are some professional painters who feel that a fine custom paint job cannot be applied over anything but bare metal. Most painters find this view a little extreme, but if you insist on a ground-up, restoration-type paint job, stripping is necessary.

Paint stripping is best reserved for very old cars with many layers of old and damaged paint. The bad news about paint stripping is that there is no easy or inexpensive way to do it. Either you do it yourself, which is very tedious, or you can have it done at a commercial stripper, which will still involve a fair amount of disassembly work on your part.

Home paint stripping requires the use of caustic chemicals. They can be very harmful to your skin and the fumes are also quite hazardous. The paint stripper is applied with a brush and left to attack the paint. After the paint bubbles up, it is scraped off with a putty knife. Depending on the amount of paint, you may need to apply more than one coat of paint remover. Even after several coats, there will be areas that just don't want to lift. These areas will have to be sanded.

Commercial paint strippers (also known as rust strippers) are the easiest and most thorough way to remove paint, although the cost is considerably more than home paint stripping. Either individual parts or the whole

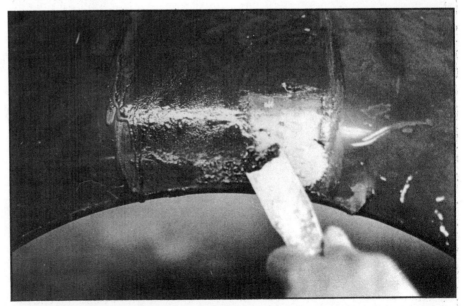

Chemical stripper will soften and loosen old paint so that it can be scraped away with a putty knife, wire brush, or a jet of hot water. Always wear rubber gloves and safety goggles when using strippers.

One big difference between a first-rate paint job and a one-day "quickie" is that all parts not to be painted are removed rather than masked off. Strip the vehicle of bumpers, lights, handles, and all chrome trim or nameplates that are readily accessible. This step not only makes sanding and painting easier, but yields a more professional-looking finish in the end.

After cleaning the surface with wax and grease remover, wet sand the entire car with 320 wet-or-dry paper. Keep a bucket of water nearby to keep the surface liberally covered with water.

vehicle is dunked in a variety of chemical solutions to remove the paint and rust.

Another method of removing paint is by sandblasting. Sandblasting is usually reserved for heavy chassis parts that will not be warped by the force of the abrasives. Professional sandblasters that specialize in old cars can remove paint without damaging the body, but be sure you take your car to a shop that is experienced with fragile sheetmetal. There are also home sandblasting units that are suitable for small parts. However, sandblasting can leave a mess that will take weeks to clean up (the dust and sand will get into every little corner of your garage), so it is generally best to leave sandblasting to the professionals.

Paint can also be removed by sanding but this is the most tedious and time consuming method of all. And, if you are not careful, sanding with a power grinder can leave deep

scratches in the metal. Paint stripping is neither fun nor absolutely necessary, so avoid it unless you are willing to undertake a difficult and time-consuming job, and the end results will justify the efforts.

PREPARING FOR PAINT

Once you have completed any necessary bodywork, you are ready to prepare the surface for paint. If you didn't clean the surface before starting the bodywork, do it now. Start with soap and water and finish with an application of wax and grease remover. Follow the directions on the wax and grease remover container. Some types call for applying the wax and grease remover with one rag and wiping it off with another. Don't skip any steps, you may leave a coating of residue on the surface that will prevent proper application of the final paint.

Remove as much trim as possible.

The less masking you have to do, the better the paint job will be. Masking paper can trap dust and debris which will later fall on the wet paint. Remove the bumpers, grille, and anything else that comes off easily.

The amount of sanding required will depend on the age and condition of the underlying paint. If you are applying a mural to a new van, all that is necessary is a light sanding to rough up the surface, but if the paint is old and peeling, all the damaged paint will have to be thoroughly sanded. Whether you sand by hand or by machine, whether you wet or dry sand is up to you. As a general rule, it is a good idea to sand from the top of the vehicle to the bottom. This is par-

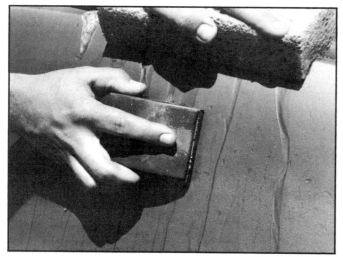

For an ultra-smooth finish, use a rubber sanding block while preparing the surface. You can dip a large sponge in water and let it trickle down on the sanding area to keep it well lubricated and to keep the paper free of accumulated sanding debris.

On concave surfaces, you can wrap the paper around a short length of radiator hose. On convex surfaces, you could use something like a rubber squeegee as a sanding block.

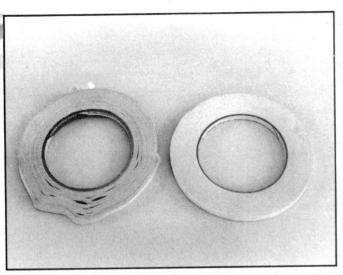

Masking tape is cheap compared to other painting supplies. Get plenty of fresh tape before you start masking. Old tape (on the left) is yellow, brittle, and won't stick securely to the surface.

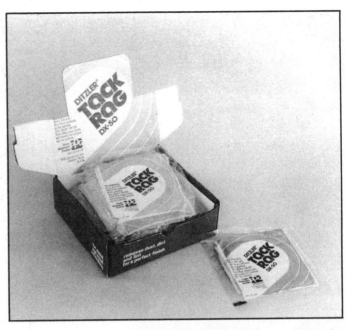

ticularly useful when wet sanding because the water carries away the sanding debris, leaving a clean, sanded area. If you choose to sand with air-powered tools, keep an air nozzle handy to blow away the debris. It isn't a bad idea to follow the machine sanding with a final wet sanding. To help keep the sandpaper clean and slippery when wet sanding, many painters put a little household detergent in the water.

When you think you've sanded everything as well as possible, let the surface dry and then check it out with the palm of your hand. If any areas need additional sanding, now is the time to catch them. Remember that any area where bare metal shows through must be featheredged.

MASKING

Once all the initial sanding is finished, it is time to mask the vehicle with masking tape and paper. It is important to realize that there is a difference between types of masking tape. Only use top quality, fresh masking tape. Old, cheap tape won't hold well and will let overspray creep into unwanted areas. The expense of redoing oversprayed areas is much more than the cost of quality tape. Old tape usually has a distinct yellowish color and the edges are often brittle.

Small areas and trim pieces can be covered with just the masking tape. Large areas, like windows, should be covered with masking paper. Masking paper is made by 3M and other companies, and is available at paint supply stores. You can use butcher paper or heavy wrapping paper, but masking paper is best. Newspaper will work in a

Masking paper is best for covering large areas, such as windows. This paper is inexpensive and protects against paint seepage (which can occur with other masking substitutes such as newsprint). It is available at most automotive paint stores.

When you are buying paint products, be sure to buy several fresh tack rags. After the car is masked, just before applying the paint, go over the entire surface with the tack rag to pick up any dust, lint, or other debris which could spoil the new finish. Refold the rag and turn it often so that will effectively pick up as much dust as possible.

If you are recovering a paint job that was in fairly good shape with a similar type of paint (e.g., enamel over enamel), primering might not be necessary. After bodywork, however, or over old and weathered finishes, a complete coat of primer is always a good idea. If you are changing paint types, or if the underlying surface is at all questionable, apply a coat of sealer or a combination primer-sealer.

Not only does a complete primer coat provide the best protection for the topcoat, but it also allows you to spot any dips, waves, pits, or scratches and fix them before proceeding any further. After the final primer coat has been applied, let the car sit for as long as practicable to let the primer shrink and "cure."

pinch, but it isn't recommended because it may become saturated with paint, causing the newsprint to bleed.

When applying masking paper, do your best to avoid folds that can catch dust and debris. Make the folds go under, or if there are outside folds, seal them with masking tape. After all the masking paper and tape is in place, go over it to be sure there are no loose edges or gaps where paint can enter.

PRIMING

With the masking out of the way, blow away any debris with an air nozzle. Then wipe down the whole vehicle with a fresh tack rag. The tack rag will pick up dust and sanding debris that the air nozzle missed. Mix the primer according to the directions on the can. Either enamel- or lacquer-base primer can be used (consult your local paint store and tell them what type of final finish you will be using). Some professional painters prefer enamel primer because they feel that it offers the best adhesion. Lacquer primer is preferred by high-volume shops because it is fast drying.

Don't apply primer in heavy coats. It is better to use light coats. Remember to apply a thorough coating because part of the primer will be sanded away during subsequent preparation steps. Primer has a tendency to shrink, so the longer it has to cure, the better. This isn't a critical problem but if you have the time, let the primer cure for a week or two. This is just one of those little tricks that can make a difference in a top-notch custom paint job.

After the primer has dried, block sand it with 320 or 400 grit paper. You can sand the primer either wet or dry, although wet is preferred. If you choose to wet sand, let the porous primer dry thoroughly before covering with paint, otherwise moisture can get trapped under the surface. Be careful not to sand through to bare metal. If you let the primer set for more than a few days, it will be necessary to remove all masking tape and reapply it before spraying the final coats of paint. Masking tape that is left in place too long gets brittle and is very difficult to remove.

The final step before applying the top coats of paint is to make sure the surface is completely free of debris. Blow it clean (especially the little crevices), wipe the surface with wax and grease remover, and go over everything with a new tack rag. Surface preparation is time consuming but effort invested here will result in a professional-looking job.

HOW TO PREPARE DOOR JAMS

An important detail that separates professional paint jobs from the "one-day wonders" is careful preparation and painting of less obvious areas, such as the door jambs, the engine compartment and the undersides of the hood and trunk. Clean, sand, and primer these areas when you prepare the rest of the car. After the entire vehicle is ready for paint, spray these "enclosed" sections first, allowing them to completely dry (a day or two) before closing the doors, hood, and trunk for final spraying of the exterior. It adds a day or two to the process, but it gives top-quality, professional results.

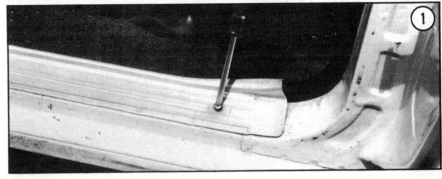

As on the exterior, begin by removing any trim or other parts that won't be painted.

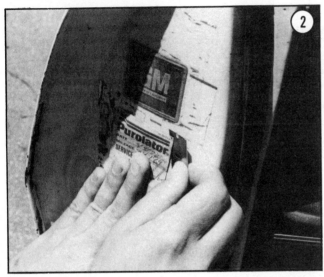

Peel off service stickers with a razor blade and clean away the glue residue with solvent or sandpaper. You can either remove rubber weather stripping and replace it with new rubber after the paint job is finished or, if necessary, you can carefully mask it off (new weather stripping may be quite expensive or difficult to find for some older vehicles).

Be sure to very thoroughly clean the door jambs and the underside of the hood and trunk with a good wax and grease remover. Lubricants and wax residue tend to collect on these surfaces.

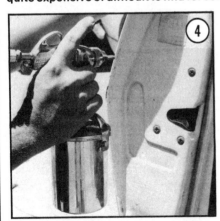

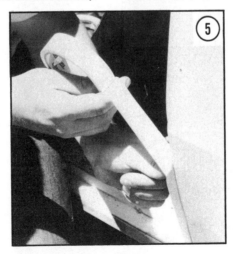

After thoroughly sanding down all surfaces to be painted (don't overlook those hard-to-reach creases and corners), mask off the interior and all areas that must be protected from overspray. Spray the surface with primer (if necessary), let dry, then shoot with a finish coat. A touch-up gun works beautifully for painting small areas like the door jambs.

If for some reason you do not want to paint the door jambs or underhood (e.g., you're repainting a car the same color or you are just adding some custom-color panels over the existing paint on a vehicle), you can keep the paint from penetrating into door, hood or trunk seams by "backtaping." Use tape at least one inch wide, run it along the jamb so that half of it protrudes, then fold it backwards and carefully close the door or hood so that the tape effectively seals the crack from the inside.

CHAPTER 5

PAINTING FUNDAMENTALS

- FINDING WHAT YOU NEED
- PAINT MIXING MADE EASY
- USING THE RIGHT AIR PRESSURE
- CORRECT SPRAY GUN TECHNIQUE

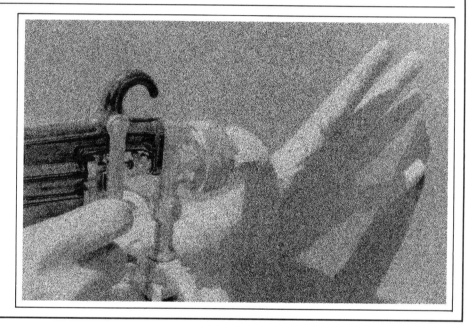

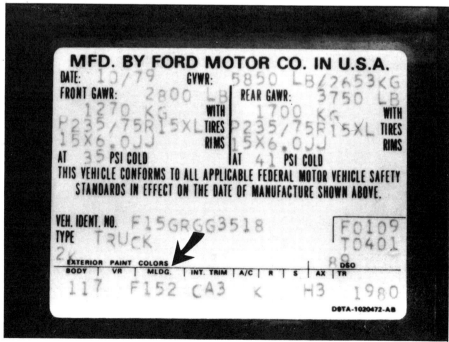

If you're restoring a vehicle and want to repaint it with the same factory color, find the i.d. or body trim tag that lists the paint code (as shown on the bottom line of this late-model Ford tag). Take this number to your paint supplier and he can order or mix a matching color for you.

THE MECHANICS OF PAINTING

Regardless of how "individualistic" a specific custom paint job may be, there are some basics steps that are part of every paint job. We call these steps the fundamentals of painting. The fundamentals include spray gun techniques, mixing paint, and setting up your equipment properly.

Most painting fundamentals are just good common sense. Others, like spray gun control, are easily learned and mastered with a little practice.

OBTAINING SUPPLIES

Before you begin, you should collect all of the needed supplies. If you are using custom paints, the type and color of the paint will very likely determine whether or not you use lacquer, enamel or a two-part paint. If you are repainting a car the same color as it was originally painted, check the code on the paint and color I.D. tag. This tag is usually located somewhere on the front portion of the car, usually on the firewall or front door jamb. If you take the paint number code to your local paint dealer, he will be able to give you paint that exactly matches the original. Even if you aren't doing a duplicate repaint, the paint number code can tell you if the car was originally painted in enamel or lacquer.

Another way to determine the original paint type is to place a large drop of lacquer thinner on the paint. Do this in a place where it isn't readily noticeable, e.g., the inside of the trunk or in a door jamb. If it starts to dissolve the paint, then the paint is lacquer. Otherwise, it is enamel.

The best way to select the type of paint you prefer is through experience. After a couple of paint jobs you will develop a preference for a certain paint. This is often based on the prevailing conditions where you are doing your painting. However, until you have enough experience, rely on that of others. The best place to get advice on paint selection is your local paint dealer. It is his business to know paint. He knows what is popular with local professional painters, what is new, and what should be best suited for your equipment and abilities.

It is a good idea to get all of your painting supplies at the same place. This way you will be assured of receiving products that are chemically compatible. Buying all of the required paint at one time will insure that it is from the same "master batch." Quality control by paint manufacturers is excellent, but there is a remote chance of there being a slight difference between batches of paint. And, there is likely to be a slight color variation between different companies that make the same factory color, so stick with one manufacturer.

When buying your paint, get the right solvent for the job. Tell the counterman what time of day you plan to paint. The temperature at the time of application is important in selecting the best solvent. The counterman should also be able to help you estimate how much paint you will need (depending on the size of the vehicle and the number of coats you intend to apply). It is always a good idea to purchase a little too much paint, rather than not enough. If you run out of paint, it is very difficult to stop and go get more. On the other hand, you can always use the leftover paint for touchups.

Remember to pick up all related supplies while at the paint store. Get fresh masking tape, a good assortment of sandpapers with various grits, a couple tack rags, and several paint

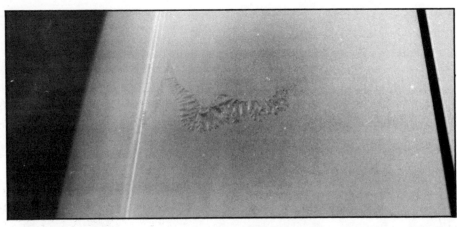

If you are painting over an already-painted surface, be sure the paints are compatible. Lacquers and certain catalyzed urethanes or acrylics can attack underlying enamels, causing them to lift and wrinkle.

strainers and mixing sticks.

MIXING PAINT

It may seem silly, but many paint jobs are less than satisfactory just because the paint wasn't properly mixed and strained. The importance of stirring paint can't be stressed enough. Paint pigment has a natural tendency to settle to the bottom of the can. Most paint stores have special racks that keep the paint well stirred or they have mechanical paint shakers. If you use the paint as soon as you get home, there should be no problems. If much time elapses, take the extra care necessary to be sure the paint is well

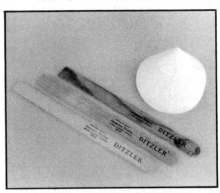

Mixing sticks and paint strainers are cheap, but very essential to a good paint job—never reuse dirty ones. Most paint stores will give you a free supply when you buy the rest of your materials.

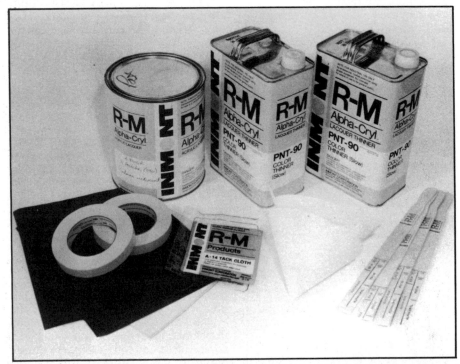

To assure compatibility of products, it's best to get all paints, thinners, sealers, and primers from the same manufacturer (especially if you're using modern two-part paints). To avoid bothersome trips in the middle of the job, get all the materials you'll need to complete the job: mixing sticks, strainers, sanding paper, masking paper, tack rags, and plenty of tape.

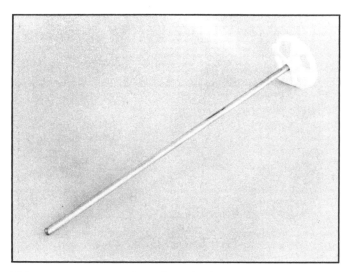

If the toner separates from the paint in the can, you won't get the proper color. Be sure to mix it thoroughly before thinning. This "mixer" fits into a drill motor for stirring gallon cans.

mixed.

Shake the can or turn the can upside down for a while to let the pigment mix with the binder or base materials. Open the can and use a stirring or mixing stick to thoroughly stir the paint. Be sure to scrape all pigment off the bottom of the can. Keep stirring until all the pigment is completely dissolved. All paints need stirring, even primers. Primers have a heavy pigment content and are very prone to settling. Metallic and flake paints also need extra attention to insure thorough mixing.

Mixing sticks are usually made of wood. Change sticks when you change colors. Or get a metal mixing stick that can be wiped clean with solvent after every use.

After the paint has been thoroughly stirred, you will need to dilute it with

Mixing is especially important with custom paints like pearls or metallics. These paints are infused with suspended particles that quickly settle to the bottom of the can.

Before spraying paint, you must reduce it in correct proportions with the proper thinner. Use a separate, clean container (such as an empty coffee can) to mix the paint and reducer. If you are painting an entire car, it is wise to reduce at least a gallon of paint before you begin, so you can refill the paint gun quickly without having to stop and mix more paint. You can probably obtain empty gallon containers for this purpose at the paint store. Keep the extra mixed paint covered while you're painting, and restir it before loading the gun.

either thinner or reducer (depending on the type of paint used). Read the directions on the paint can and follow them as to the type and amount of thinner. Use top grade solvents for the best gloss and paint flow-out.

You can either mix the paint in a separate container or in the paint cup. Drips can be avoided if you place a piece of masking tape on the rim of the paint can, or use inexpensive snap-on spouts for standard size paint cans. Regardless of where you mix your paint, always pour any paint that goes into your spraygun through a strainer. Even if you use a strainer on the pickup tube, it is still essential to strain the paint as it enters the paint cup. Conical strainers are available at your paint dealer. They fit neatly on top of one- or two-quart spray gun cups, so it is most practical to mix the paint with thinner in a separate container, then strain it as you fill the cup.

If for any reason paint should sit in the paint cup for any length of time, re-stir it. This is especially important with metallic paints. There are paint cups with built-in agitators for use with flake and metallic paints or you can put a couple of ball bearings or marbles in the paint cup. Shake the gun periodically and the marbles will help agitate

the flake particles.

After completing a paint job, keep the diluted paint separate from the unthinned paint. If you put the thinned paint back into the original container, the proportions won't be correct the next time you thin it.

AIR HOSES AND AIR PRESSURES

To get a good paint job, you need the right amount of compressed air. The length of the air hoses will affect the operation of the gun. The length affects the amount of pressure loss between the compressor and the spray gun. The length also affects the temperature of the air.

Just because the regulator on your compressor reads 50 pounds of pressure doesn't mean you have 50 pounds at the nozzle. The pressure delivery will drop (proportionally) as the hose length is increased. Smaller-diameter hoses lose more pressure than larger hoses (see the chart on page 33 for a comparison of pressure

losses at various lengths).

You could avoid pressure loss by using a very short air hose, but then the air temperature would also increase. Compressing air generates heat, so it is a good idea to have at least 25 feet of hose. You will also need at least this length to work around a full-size car without moving the compressor. Lay this hose out flat and it will aid in cooling the air.

If you would like to make a semi-permanent setup in your garage, you can use ordinary pipe to carry the air from the compressor to an air transformer (combination regulator and moisture trap). Then use a shorter length of hose between the transformer and the spray gun. Regardless of how your air hoses are set up, you should employ some type of moisture trap relatively close to the spray gun. Moisture can ruin an otherwise excellent paint job.

Besides using a pressure-drop chart, it is possible to determine the air pressure at the spray gun with a

Pouring paint smoothly from a full gallon container can be tricky, if not downright impossible. A snap-on lip for paint cans, or a screw-on spout for thinners, will make this task less bothersome and messy.

Although strainers are designed to fit neatly in the mouth of most paint-gun cups, a strainer stand makes refilling the cup a quick and easy job. It also lets you see when the cup is full.

remote pressure gauge. This gauge attaches to the base of the spray gun where the air line connects to the gun.

When determining pressure drops from our chart, remember that the air hose diameter is based on the smallest restriction in the system. If you use quick connectors of a small diameter, then this is the diameter to use, rather than the diameter of the air hose. As a general rule, a standard-size quick connector will reduce the air pressure at the spray gun by about one pound. Check all fittings and connections to be sure that there aren't any air leaks.

For air pressure settings, check the instructions on the paint can. If possible, keep pressures on the low side. This reduces overspray and places less strain on the compressor. And, to minimize overspray while doing small spot repairs, use less air pressure than you might normally use for a complete paint job. Generally speaking, primers should be shot at 40-45lb (pressure at the spray gun), sealers at 35-45lb, acrylic lacquer at 25-35lb for spot

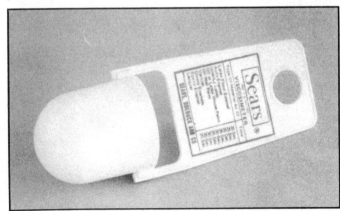

Most painters thin paint according to the directions on the label, but you can also use an inexpensive viscometer to thin paint to the recommended "drip rate." Such a tool is helpful if you must paint during weather conditions that can adversely affect the normal paint viscosity.

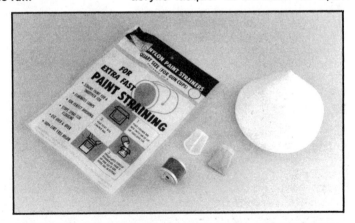

Always strain mixed paint before pouring it into the paint cup. Either the throw-away type (right) or the resuable nylon strainer (left) are suitable. For extra protection from impurities, you can attach a small strainer (center) to the pickup tube in the spray gun.

AIR PRESSURE RECOMMENDATIONS	
MATERIAL	PRESSURE AT GUN (PSI)
PRIMERS	40-45
SEALERS	35-45
ACRYLIC LACQUER	SPOT REPAIRS: 25-35 COMPLETE JOBS: 40-45
ENAMEL	COMPLETE JOBS: 50-60
ACRYLIC ENAMEL	COMPLETE JOBS: 60-65

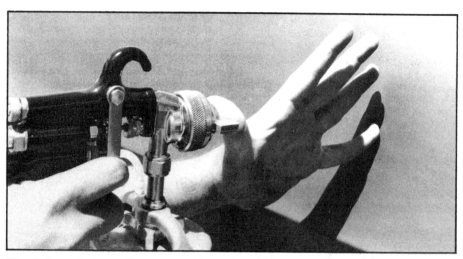

The distance between the gun and the surface is critical and depends on the type of paint you are using and the air pressure at the gun. For most automotive paints, the span of your hand is about the proper distance.

repairs and 40-45lb for complete jobs, enamel at 50-60lb (complete jobs), and acrylic enamel at 60-65lb for complete jobs. Remember that air pressure figures aren't valid unless the paint has been thinned according to the manufacturer's directions.

SPRAY GUN TECHNIQUE

The spray gun is where it all comes together. All of your preparation work is either worthwhile or wasted time, depending on how you handle the gun. It's true that color sanding can remove mistakes from a lacquer paint job, but the best way to get a perfect paint job is through excellent preparation combined with the proper spray gun technique.

The standard spray gun is a precision instrument, and you will have to make a few adjustments to insure a proper pattern as the paint leaves the gun. As long as you take good care of your spray guns and keep them clean (see the chapter on equipment maintenance) you should only need to make minor pattern adjustments each time you paint.

At the back of the spray gun above the handle, there are two adjustment screws. The top one is called the air-adjustment screw and the bottom one is called the fluid-adjustment screw. The air-adjustment screw controls the shape of the fan (you must also adjust the incoming pressure with the air regulator to maintain correct volume proportional to the fan shape.) The amount of air determines the spray pattern of the paint. For this reason the air-adjustment screw is also known as the pattern control. The farther the knob is turned in (clockwise) the smaller and rounder the pattern gets. By turning the knob counterclockwise, a fan shape will appear. Practice setting the control knob and spraying patterns on a piece of cardboard. Generally speaking, if the area to be painted is large, you will want a larger pattern.

The lower knob, or fluid-adjustment screw, controls the amount of paint that flows through the gun nozzle.

Turning the knob as far clockwise as possible will shut off the fluid. Turning the adjustment screw counterclockwise will open the fluid valve and let more paint pass. As the pattern size is adjusted wider or bigger, more fluid will be needed. Accordingly, open the fluid valve for large-area patterns and close it down for small-area spot repairs. The air and fluid adjustments work together, so practice coordinating both controls for large and small patterns.

There are a few other items that affect the paint pattern. The distance that you hold the spray gun from the surface is important. This distance is affected by the type of paint, the temperature, and the amount of thinner being used. The ideal distance is one that allows the paint to cover well, without runs and with a minimum of overspray. Each paint job is slightly different, so you will need to experiment a little. As a starting point, though, hold the gun between 8 and 10 inches

No matter how good your equipment, materials and surface preparation, the crux of a paint job rests in the handling of the spray gun. It takes practice to develop the right technique, so practice on something other than a Rolls Royce. Develop a comfortable feel for the gun, releasing the trigger, and keeping the hose out of the paint. After a few paint jobs, it becomes second nature.

from the surface. With lacquers you can usually hold the gun closer to the surface.

The condition and position of the air cap or nozzle also affects the paint pattern. We will assume that the air cap is completely clean and free of debris. Otherwise you will get very irregular spray patterns. Never attempt to clean the holes in the air cap with any metal object. This will cause permanent damage and pattern distortion. The other pattern adjustment that relates to the air cap is whether it is in a horizontal or vertical position. The standard position is horizontal, which yields a vertical pattern. This pattern is best for the typical side-to-side motion used to cover large surfaces. By loosening the knurled outer ring you can turn the air nozzle to a vertical position (remember to retighten the outer ring before painting), which gives a horizontal pattern. This pattern is good for areas like door jambs or other surfaces that require an up-and-down motion of the gun.

The actual control of the spray gun is something that can be learned with a surprisingly small amount of practice. The more you paint, the sooner gun

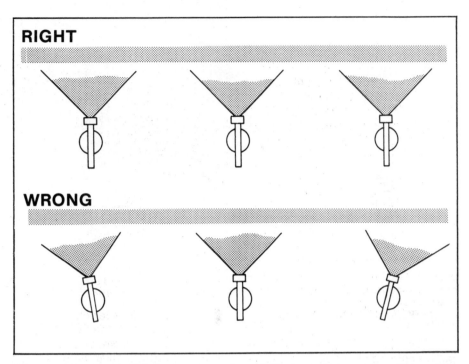

RIGHT

WRONG

When making a pass with the spray gun, keep it the same distance from the surface at all times, and do not swing it in an arc at the start and end of the pass. If you move the gun away from the surface, thin spots will result. If you arc the gun too close to the surface in the middle of a pass, a run or sag may occur.

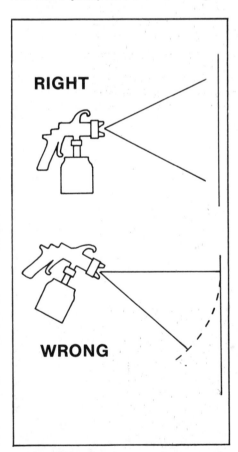

RIGHT

WRONG

Do not tilt the gun up or down as you spray. Keep it parallel to the painting surface at all times so that the fan will provide equal coverage over the entire pattern.

control will become second nature to you. When spray gun technique becomes a natural habit, you can devote all of your attention to other factors that affect the paint job. The main concern with spray gun control is uniformity. You want to spray the same amount of paint on all parts of the vehicle. The spray gun should be kept parallel to, and a uniform distance from, the surface at all times. The spray should always hit the surface at a perpendicular angle. In other words, don't arc the gun and don't tilt it.

Arcing or swinging the spray gun is one of the most common mistakes. This technique will give a paint coating that is too thin on the ends and too thick in the middle. Arcing can be caused either by arm movement or by moving your wrist at the start and finish of each stroke. It is best to keep your wrist still. Instead of moving your wrist to control the start and finish of each stroke, use the trigger. Start each pass off the panel and smoothly pull back on the trigger so that when the gun reaches the panel, paint is being emitted from the gun. Release the trigger at the other end of the panel but continue the stroke a little further.

Besides the importance of not arcing the spray gun, it is also important not to tilt the gun. When you tilt the spray gun the top part of the pattern is heavier than the bottom part. Tilting the gun is also conducive to runs. It may seem very difficult to spray a roof or hood without tilting the gun,

but this is where dripless paint cups help. Even if your spray gun didn't come with a dripless cup, you can buy such a cup at your local paint store. Usually, you can remove your present paint cup and substitute the proper dripless model. If you must work with a standard paint cup, it is a good idea to tie a clean rag around the lip of the cup to catch any drips.

Each stroke of a typical pattern should overlap the previous one by 50%. The gun should be moved at a rate of approximately one foot per second. Never stop or hesitate in the middle of a pass or else you are likely to get runs in the paint. Paint from the top downward. This will help to avoid overspray on a previously painted area. Since each pass is overlapped, the first stroke should either hit the masking paper or be shot partially into the air. The last stroke of a panel will also be shot half off the vehicle. This way the edges also receive a full coat of paint, avoiding light spots.

Always try to work in a manner that insures you are painting next to wet areas instead of dry ones. Don't start at the front left corner of a vehicle and work around in a 360° circle, because by the time you get back to where you started you will be spraying wet paint next to paint that is already dry. Remember to spray door jambs and hood and trunk edges before you start on the rest of the vehicle. In fact, most painters do these areas a day before the rest of the job so that the vehicle

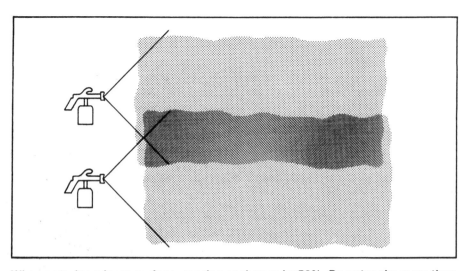

When spraying a large surface, overlap each pass by 50%. Do not make more than one pass in the same place. If the area needs a second coat (or more), repaint the entire section, or the whole car, so that one area does not get a thicker coat than others. If you are applying several coats of light-colored or transparent (candy) paints, you can "cross coat" to gain even coverage: apply one coat horizontally, the next one vertically and so on.

can be painted with doors, hood, and trunk closed.

There are several ways to work when painting a whole vehicle. An example is to start on the roof and then go to the right door, right rear fender, trunk, left rear fender, left door, right front fender, hood, and end with the left front fender. Another sequence is: roof, hood, left front fender, left door, left rear fender, trunk, right rear fender, right door, and right front fender. Always start at the top, then work around the vehicle painting each section completely in turn.

There are several types of paint coats. Follow the directions on the paint can for the type needed for each specific paint job. A pattern where you apply the standard 50% overlap just one time around the entire car is called a single coat. A double coat is where you repeat the single-coat procedure immediately. Usually enamel is applied in single coats and lacquer is applied in double coats.

Paint coats are also distinguished as light, medium, and heavy coats. This relates to the amount of paint applied with each pass. You will also see the terms mist coat and dust or tack coat. A dust coat or tack coat is a very light one that is applied before any other paint is applied. It will not cover the surface with an opaque layer, but it produces a "sticky" surface to help keep the next heavy coat of paint from running. A mist coat is a final coat that is mostly thinner. A mist coat will produce gloss by reducing any overspray left on the surface.

A term that often comes up in relation to types of paint coats is "flash time." The directions will say "allow the paint to flash," which means the time it takes for most of the solvents to evaporate. You can usually tell when paint has flashed because a slight dulling occurs.

Another term that is often used with certain types of paint is cross coating or cross hatching. This refers to the practice of applying half of the coats perpendicular to the other coats. With candy paints this technique helps prevent streaking.

The spraying techniques used for full-size spray guns also apply to touch-up guns and airbrushes. The fluid- and air-adjustment controls are even the same on most touch-up guns. Airbrushes have their own adjustment systems.

The two important things to keep in mind are uniformity and practice. Keep your motions smooth and uniform; practice a lot and before you know it, you will be handling a spray gun like a pro.

SHOP SAFETY

The idea of shop safety is about as popular as flossing your teeth, but like the dentists say, it's for your own good. Shop safety should never be overlooked because painting involves some potentially harmful conditions. Paint and many related supplies are quite flammable. Paint fumes can also be quite toxic. For these reasons it pays to have a clean, safe painting area.

Fire can be a very real hazard. Keep paint in a safe location. It is a good idea to store supplies in a metal cabinet. Any large quantities of paint and thinner should be stored away from your work area, preferably in a separate metal shed. Keep all containers properly sealed when not in use. Never smoke or allow open flames near painting areas or paint storage areas. Keep all electrical connections and tools in good condition so there is no possibility of an electrical spark. Don't create an environment for spontaneous combustion by leaving piles of dirty rags or trash lying around your shop. Be sure to have at least two or more fully charged fire extinguishers in handy locations, just in case a fire should occur.

Ventilation is important for fire

When you are painting a whole car, decide how you're going to do it before you start. To keep overspray from falling on unpainted areas, it's best to start at the top and work down; but always paint entire sections completely before moving to the next. For example, paint the top, then the hood, then a front fender, then a door, and so on, until you have worked around the whole car.

prevention and your personal health. A large buildup of solvent fumes can be ignited by a small spark. Fumes can also be toxic and damage your respiratory system.

A top quality respirator or spray mask is the most important piece of painting equipment you can buy. Respirators may be clumsy to wear and not particularly comfortable, but they keep dust and harmful chemicals out of your lungs. If you do not wear a mask, fumes may only seem to irritate your throat, but over a period of time these "irritating" chemicals can cause serious lung problems. The fumes from two-part paints and clears are especially dangerous. Always wear a respirator, preferably one with replaceable filter cartridges. Renew the cartridges often and don't rely on the cheap surgical-type, paper masks. Remember that it is also important to wear a respirator when doing heavy sanding and when working with fiberglass.

Eye protection is also important, especially when doing surface preparation and bodywork. Whenever you do any grinding or hammering you should wear safety glasses or goggles. Of course, eye protection is mandatory when welding. Eye protection is also mandatory when using corrosive chemicals for metal conditioning or paint stripping. Be sure to wear rubber

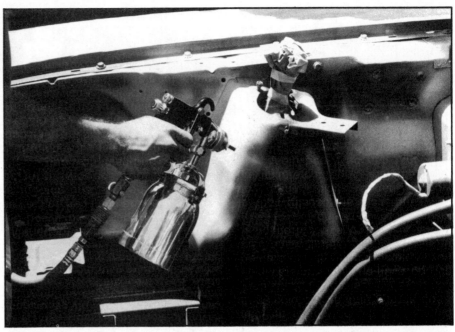

Wrist action is not conducive to good spray gun technique. Hold the wrist firm and move the entire forearm and upper body to make an even pass.

gloves when using hazardous or corrosive chemicals.

Keeping your work area clean and neat will also promote safety. Don't leave things where you are likely to trip on them. Avoid spills that may make the floor slippery. A clean work area is not only safer, it will also reduce the chance of airborn debris ruining an otherwise fine paint job.

No paint shop should be without an adequate, fully charged fire extinguisher, especially where welding might also be done. If you're using paint products at home, keep a reliable extinguisher handy.

If you're adding several custom colors to make a creative pattern on a car or van, you'll end up with a clutter of cans on your workbench. This makes the job seem more difficult, leads to dirt in the paint and is a possible fire hazard. Take a couple of extra seconds to close cans tightly and store them out of the way.

CHAPTER 6

WHAT TO DO ABOUT MISTAKES

- OPPS!...RUNS, DRIPS, AND SAGS
- ORANGE PEEL, FISH EYES AND DEBRIS
- BLUSHING AND BLEEDING
- PIN HOLES IN FILLER
- SANDING SCRATCHES
- EXCESSIVE OVERSPRAY

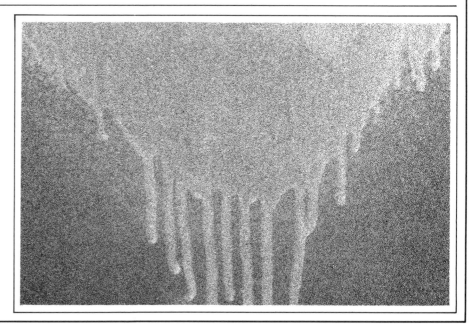

COMMON PAINTING MISTAKES

The ability to deal with painting mistakes separates professional painters from amateurs. The pro realizes that mistakes are a part of painting. They are costly from a time standpoint, but they happen.

Professional painters know how to handle small mistakes, but beginners tend to panic when even the most basic problem surfaces. This usually leads to further, more complicated problems. The best advice for beginners is to take extra precautions in the first place so you don't have to deal with problems at all and if you encounter a problem, stay calm so you don't ruin the rest of the paint job. The idea is to identify the problem as soon as possible and remedy it, if possible, without having to start the job over from the beginning.

When it comes to problems the beginner has one big advantage over the professional: time. A pro usually has a tight schedule and down-time is lost money. Shop overhead (rental,

One of the best and easiest ways to avoid mistakes is to use materials the way they were designed. Read and follow the directions on the labels of all paint products. Many paint and equipment manufacturers also offer helpful brochures for the use of their products.

insurance, wages, etc.) is high no matter if the painter is producing income or not. This means that pros will often be forced to paint under less-than-favorable conditions. They have professional equipment but even a spray booth won't overcome temperature or humidity problems (unless it's

a super-expensive, controlled-environment booth). To keep production going all the time pros often ignore the manufacturer's instructions and use their own "trick" techniques. For their specific conditions these non-conventional techniques may (or may not) work, but the beginning painter should always follow instructions to the letter. In a way, the amateur is very lucky. Without high-volume production demands, you can wait until conditions are most favorable to produce a top quality job.

One of the best ways to deal with mistakes is not to make them in the first place. Dirt is one of the most common and most easily avoided problems. Dirty equipment, especially the spray gun, will cause poor paint application. A dirty painting area is an inexcusable source of debris that can get into the paint job. Any dirt, wax, or grease left on the vehicle through improper surface preparation will surely spoil a paint job. Keeping every aspect of your painting operation as clean as possible is the best way to

If you get a run like this, stop painting immediately. You're doing something wrong! The most probable cause of runs is holding the gun too close to the surface or not passing the gun evenly across the surface.

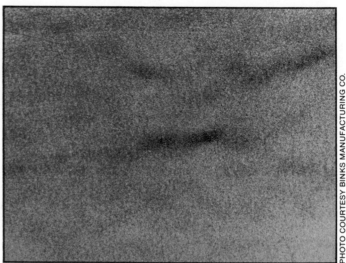

Sags are harder to detect and sometimes do not appear until after the job is almost done. The usual cause is application of too much paint in one area. Sags occur most often on vertical surfaces.

avoid mistakes.

Reading labels is another excellent way to avoid common mistakes. An alarming number of beginning painters assume they know more about paint than major paint companies and they don't take the time to thoroughly read (and follow) the manufacturer's instructions. You will avoid many of the so-called "stupid" mistakes if you just read the complete instructions on every container of painting product you apply to your car. In fact, you would be well advised to read as much as you can about painting in general, including the information catalogs available from several of the various paint manufacturers.

Taking your time is another vital step in avoiding common painting mistakes. Don't rush any step of the job. If the recommended drying time between coats is two hours, wait the two hours, rather than trying to get by with a one-hour wait. Paint manufacturers want their products to be as easy and quick to apply as possible, so they wouldn't suggest a specific waiting period unless it was necessary.

Lots of practice will help you avoid mistakes. Take as much time as necessary to learn how your spray gun functions. Practice adjusting the controls while painting on pieces of cardboard or scrap material, or if possible, practice on an old fender or similar sheet metal. Experiment with the distance you hold the spray gun from the surface. Find out just how close you can get before the paint runs. When experimenting with runs, remember that factors like paint thickness, type of thinner, and weather conditions also affect whether or not paint will run. Vary the air pressure from the com-

pressor to see what effect it has on painting. The more you know about what causes a problem, the easier it is to avoid or rectify. Practice is really the key to consistent results because the more experience you get, the more confident you will become and the less likely to make mistakes.

The final tip on avoiding mistakes is to stay calm. Don't automatically assume that a tiny mistake means the downfall of your custom paint job. As soon as you spot a mistake, stop applying paint to the vehicle. Play with the spray gun on some scrap material to find out if the problem is in the gun or on the surface. If it is the spray gun, rectify the problem before resuming your work. If the problem is caused by the environment, stop painting until you figure out what is wrong. Often an environmental problem can be solved with a simple change in the type or amount of thinner used. If the problem is in the surface, you will probably have to stop and wait until the paint is dry.

Then solve the problem, fix the area, and start painting again. By using the right materials, what seems like a major problem can actually be fixed very easily. For instance, runs can plague beginning painters, but by using lacquer paints you can stop worrying about runs because they are easy to sand out and repaint.

The following is a rundown of typical problems and how to prevent and correct them.

RUNS, DRIPS OR SAGS

Regardless of what you call them, runs or sags are a common problem for novice painters. Technically speaking, you could say that a run is longer than a sag. In any case, they are both caused when the paint slides away from where it is supposed to be, either because of poor adhesion or because the paint is applied too heavily. The excess paint breaks away from the surface and sags downward.

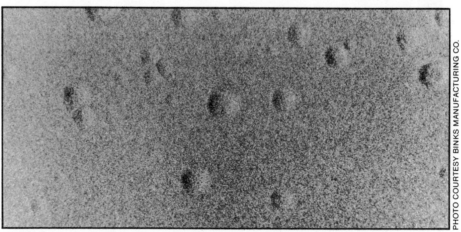

A severe case of orange peel looks just like an orange peel. The cause is usually insufficient reduction of the paint or use of an improper thinner.

Most enamel paint jobs will exhibit some degree of orange peel because the surface is not rubbed smooth as are most lacquer paint jobs. By using a reducer with the correct drying "speed," the proper air pressure and a deft spray gun technique, a good painter can lay on enamel that will flow out like glass...but it's not easy to do. The owner of this vehicle obviously approved of the slightly orange-peeled finish before adding the delicate brush work.

The causes of runs or sags may be related either to painting technique or improper preparation. One of the most common causes is not using enough thinner or reducer. As a result there is too much paint in relation to the amount of evaporative materials. Insufficient air pressure will cause sags because the paint isn't able to properly atomize. Applying too many coats of paint, too quickly, will cause drips. Very slow thinners are quite run-prone. Improperly cleaned surfaces cause runs because the paint can't adhere as it should. Temperature extremes, especially extreme cold, can cause runs. An improperly adjusted spray gun that shoots a distorted pattern can cause sags because part of the pattern will be applying more

paint than the rest of the pattern. Likewise, a gun adjusted for too much material flow in relation to air can cause runs. Holding the spray gun too close to the surface is another common cause of this problem.

The prevention for these ills is virtually self-explanatory: use the right thinner; reduce the paint properly; start with a clean surface; beware of temperature extremes; apply the paint in thin to medium coats; allow proper drying time between coats; properly adjust the spray pattern; keep the spray gun moving and held at the proper distance from the surface; and work in a well-lighted area so that you can see your work.

It is possible, though difficult, to repair a sag that is still wet. The sag can

be lightly brushed out with a very fine artist's paint brush. Another coat of paint must be applied over the mistake to hide any brush marks. The best way to repair sags, however, is to let them dry, sand the damaged area, and then repaint. This is much easier with lacquer-based paints than with ordinary enamels, but catalyzed acrylic enamels can be sanded and recoated after a drying time of 12 to 24 hours. Straight enamels, however, take a week or two to dry sufficiently for sanding and repainting.

ORANGE PEEL

Orange peel is another very common problem. In many ways it can be considered the opposite of a sag or run. The conditions that cause sags, when taken to the opposite extreme, cause orange peel. Orange peel looks just like its name. The surface is rough and pitted instead of smooth and glossy. It is primarily a problem with enamel paints, since most orange peel can be rubbed out of a lacquer finish.

Orange peel is created when the paint droplets fail to flow together properly after they land on the surface. The paint droplets must flow together to achieve a smooth gloss. Too much flow produces sags; not enough flow creates orange peel.

The use of very fast thinners or reducers will cause orange peel because the thinner evaporates before the paint gets to the surface, leaving a rough, orange peel effect. Holding the spray gun too far from the surface will also cause the paint to dry too soon, as

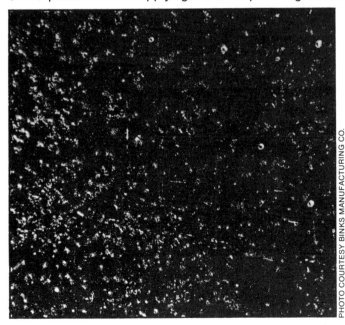

This is obviously a severe example of debris underneath the paint surface. A spot or two of dust, a hair, or an errant bug can spoil an otherwise-perfect panel on your paint job.

Just before the vehicle is ready to paint, blow off the entire surface with an air nozzle. Be sure to direct the airstream into all cracks and crevices, such as vents or hood seams where water, sanding dust or other debris may have collected. If you don't blow it out now, your spray gun will probably blow it into the paint. Follow this step with another pass of the tack rag.

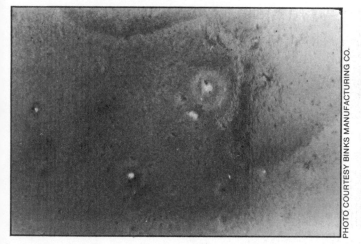

Fisheyes are small pinhole separations where the paint refuses to stick to the underlying surface. The usual cause is traces of silicone—a substance that is very difficult to remove—on the subsurface.

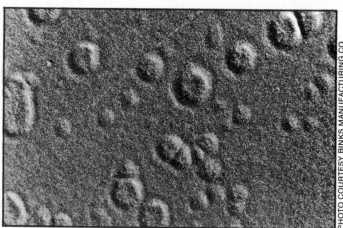

Severe fisheyes may be caused by an accumulation of grease or some similarly oily substance that will not allow the paint to adhere properly to the surface. The sure cure for this problem is to clean the surface thoroughly with wax and grease remover.

will the use of an excessively wide spray pattern or too much air pressure at the gun. Since this problem is related to the evaporating time of the solvents, temperature is also a factor. Painting on a very hot day is likely to cause orange peel, unless a slow-evaporating thinner is used. Another cause is spraying in a draft, because the wind will blow the paint away from the surface.

Orange peel is a relatively easy problem to cure. If the condition is severe, sand down the paint with 320- or 400-grit paper (wet) and apply another coat. In many cases, however, you may follow the orange-peeled coat with a second, wetter coat of paint that will flow out properly and fill the orange peel. With solid color lacquers or catalyzed enamels, you can sand out orange peel with 600-wet paper after the paint has dried thoroughly. Follow with rubbing compound for a smooth shine. Metallic or other trick colors, however, can produce "blushes" or color variations if color sanded too much. Such paints should be covered with clear before vigorous color sanding and rubbing out.

Prevention of orange peel includes the following precautions. Make sure your spray gun and air source are properly adjusted. Hold the spray gun the correct distance from the surface. Use the right thinning solvents for the prevailing conditions. Spray in a draft-free area. Use the lowest air pressure that still gives good paint atomization. Apply the paint in coats as wet as possible without getting sags. Try to keep the painting surface and the environment between 70° and 90°F.

DEBRIS IN PAINT

It is quite common for airborn particles to land on a newly painted car and create surface blemishes (especially if you are doing the work in your garage or driveway). When the paint dries, the surface looks rough and pock-marked. The main cause of debris in a paint job is the failure to thoroughly clean the painting area before starting the job. Professionals often work in an enclosed, well-ventilated spray booth, but home painters are forced to take extra care to maintain a clean painting environment.

Dirt can hide in a variety of places and it doesn't take much airborn debris to ruin a good paint job. Every seam, crack, and door jamb of a car is a potential source of dirt. Paint that either isn't strained or is improperly strained can be a source of debris. A dirty spray gun can eject particles of dried paint left in the gun from a previous paint job.

Small amounts of dirt in lacquer-based paint jobs can be rubbed out with rubbing compound. Debris in an enamel job is harder to remove. Let the enamel dry thoroughly. Then wash with water and try to dislodge small particles with a fine hand-applied polishing compound. Stubborn particles will have to be sanded out and the area repainted.

The best way to avoid dirt in a paint job is to keep everything connected with the paint job as clean as possible. This includes the shop, the equipment, and the vehicle to be painted. It is best to do your sanding and bodywork in an area separate from where you will be painting. For instance, sand the car and do bodywork in the driveway, then paint inside the garage. Before masking, thoroughly blow off the entire car with an air nozzle, being sure to get all dust, dirt, or water out of all seams, vents, door jambs, etc. After the car is masked, blow if off again, then go over the surface with a fresh tack rag. Always strain paint carefully and use a strainer in the paint cup. Sometimes it helps to lightly wet down the floor of the area where you are going to do the painting to keep down dust, but don't use too much water or the evaporating water can add humidity to the air and cause the paint to blush.

FISH EYES

Fish eyes are small separations in the paint surface, leaving little spots or craters where the subsurface shows through. Fish eyes don't always occur immediately. They usually appear as the paint is drying.

The major cause of fish eyes is silicone residue on the paint surface. Silicone is in many waxes and if all traces of wax aren't removed from the vehicle fish eyes are very likely to appear. Silicone and other surface contaminants can also be created by sanding dust, dirty rags, or greasy hands that touch the surface before painting.

The best way to prevent fish eyes is to thoroughly and properly clean the painting surface. Use a good wax and grease remover. Use clean rags (not commercial shop rags; they are cleaned in solvents that stay on the rags). Many commercial painters use a product known as fish eye eliminator in their paint, but this is not a proper substitute for thorough surface preparation.

If the surface is clean enough you shouldn't have to worry about fish eyes, but it is possible to test for fish eyes before you start painting. Cover a small test area with black enamel applied in a thin wet coat. If fish eyes appear, more cleaning work is re-

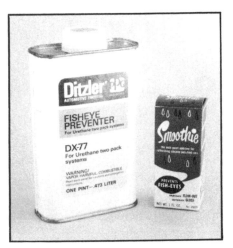

Since the advent of silicone polishes, fisheyes have become an increasingly difficult problem for all professional painters. The new two-part paints seem especially vulnerable to this problem. If you encounter them once you've begun painting, you could try adding some "fisheye eliminator" to the paint; but this is not a suitable alternative for thoroughly cleaning the surface before you begin.

quired. Wipe off the paint before it dries, and reprepare the area for paint.

There is no single solution for fish eyes if you encounter them while painting. You can stop and try to wipe the area clean with thinner or reducer if the paint is still wet, but you will have to clean and repaint the area. If the fish eyes aren't severe you can often let the affected area tack dry and then cover it with a second coat of paint. This will often fill in the fish eyes. (You might also want to add fish eye eliminator for the second coat.) If the fish eyes are really severe you will need to thoroughly sand or remove the paint, reclean the area, and start anew.

BLUSHING

Blushing occurs when a finish turns milky right after it has been applied. The milky, dull look is usually caused by moisture that condenses on the wet paint and reduces the normal glossiness.

Blushing very often occurs when you paint during humid weather conditions or if you create your own humidity in the spraying area. This can happen on a warm day when the floor is sprayed with water to hold down dust. The heat causes the water on the floor to evaporate and create an artificially humid condition. Too much air pressure can also cause blushing because air always contains some moisture. This is a good reason to use a water trap in your air line and to drain the accumulated moisture from the compressor air tank daily. Moisture can

also remain on the vehicle if it has been wet sanded. Be sure everything is completely dry (blow out all cracks and crevices with an air nozzle) before painting.

If you encounter blushing it can be remedied by adding a retarder to the paint or switching to a slower reducer. Small cases of blushing can be cured by spraying a coat of retarder or high-grade thinner over the blushed area. This should dissolve the blushing. In extreme cases it will be necessary to sand the area and repaint.

Blushing can be prevented by not painting during humid conditions. (Rainy days are a bad time to paint because of the higher risk of blushing.) The proper use of a retarder will also help eliminate this problem.

BLEEDING

Bleeding occurs when a former color shows through new paint. This is caused when the pigment in an old color dissolves in the solvent of the new paint. The result is the same as spraying two colors at one time—the final color becomes a blend of the two colors. Certain color combinations are very prone to bleeding. Shades of red and maroon are the worst offenders, especially when covered by a light color.

A good coat of primer/sealer over the previous paint, allowed to dry thoroughly, will usually prevent any bleeding. (There are special sealers that can be sprayed over a possible bleeder color before applying a new

Unless you're certain the underlying paint is very stable, it is wise to apply a sealer over the surface before repainting. Your paint dealer can help you choose the right type for the job. Most come in quart cans, premixed and ready to paint.

color.) However, the surest way to prevent bleeding is to remove all previous color coats before applying new paint.

When bleeding occurs, you will probably have to sand away the bleeding color and start over. After the bleeding dries, however, it is sometimes possible to apply a sealer and then repaint the area. But, it is better to apply the sealer at the start of the job so that you don't end up with an excessively thick layer of paint. Paint that is excessively thick has a greater tendency to crack.

PIN HOLES OVER BODY FILLER

Tiny pin holes can appear when paint is applied over areas of body filler. This is caused by improper use of the filler. The major mistakes are using too much hardener, not thoroughly mixing the hardener into the filler, or mixing the filler so vigorously that air bubbles form in the filler. Also, hardener that does not mix with the filler will form soft lumps that can fall out of the filler after it dries.

If pin holes appear in body filler as it is being sanded down, fill them with a light new coat of properly mixed filler. Often the pin holes will not show up until after the repaired area has been primered. If so, fill them with spot putty, block sand, and reprimer the area.

If the surface is not carefully sanded and primered, pin holes can appear when the paint coat is being applied. If this happens the only solution is to sand down the area and reapply the filler, or try to fill the pin holes with successive coats of primer-surfacer or a light coat of body putty.

BODY FILLER BLEED-THROUGH

Occasionally the body filler used in the subsurface will discolor the new paint. These areas usually leave a distinct outline showing where the body filler was applied. This problem is especially noticeable if it occurs with translucent colors.

Body filler bleeding is caused by applying the new paint before the filler has had sufficient time to cure. Using too much hardener can also cause this problem.

The way to prevent this problem is to fastidiously follow the directions supplied with the filler. Use the correct proportion of filler and hardener, and allow ample time for the filler to cure. Problems like this can usually be avoided entirely by letting a vehicle sit for at least a week (after the bodywork and prime coats are finished) before

PAINTERS' TROUBLESHOOTING GUIDE

Common mistakes and how to correct them

PROBLEM	CAUSE	CURE
Runs, Sags	1) Holding gun too close; spraying too much paint in one area; applying second coat too soon. 2) Too slow of thinner 3) Reducing in improper proportions 4) Faulty spray gun pattern; too little air pressure.	Allow paint to dry, wet sand with 220 paper, repaint area
Orange Peel, Rough Suface, Overspray	1) Using too fast a thinner 2) Applying paint in too few, thin, or "dry" of coats 3) Improper reduction 4) Holding gun too far from surface 5) Improper spray gun mixture control; too much air pressure 6) Painting in a breezy area	Mild cases: wet sand with 600 paper and rub out Enamel or severe cases: wet sand with 400 or 320 paper and reshoot with slower thinner or add retarder to paint
Fisheyes, Separations, Craters	1) Improper cleaning or contamination of surface 2) Oil or impurities in air source or wipe-down rag; touching surface with oily hands 3) Insufficient sanding of surface; poor prep	Mild cases: (1) add "fisheye eliminator" to paint and reshoot when first coat is tacky; or (2) let dry and color sand and rub out Severe cases: wipe off paint with thinner while still wet, thoroughly clean area with wax and grease remover, resand, and repaint
Streaking, Mottling	1) Improper overlap or poor gun technique 2) Improperly adjusted or faulty spray gun fan pattern 3) Applying paint too thin 4) Applying metallics too heavily or "wet"	Check spray gun pattern; recoat in even overlapping strokes. If problem persists, "crosscoat" at 90 or 45 degrees
Crazing, Blistering, Lifting	1) Applying paint over incompatible substrate (i.e., lacquer over enamel) 2) Not allowing enough drying time for primer or between paint coats 3) Thinner too slow; coats too heavy	Mild cases: sand down area, apply sealer, repaint in light coats with plenty of drying time Severe cases: strip or sand to bare metal and start over
Checking, Cracking	1) Not enough drying time for primer or between paint coats 2) Excessive paint layer build-up; too thick of coats	Allow thorough drying time; sand smooth and refinish
Sanding scratches, Putty swelling	1) Poor surface preparation 2) Not allowing primer to dry thoroughly; too much primer	To avoid problem: prepare surface thoroughly with 320 paper; use minimum of primer and spot putty To correct problem: sand smooth, coat with sealer, refinish; use faster thinner if possible
Bleeding	1) Incompatible or uncured underlying paint 2) Too slow of thinner 3) Top coat too thin	Apply sealer and recoat area using fast thinner; if severe, strip original paint

applying the final color coats.

If body filler bleed-through occurs, the only sure remedy is to grind out the filler and begin again.

STREAKING

Unfortunately, some paint jobs more nearly resemble a zebra, rather then a fine custom finish. The color is uneven, with off-color light and dark areas. This problem is generally called streaking.

The main cause of streaking is improper spraying technique. Failure to properly overlap successive passes with the gun or an improperly adjusted spray pattern are usually the primary problems. This often results in an uneven pattern with more paint in some areas than in others. Improper application of base coats under translucent colors can also make the top coat appear streaked.

The way to avoid streaking is to fully master gun control and technique. (If you are a beginner, practice on a large piece of scrap material before painting an actual car.) Most painters try to overlap each pass about 50%. Make sure the gun sprays a uniform fan pattern from top to bottom. Streaks or tone variations in undercoats will show through translucent top coats, and can sometimes even affect light, opaque colors. Candy top coats are very susceptible to streaking and color variations, especially on large panels, and must be applied very evenly for uniform coverage.

If you notice streaking occuring during a paint job, first check the fan pattern of the spray gun. It may need adjusting, or the nozzle may need cleaning. Second, try altering your overlap technique while spraying. If you still can't get even coverage, try spraying each panel with horizontal passes, then going back over it with vertical passes.

Metallic paints, especially lacquers, are more prone to streaking than straight colors. Use a good quality, slow thinner for the top coat so that the paint will flow evenly. If streaking or discoloration still occurs, try mixing 1/2 color with 1/2 clear for the final coat, or spray the last coat fairly dry and follow it with one or two coats of straight clear.

SAND SCRATCHES

When scratches appear under freshly dried paint the condition is known as sand scratching. Sometimes the scratches can show up days after a paint job is finished because solvents

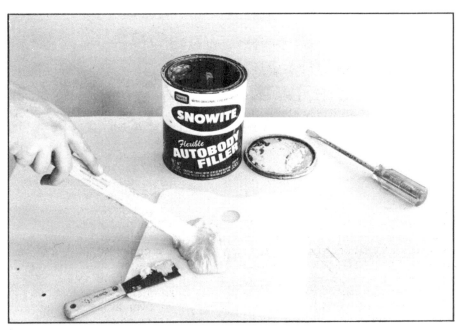

When you mix a batch of body filler, be sure to eliminate any pockets of catalyst and don't stir so vigorously that you create bubbles, otherwise you will uncover many small holes when you sand the surface. Also, be certain to add catalyst in the proper proportion or else the filler may never harden completely, causing it to bleed through the paint or pull away from the surface.

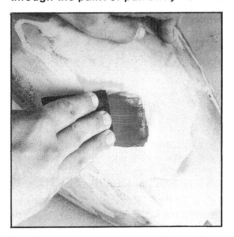

Sandpaper scratches or other minor surface imperfections should be discovered at the primering stage and either sanded smooth or filled with a light coat of spot putty.

will continue to evaporate from the paint or undercoat, causing it to shrink.

The prevalent cause of sand scratches is improper surface preparation. Scratches may be left on the surface when the sanding process is rushed. If you try to get by without using fine sandpaper to smooth the surface, you are likely to get sand scratches. Areas that have been ground down to bare metal with a body grinder need to receive further sanding with progressively finer sandpaper so the coarse scratches won't show through the top coats. If scratches show up after an area has been primed, you can be sure that the top coats will only amplify those scratches. And, deep scratches that have been "filled"

with primer can reappear later as the primer shrinks. This is another reason why it is best to let a primed surface dry as long as possible (up to a week) before the top coats are added.

The best way to prevent sand scratches is to properly prepare the painting surface. Clean the area thoroughly, use the correct thinners in the primer and do the final sanding properly. After grinding or doing bodywork on an area, feather-edge any surrounding paint, primer the area, allow it to dry thoroughly, and then block sand with 180- and then 220-dry paper. If any sanding scratches still show, primer and sand again. Primer-surfacers are better at filling small scratches than regular primer. The use of 400-grit sandpaper for the final sanding of the primer coat will help insure a smooth finish.

Sand scratches are often found around feather-edge repairs. In areas where there are feather-edge repairs fog the first coat of color. This will keep the solvent-content of the paint low when it first hits the feather-edge area, and provide a barrier between the feather-edge repair and the subsequent coats or paint. Sealers can be used on old paint to prevent the new solvent from penetrating and creating sand scratches.

If you encounter sand scratches during a job, let the paint dry, wet sand with fine paper, and repaint the area. If severe scratches show up, the area may have to be spot-painted with primer-surfacer before sanding. Minor sanding scratches in lacquer finishes may rub out, but they can reappear later as the paint continues to shrink.

CHECKING AND CRACKING

Checks and cracks are created when the paint separates in a series of lines. An irregular separation is known as cracking and a crowfoot-like separation is known as checking.

A major cause of checking and cracking is extreme temperature changes. If paint is applied when the surface is very hot and then shortly thereafter the surface temperature is allowed to drop dramatically, there is an excellent chance of checking or cracking. Applying paint over a surface that shows signs of previous checking will seldom hide the checking. Previously checked areas must be thoroughly sanded or stripped before painting. Color coats that are applied too thickly are more prone to cracking

than thinner coats. Cars that have clear applied on colored top coats very often check or crack (especially if left out in the sun, causing repeated expansion and contraction of the metal/paint interface). Paint that isn't properly mixed can crack because the paint film doesn't bond properly to the surface. If underlying coats of paint aren't allowed enough drying time, cracking can occur. The different rates of shrinkage between the coats will pull the layers apart, causing cracks. Incompatible products can also result in cracking and checking due to adverse chemical reactions.

The only solution after cracking appears is to completely sand down or strip the damaged area. Then clean, prime, and repaint the area.

To prevent checking and cracking, don't paint over areas that already show signs of damage. Don't apply heavy primer or top coats. Be especially careful of applying heavy clear

coats with two-part paints that use a catalyst, follow the directions explicitly—too much catalyst will promote cracking. Moderate the temperature of your painting area so that there are no violent extremes. (Don't paint on a hot sunny day and let the car cool rapidly during the evening.) Stir and mix all paints thoroughly. Allow sufficient drying time between coats of paint and primer.

EXCESSIVE OVERSPRAY

Overspray is expected in most painting conditions, but when too much overspray occurs it becomes a problem. This problem is also sometimes called "dry spray." If overspray spreads over the car as you paint, it will contaminate successive coats, causing a rough finish. This condition also wastes paint and greatly increases cleanup time.

There is an optimum time in which paint should travel from the spray gun to the painting surface. Anything longer usually results in excessive overspray. Holding the spray gun too far from the surface is the major cause of this condition. Too much air pressure can also cause overspray. Too little thinner will cause dry spray because there is not enough solvent to make the paint flow properly. A poor quality thinner, or one that is too fast for weather conditions will also hamper flow-out and cause dry spray. Painting outside on a windy day makes it very difficult for the paint to reach the car, the result is a lot of overspray.

Most overspray problems can be corrected at the time of application by switching to a slower thinner, reducing air pressure, or correcting your spray gun technique. If the overspray or dry spray isn't too severe and the paint has a lacquer base, it is possible to rub out the flaws. If you are using enamel or metallic/flake-type custom paints, avoid excessive overspray at all costs. It is extremely difficult to successfully rub out these paints. A trick that sometimes works on lacquer-based paint is to spray a coat of heavily diluted paint over the dry spray. A top quality, medium-slow thinner should be used in a ratio of approximately six or seven parts thinner to one part paint.

Remember a few simple rules and you will avoid most mistakes: follow directions to the letter, take your time and never skimp on any preparation work. Mistakes are an unplesant part of learning to paint. Don't become discouraged when you run into problems. The more you paint, the fewer mistakes you will make.

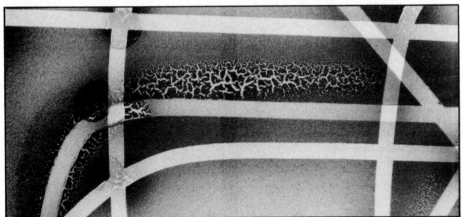

This may look like a trick finish, but the painter didn't intend it to look quite this way. This cracking was caused by not allowing the underlying coats of paint proper time to dry before adding more color.

If the paint surface looks more like sandpaper than glass, the problem is "dry spray" or a severe overspray problem. It can be caused, among other things, by thinned paint that dries too quickly, excessive air pressure or holding the gun too far from the surface.

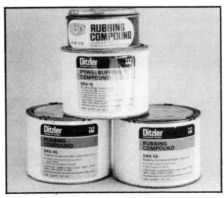

PHOTO COURTESY BINKS MANUFACTURING CO.

Rubbing compound and 600 wet-or-dry paper can save many a paint mistake, provided it's not too severe. Compounds come in different grits, just like sandpaper, and the finest types can even be used on enamels if you work in small areas. If, after wet sanding with 600 paper and polishing with compound, the flaw still persists, you can repaint the area (compounds contain no polish or silicones).

CHAPTER 7

AIRBRUSH TECHNIQUES

- **AIRBRUSH BASICS AND TRICKS**
- **MURAL PAINTING**
- **WHEN NOT TO USE AN AIRBRUSH**
- **AIRBRUSH MAINTENANCE**

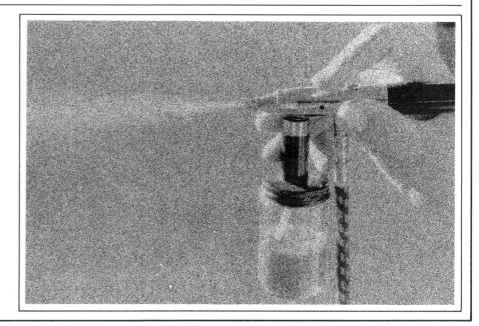

AIRBRUSH TECHNIQUES AND MURAL PAINTING

The airbrush is the little giant of custom painting. Although small in size, the airbrush is one of the biggest assets for a custom painter. The airbrush is a precision, miniature spray gun capable of a wide variety of painting tricks. The versatility of the airbrush is only limited by the imagination of the user. In the hands of a skilled artist the airbrush can produce results that appear virtually photographic in detail. Even in the hands of a beginner, an airbrush can produce a wide array of interesting custom painting effects.

The fact that airbrushes are small and light makes them easy to handle. It is much easier to concentrate on what you are painting when your arm doesn't have to support the weight of a

quart of paint and the attendant heavy air hoses of a standard production spray gun. In addition, an airbrush produces very little, if any, overspray. This is important in finely-detailed mural work.

Airbrushes have been around since the 1800's. Thayer & Chandler, a major supplier of high-quality airbrushes, has been making airbrushes in the

United States since 1891. The company claims that some of their airbrushes have been in use for more than 50 years—proof that a well-maintained airbrush can be a lifetime investment.

Before the 1960's airbrushes were used primarily by commercial artists, photo retouchers, and model builders. When custom painters started using

Airbrush murals came into vogue during the van craze. It was natural, since the broad side of a van makes a perfect canvas for such scenes.

airbrushes on cars and vans the whole field of custom painting really revolutionized. In recent years the use of murals on vehicles has subsided somewhat, but the airbrush is still a very popular and useful painting tool. The airbrush is inexpensive and easy to use, and makes an excellent starting point for a beginner wishing to enter the custom painting field.

AIRBRUSH EQUIPMENT

A tremendous variety of airbrush designs are currently available. They range from very simple, inexpensive beginner models to precision professional models that are capable of painting a line as fine as one drawn by a pencil. Some airbrushes are almost the size of a touch-up gun and use 4-ounce fluid jars, while other airbrushes are the size of a fountain pen with paint thimbles that hold as little as 1/16 ounce of paint.

All airbrushes are reasonably priced. You can buy very basic, single-action, external-mix models for as little as $10 to $15, or you can buy top-of-the-line professional models for under $100. Even a professional favorite like the Thayer & Chandler Model C kit, which includes a double-action Model C airbrush, three fluid jars, brush hanger, and cloth-covered airhose, lists for less than $85. Two good choices for beginners (and professionals as well) are the Thayer & Chandler Model E and Model G airbrushes. Both are single-action, internal-mix airbrushes. They range in price from about $35 to $50, and either model is an excellent compromise between the "cheapie" airbrushes and the more sophisticated double-action professional models.

An explanation of the terms single-action, double-action, internal-mix and external-mix is in order here. On a single-action airbrush a single trigger movement controls both the air and paint. When you depress the trigger, you get atomized paint. This is the easiest type of airbrush to master. Double-action airbrushes offer greater versatility. The air and fluid are controlled by separate movements of the trigger. Airflow is controlled by pushing downward on the trigger and fluid is controlled by pulling back on the trigger. By manipulating the trigger you can greatly vary the air-paint pattern. (With single-action airbrushes

The Thayer and Chandler Model E is a good example of a quality single-action airbrush, and sells for less than $50. It is an internal-mix design, and comes with three screw-mount paint jars.

Airbrushes have existed for a century, but only in the last few years have custom auto artists considered using them to create rolling masterpieces. The results, as evidenced by this surrealistic Camaro, can be quite striking.

Top-of-the-line airbrushes, like this Thayer and Chandler Model C, are usually of the dual-action design. This airbrush comes with paint jars in three sizes and a good quality cloth-covered hose.

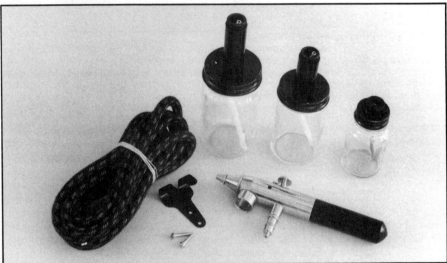

you must turn the fluid control knob to increase the amount of paint.) This control makes the double-action airbrush an extremely versatile tool, but it is more difficult to maintain a consistent pattern with a double-action airbrush. Double-action airbrushes are the ultimate creative tool, but single-action airbrushes are still very versatile and easier to handle.

As a general rule less expensive airbrushes are external-mix while the top models feature internal paint and air mixing. The least expensive of all airbrushes are single-action, external-mix models without a control needle. These units generally can't spray a pattern less than 3/4-inch wide and are not suited for fine detail work. They are suitable for large panel patterns rather than mural work. The next step up the ladder includes single-action, external-mix airbrushes that have interchangeable paint tips. The Bad-

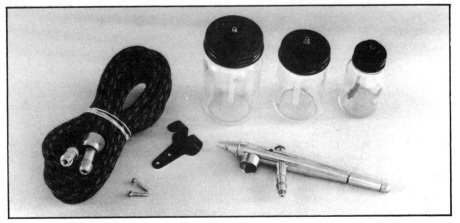

Inexpensive external-mix airbrushes, such as this Badger Model 250 (which comes with a can of aerosol propellant), are intended more for hobby painting than fine-line detail work. However, they can be used for simple custom paint tricks, such as stencil painting, that do not require fine lines or dot patterns.

ger 350 is a good example of this type of airbrush. With a fine paint tip, airbrushes like the Badger 350 are capable of spraying 1/8-inch wide patterns.

Internal-mix airbrushes mix air and fluid inside the head of the airbrush. All internal-mix airbrushes use a control needle that allows much finer control of the paint pattern. Even the moderately priced single-action, internal-mix airbrushes, like the Thayer & Chandler Model E and Model G, are capable of spraying lines as thin as

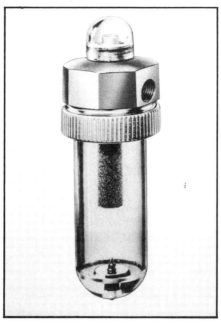

Airbrushes are delicate instruments, highly susceptible to clogging if impurities get in the passages. Thayer and Chandler offers this miniature air filter, which attaches in the air line between the brush and the compressor.

1/16-inch. The Model G has a range of 1/16-inch to 1-1/4-inch while the Model E can spray patterns from 1-1/16-inch to 2 inches wide.

At the top of the price scale are the double-action, internal-mix airbrushes like the Thayer & Chandler Model C. The thing to consider when shopping for a fine instrument like a double-action airbrush is whether or not the unit is suited for automotive use. As an example, Thayer & Chandler makes a very fine artist's airbrush called the Model A. It is designed for very minute

detailing but it isn't a good choice for general automotive work. They also make a Model AA which will spray twice the amount of paint as the Model A. This model is suitable for advanced mural work but the venerable Model C is the most versatile model for automotive applications. It has a pattern range from 1/16-inch to 2-1/4 inches. It uses 1-, 2-, and 4-ounce fluid jars, as opposed to the tiny paint thimbles used with the Model AA airbrush. Choose wisely when shopping for an airbrush and you will end up with a very versatile custom painting tool that will provide years of tireless service.

Besides the actual airbrush, accessories like airhoses, filters, fluid containers, and regulators must be considered. There isn't a tremendous amount of interchangeability between different brands of airbrushes so you will usually have to get your airhose from the manufacturer of your airbrush. The two main types of airhoses are the clear plastic hoses and the braided, cloth-covered hoses. The cloth-covered hoses are far stronger and really the only type to use for automotive applications.

In any type of automotive painting it is very important to keep moisture out of the airhoses. This is especially true with airbrushes, and there are compact moisture filters made especially for airbrushes. One of the better models is the Thayer & Chandler #811 air line filter. It is easy to clean and has a handy manual drain based on a simple tire valve stem. Paasche also makes a very compact inline moisture trap.

Fluid containers come in a wide variety of shapes and sizes. Capacities vary from 1/16-ounce "thimble" color cups to 4-ounce jars. Paint containers are available in plastic, metal, and glass. Clear containers are favored by most custom painters and the glass containers are easier to clean and maintain, although the plastic containers are less expensive. Depending on the design of the airbrush, fluid containers either have threaded attachments or slip-fit friction fittings. The slip-fit containers are easier to change but there is the possibility of a slip-fit paint jar getting knocked loose and spilling paint on the car. It is a good idea to have several paint containers when doing any multi-colored work. You can quickly and easily jump from one color to another without cleaning the container. (Keep a container of thinner handy to clear the airbrush between color changes.)

Although your compressor should have a regulator, an inline air valve or

Since airbrushes require considerably less air pressure than regular spray guns, a small adjustable regulator can be a helpful accessory.

Most airbrushes will work with cans of compressed propellant. These canned propellants are fine for a beginner, but they are fairly expensive and don't last long. If you're serious about doing airbrush work, a small compressor will become a necessity.

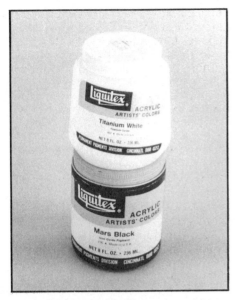

Before you begin to use an airbrush on a vehicle, you will have to practice quite a bit. Water-soluble artist acrylics are excellent for practice. These paints clean quickly and easily with water, but don't use such paints on a car because they are obviously not very durable.

regulator is a good idea when using an airbrush. By placing a regulator or air valve inline with the airbrush you can easily and precisely control the air pressure. This is important. The more control you have, the better work you can do. Simple inline air valves (without a pressure gauge) are actually screw valves that vary the pressure delivered to the airbrush. Adjusting one of these valves is largely a trial-and-error procedure. A better choice is a regulator that also has a pressure gauge. With the pressure gauge you can precisely control delivery pressure and you can adjust pressure to exact requirements for special patterns and effects. A good example of a regulator made for airbrushes is the Thayer & Chandler #810 regulator and air gauge. The #810 is a compact version of the type of regulator used with production spray guns.

All airbrushes have one thing in common: they need some type of air source for their operation. Airbrushes can use a wide variety of air sources, ranging from a spare tire to an industrial compressor. Since airbrushes have such small spray patterns, they have small cfm requirements (cubic feet of air per minute). This means that even the smallest compressors can meet the air demands of most airbrushes. For all types of custom painting the best air choice is an electric compressor. A standard compressor (1-5hp) with the proper regulator will operate any airbrush. If you don't want to spring for a full-size compressor, a

Custom automotive finishes, like Metalflake Candy Apples, are excellent for airbrush work. They come in small cans, pre-mixed and ready to shoot. This makes reloading easy and facilitates changing colors when painting complex designs.

compact electric compressor will be fine. These are diaphragm-type compressors and they are usually rated between 1/10 and 1/2 horsepower. These units are extremely portable and they are priced well under $100. A heavy-duty model, suitable for continuous spraying is an excellent choice.

Another way to get air for your airbrush is from the local gas station. You can get connectors to attach an airbrush to portable air tanks, or even spare tires. This method has its limitations unless you live very close to a gas station. Some professional illustrators use large tanks of compressed air, nitrogen or CO_2 for power. These tanks are nice if space is limited but they must be refilled often if you use the airbrush a lot. Some brushes will also work with cans of aerosol propellant (similar to cans of spray paint but without the paint). They will work for small jobs, but the 11-ounce aerosol cans are not cheap and they can quickly add up to more than the cost of a diaphragm compressor.

Whatever source you use, the important thing is to keep the air clean with an inline filter. Paint and air mix, but paint, air, and water don't.

AIRBRUSH BASICS

If you are in a hurry to become a famous custom painter, skip over this section, but if you want to be a good custom painter, spend some time learning the fundamentals of airbrush-

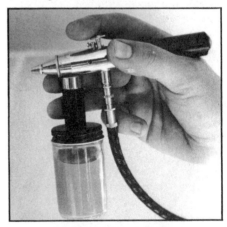

This is the proper way to hold an airbrush. Depress the trigger with the joint of the knuckle, rather than with the ball of the finger. This method is the least fatiguing when painting large or intricate designs.

Handling an airbrush is easy when you get the hang of it. Start by practicing on a tablet of paper—begin with rows of small, even dots and drawing straight lines of varying widths.

ing. The key to good airbrush work (besides natural artistic ability) is precise control of the airbrush. When you know exactly how to manipulate the airbrush, it is much easier to produce fine work. Even if you lack natural artistic talent, good airbrush technique, plus skillful use of masks, stencils, tape and other aids, will still allow you to produce top-notch airbrush work. On the other hand, if you fail to master the basic airbrush techniques, no amount of artistic talent will save your work.

Before you can begin practicing, you have to set up your equipment. Hook up all your airhoses, making sure that all connections are tight. Set the air pressure between 30 and 40psi to start, and experiment to find the best air pressure setting for your particular airbrush. Also, you will find that different paints require different amounts of air pressure, so always adjust the airbrush on some scrap material before you start to paint. Remember that the greater the air pressure, the more likely you are to experience overspray.

You can use a wide variety of paints in an airbrush but for automotive use lacquer and acrylic lacquer are virtually the only paints used. Nonetheless, there are other paints that will work very well for practice exercises. You can use water-soluble ink, concentrated water colors, liquid acrylic artists paints or model airplane paint. The important thing is to properly thin the paint. Unless the instructions are specific, you have to experiment with the different types of paint to determine how to thin them. Almost any paint should be thinned at least 50% and automotive lacquers should be thinned at a ratio of four or five parts thinner to one part paint. To keep the airbrush from clogging, you should start with very thin paint and add more paint until you get the proper consistency for even spraying.

An important point to remember about automotive lacquers is that they dry quickly. This means you must periodically flush the airbrush with thinner to avoid clogging up the airbrush with dried paint. Always flush with thinner between colors and even while using the same color for a long period of time. Clean your airbrush immediately after using automotive lacquers. The passages in an airbrush are very tiny and they can easily become obstructed with dry paint.

After you have your airbrush hooked up to an air source and have properly diluted paint in the fluid container, practice adjusting the var-

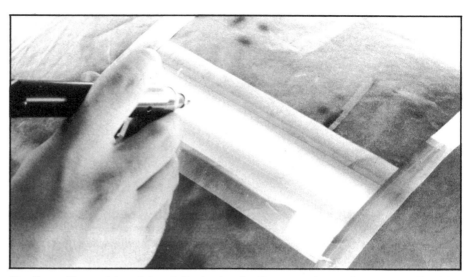

Shading with an airbrush is relatively simple. On a practice surface, tape off a thin rectangle and try shading the top and bottom so that it looks curved, or tubular (when the tape is removed). This exercise is called making cylinders without ends.

ious controls. The mechanism may vary depending on the type of airbrush you have (consult your airbrush instruction manual), but for the most part they should consist of a needle-adjusting screw and the paint tip. These adjustments, in conjunction with paint consistency and air pressure, control the spray pattern of the airbrush.

Besides the paint, air, and mechanical adjustments, the distance you hold the airbrush from the work surface also affects the pattern. The closer the airbrush is to the work, the smaller the pattern will be. Experiment until you get a good feel for how these variables affect the spray pattern.

The proper way to hold an airbrush is similar to the way you hold a pencil. Most people automatically put the ball of their index finger on the trigger. The proper grip is to slide the finger forward a little so that the first knuckle joint depresses the trigger. Even though this grip seems awkward at first, over long periods of time it is actually less fatiguing. You can hold the airbrush with just one hand, but most painters prefer to support the paint jar with their other hand. This is for additional stability and it prevents slip-fit paint containers from falling.

Operation of a single-action airbrush is straightforward—you just depress the trigger. The farther you depress the trigger the more paint is released. With a double-action airbrush there is a definite routine to follow. First, start the airbrush in motion. You want a smooth and consistent motion, like that used in all types of spray painting. Then, depress the trigger straight down to release air. The farther you press, the more air you will get. After the air is flowing, gently

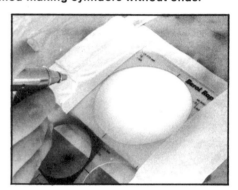

Try shading a circle so that it looks like a sphere. Use a draftsman's circle template (or a round hole cut in cardboard) as a stencil. Next, lightly shade the perimeter of the circle and darken one side of the sphere to make it look as if light is striking it from the opposite side. When you remove the stencil, the finished product looks three dimensional.

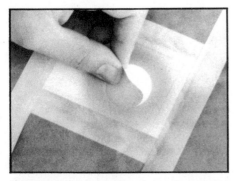

Here's an easy trick: on a yellow background, place a circular adhesive label (available at stationery stores). Fog around the perimeter with orange paint, remove the label, and you have a bright, shining sun.

This relatively simple design was created entirely with an airbrush over the base color of the roof of the car. The stars in this celestial scene are an example of using blow-ups effectively.

pull back on the trigger to release the paint. The more you pull back, the more paint will be released. At the end of a stroke, reverse the actions. The paint is always the last to start and the first to stop. This makes for neat work.

Various exercises will improve control of the airbrush. The first thing is to learn to make straight lines of various widths. You can try doing it freehand or try to follow guidelines drawn on a piece of cardboard. Strive for consistent line width and try to keep the successive lines exactly parallel. Once you are fairly good at straight lines, try drawing a variety of shapes (circles, squares, triangles, etc.) on paper and tracing them with the airbrush. Then try the same shapes freehand.

Second, learn how to make a series of consistent dots. This teaches you how to release small amounts of paint quickly and accurately. Try making rows of evenly-spaced dots. Then make the dots vary in size from pinpoints to one inch diameter.

After straight lines and dots, try making circles. It takes practice to make a perfectly round circle. Don't worry if you aren't too good. You can use templates when you need perfect circles, but these basic exercises will help you develop good control of the airbrush.

Shading is a very important function of airbrushes. The easiest way to shade is to use some type of card as a guide. Practice making a dark line that gradually fades away from the edge of the card. The color buildup must be very gradual for the most effective shading.

Shading is a difficult technique to master and the effect will vary depending on the geometric shape of the subject. However, shading is the final touch that adds realism to murals and makes lettering really stand out. It makes an object look three-dimensional.

A cylinder without ends is an easy shading exercise. Use some type of straight-edged template to make two parallel lines. Shade the edges dark and gradually lighten the shade toward the center of the "cylinder." When done properly the shape assumes a tubular look.

When you practice shading remember that all three-dimensional rendering relies on a thorough understanding of "light source." In most pictorial painting (murals, three-dimensional lettering, etc.) the light in the scene falls on the objects as if it came from a single, main light source (like the sun or an overhead spotlight). To gain lifelike realism, you must picture where this light source is located (high and to the right, high and to the left, etc.) and how the light from this source falls on the objects in the scene.

One of the best ways to study light sources and practice three-dimensional airbrush techniques is to paint a circle and shade it to look like a sphere. The portion of the sphere nearest the light source is the lightest area. As the surface of the sphere falls away from this highlight area, it becomes increasingly darker. The variation of shading is very slight in the area nearest the highlight, but near the edge (or equator), the variations become more prominent. And, on the side of the sphere away from the mainlight, the shading gets darker very rapidly because the light is blocked by the highlight side of the sphere.

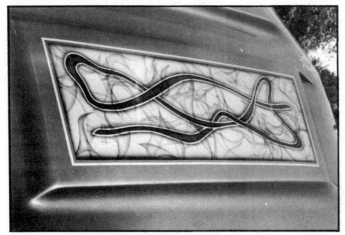

You can create patterns that appear intricate, yet are easy to apply, by using a movable stencil with an airbrush, as seen in the background of this hood panel.

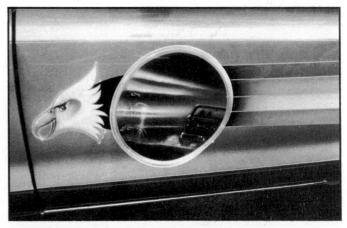

In the hands of an adept airbrush artist, designs as fine as those painted with a pointed sable brush are possible. The stripes trailing to the right of the circle in this motif are an example of airbrush blending, using candy colors.

To create a lifelike, shaded sphere with your airbrush, form the outline of a circle with a template (simple templates with circles of several different sizes are available at art supply stores). Start with the darkest shadow areas and work toward the highlight area. Lay the paint on with a smooth, circular action.

While you are practicing these shading techniques it is a good idea to find some common object to use as a model. In this case a baseball or basketball would be suitable (although a smooth, all-white object will make it easier to see the shading variations). Put the selected "model" on the workbench and shine a concentrated light source at it (a powerful flashlight or an incandescent desk lamp will be suitable) and observe the shading pattern as you move the light around the model. And, watch how the light reflected from surrounding surfaces (particularly surfaces close to the model) affect the shading patterns.

Square and rectangular surfaces that form three-dimensional cube-like objects involve a similar technique. The surface shading will vary depending upon the viewpoint and the location of the light source, and frequently the breakover from highlight to shadow along the sharp edges of these shapes is quite pronounced.

Lifelike rendering of large rectilinear shapes also requires proper control of "perspective." Like shading, perspective involves an understanding of how our eyes perceive three-dimensional objects. This is a very deep subject (no pun intended) and a full understanding requires a lot of study. However, for general purposes the main principle to understand is that parallel lines that recede into the background of the scene converge toward a common point on the horizon (called a vanishing point).

If you're one of those guys who never really "got into" art, this all probably sounds very cryptic. Rightly so, because we don't have space here to present a thorough explanation of these topics, but the point is this, nearly anyone can learn to produce outstanding airbrush art if they are willing to practice and study the basic principles of rendering and design.

But, even for the less ambitious there is a variation of shading that can be used to gain an unusual special effect with an airbrush. It is called blending, and involves a shading effect with multi-color panel painting. The airbrush is used along the dividing line between two colors to blend them together, or a solid color can be blended with increasingly lighter shading toward the line separating it from a panel of different hue or color. This simple technique can add interesting "depth" to an otherwise ordinary panel scheme. (In this case overspray can be beneficial because when a clear topcoat is sprayed over the panels, the overspray will melt and heighten the blending effect.)

And, we can't move on without restating our point, even if you don't want to become another Michelangelo, the airbrush is a valuable tool. Once you become familiar with, and spend some time mastering the basic techniques, it will allow you to produce effects and accomplish detail work that isn't possible with any other type of paint gun.

TRICK PAINTING WITH AIRBRUSHES

Most custom painting tricks that are executed with an airbrush are easier to master than pictorial murals, so we will cover the simple techniques first. Many of the tricks involve the use of some type of stencil or mask. These tricks are quite easy to learn and are an excellent place for novice airbrush artists to start.

An easy airbrush trick for beginners involves a "controlled" mistake. Freak drops are bursts of paint that are allowed to run or scatter across the paint surface. They are best formed using a double-action airbrush because you can deposit a spot of paint and then blow air onto the spot to form the tentacles of the freak drop.

Blow-ups are similar to freak drops, but the idea is to make circles without long tentacles. Blow-ups are an extension of the basic practice technique of making dots with an airbrush.

Stencils are a key element of airbrush painting, whether it be paint tricks or murals. The low-pressure pattern of airbrushes is ideal for use with stencils. Crisp designs can be made without fear of blowing paint under the edge of the stencil. Almost anything can be used as a stencil. Drafting aids like french curves, circle guides, and ellipse stencils have endless possibilities for making interesting shapes and patterns. If you can't find a stencil that suits your needs in your local art supply store, you can make your own out of construction paper or art board. The cutout part of the stencil can even be used for an outlined shape by taping it to a piece of light wire that lets you position the shape in a series of repetitive designs. To make mural painting easier, the Badger Airbrush company makes an extensive stencil kit that contains a variety of pre-cut stencils for making trees, scenery, and buildings. With this kit a beginner can produce a very professional-looking mural, even on the first try.

The ability to blend, shade, and fog

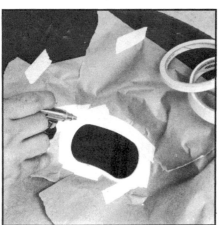

Airbrushes are also excellent for detail painting in small areas on a vehicle. Here the painter is spraying the slots in mag wheels to match the color of the car.

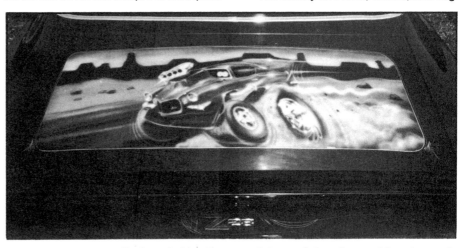

It's not always easy to find a suitable place on a late-model car for an airbrush mural scene. One trick is to set the mural in a design panel outlined by pinstripes, as on the trunk of this Z/28.

Old panel trucks come with "panels" just right for murals. This realistic scene, complete with very accurate shading, looks as if it were done in oils, but it's all airbrush work.

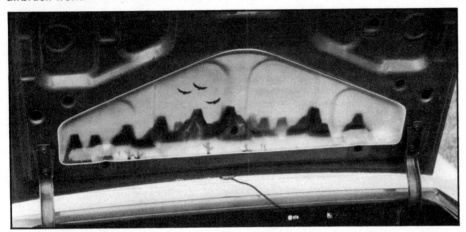

Murals are anything but subtle, and you might not want to paint one on the side of your car. However, they can also be used to advantage in otherwise-drab and uninteresting areas, such as the underside of a trunk or hood.

The Badger stencil pattern kit can be a big help to beginning airbrush artists. This excellent kit contains complete instructions, stencil-cutting paper and over 50 useful precut stencils. Extra packs of blank stencil paper are also available from Badger.

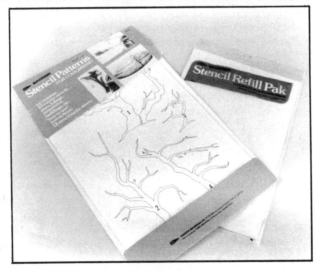

with an airbrush makes it useful in many custom painting tricks. Thin stripes can be laid out to run the length of a vehicle. By using an airbrush to blend colors, you can make a rainbow-hued stripe that gradually blends from one color to another. Fogging is great for highlighting flame paint jobs. An airbrush is perfect to fog highlight color on the trailing edges of flame patterns. An airbrush is also good for finely blended flame coloring.

The fact that an airbrush is capable of creating very thin lines makes it good for fine-line tricks. You can actually use an airbrush to pinstripe. While it is highly doubtful that you can paint a perfectly straight stripe freehand, you can use masking tape to lay out the stripe and then paint it with the airbrush. Using an airbrush for pinstriping allows you to have multiple colored striping that fades from one color to another along the distance of the stripe. Another line trick is known as endless line painting or "spaghetti

striping." Use 1/8-inch or 1/4-inch masking tape to lay a continuous, freeform line design in a panel. Then follow the pattern with the airbrush laying down a contrasting color. When the tape is removed, you have a fogged double-stripe line. This same tape technique can be used with various layers of pattern and color. Each time a new pattern and color is applied the design becomes increasingly intricate.

An airbrush is great for detailing hard-to-reach-places. It is perfect for covering scratches in the interior, such as the lower portions of doors or door jambs. Window molding and other trim is easily touched up without fear of overspray getting on the upholstery. Areas like the dashboard and glove box door are natural places to add a little airbrush embellishment. Mag wheels will look extra sharp if you paint the slotted areas a similar or contrasting color to that of the main paint job. There are plenty of uses for an airbrush under the hood of your car, too. Try painting the areas between the fins of custom valve covers for a distinctive look. Or paint designs on the inner fender wells or underside of the hood.

A relatively new technique that involves the use of an airbrush is neon tube painting. Airbrush shading is used to make the design look like a neon sign. Light highlights are added to give the tubes a glowing effect. You can give traditional stripe designs a neon look, or the neon effect can be used for wild lettering. The shading used for neon is the same technique used to make cylinder shapes. When applying the highlights use either plain white paint or white pearl. Keep in mind the main light source (just like mural painting) so that the highlights are uniform. A clear topcoat gives neon painting a brilliant, lifelike depth.

MURAL PAINTING

One of the foremost uses of the airbrush is mural painting. Unfortunately, good mural painting requires a lot of practice or enormous artistic ability, and topnotch work takes lots of both. There are shortcuts and aids for beginning muralists, so don't despair. A simple and attractive mural can be made by anyone with a little patience, an airbrush, and some stencils, but realize that the really wild, surrealistic mural masterpieces are the result of large quantities of talent and years of practice.

The two main types of murals are freehand and stencil styles, although most painters use a combination of

75

Another way to make stencil art on vehicles is to use Metalflake Spray Mask. This water-soluble paint dries to a rubbery film, which can then be cut with an X-acto knife and peeled away in areas to be painted. It's clear, so you can see what's underneath while adding different colors to a design. Spray Mask is excellent for stencil painting on curved areas, where other types of stencils won't work.

both. The best bet for beginning muralists is to use as many stencils, masks and other aids as possible, and use a little freehand work for added embellishment. There are pre-made stencils that help a lot. The Badger Airbrush Stencil kit contains 53 master stencils and 12 stencil sheets for making your own shapes. Badger also sells refill packs of the plain stencil sheets.

If you desire some specific shape you can make your own stencil. You can draw your own shapes on blank stencil sheets and cut them out with an X-Acto knife. You can cut pictures out of magazines and trace them on sten-cil paper, or if you have access to an opaque projector you can tape the blank paper to a wall and project the image so that it can be enlarged and traced. An opaque projector can also be used to trace a design right on the work surface. You can later trace the design freehanded with an airbrush. This method is obviously more difficult than using a stencil but it can be effective.

Another big aid in mural work is masking. With a masking technique the entire area is covered with a protective coating and the area to be painted is cut away with an X-Acto knife or razor blade. Regular masking tape can be used, but it isn't the best choice. The best masks are either clear adhesive paper or spray mask. Metalflake's Spray Mask is especially useful for masking because it will cling to even the most irregular surfaces. (Unlike masking paper which can be difficult to form to compound curves). Metalflake's Spray Mask is applied with a spray gun. It is translucent when it dries and you can draw on it with a grease pencil or a Stabilo pencil. Cut out the areas to be painted with a sharp knife and peel away the mask film.

Paper masks can be made from "Frisket paper," which is a transparent adhesive-backed paper available at art supply stores. An alternative to Frisket paper is clear plastic adhesive shelf paper.

There are some simple tips that will make mural work easier. Many murals employ cloud formations. An easy way to make clouds is with a piece of torn paper. The randomly torn paper gives a ragged edge that, when used as a stencil or mask, gives the effect of clouds.

Foilage can be made with a piece of natural sponge. Dip the sponge in undiluted green paint and daub it on the mural. A setting sun can be made by using a circle template and a straight-edged piece of paper. Spray a semi-circle using the paper as the bottom guide. For a solid sun that comes through colored clouds, use an adhesive circular label (available in art and stationery supply stores) as a mask. Position it before painting the clouds. When you are through with the clouds remove the sticker and you will have a perfectly round sun. The same technique can be used for a moonlight scene.

Regardless of the type of mural you create, there are a few basic rules to keep in mind. Always try to imagine the finished mural in your mind before you start. It may be helpful to draw a rough sketch of the mural. You need to have a good idea of what elements will be in the mural so that you can put them in the proper sequence. Murals need to be painted from background to foreground in a building block process. If you forget a major background item until the last, it will be much more difficult to properly execute than if it was placed earlier in the painting sequence.

The sequence of color application is also important. As a general rule most custom painters apply the lightest colors first. It is much easier to gradually darken an object rather than trying to lighten something that is too dark. Be careful what colors you put next to each other, especially when using candy colors. The wrong combination of colors will produce a muddy

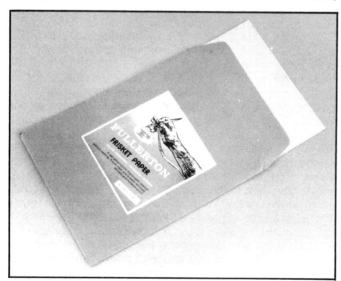

Frisket paper, found in art supply stores, is an adhesive-backed type of masking paper. Spread it smoothly over a design area, draw a pattern on it, cut it out with an X-acto knife and peel away the area to be painted.

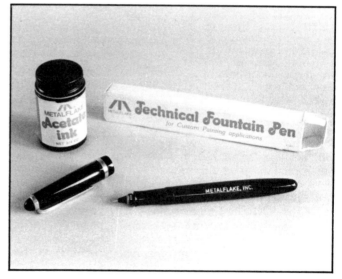

When you want to add some super-fine detail lines to a mural, you will find the Metalflake technical fountain pen and black acetate ink very useful. It's easier to use for fine line work than an airbrush. You can also fill it with automotive-type paint.

look.

Save the fine detail work until the end. Black paint can be used to add crispness, while white is usually used to soften areas. Pearl paint is especially good for softening and adding highlights.

If you don't feel you can manipulate an airbrush adequately for the fine detail work, there are other ways to achieve the detailing. Careful use of a scribing tool or an X-Acto knife will allow you to etch details into a mural. Etching works best for things like lines in a brick wall, grass blades, hair, or details in tree leaves. You have to be careful not to scratch too deeply or you will expose either the undercoat or bare metal. When etching details, you have to plan the underlying colors so that the exposed paint is the right color.

Etching adds detail by removing paint but you can also increase detail by applying more color. One way to add fine detail is with a technical pen made just for mural work. Metalflake also makes black, opaque Acetate Ink which is ideal for fine line rendering. Acetate Ink flows well and won't spread or fade.

The final touch for all murals should be a protective covering with clear. Murals are made with very thin coats of paint and and they are easily scratched. Clear also gives added depth to murals. Never judge the success or failure of a mural until you have applied the clear topcoat. On the other hand, don't spray the clear until the mural is exactly the way you want it, because you can't touch up the scene afterwards.

Virtually anything you can see, copy, or imagine can be recreated with an airbrush. All it takes is careful planning, precise execution, and lots of patience.

AIRBRUSH MAINTENANCE AND TROUBLESHOOTING

Airbrushes are fine instruments that require fastidious care to stay in top working order. Cleanliness is vital with airbrushes. The tiny passages in airbrushes won't tolerate any debris or dry-paint buildup. It is mandatory that you flush your airbrush often with good, full-strength thinner.

Check the instruction sheet that comes with your airbrush for specific maintenance recommendations. There are several general procedures that apply to most airbrushes. Besides spraying thinner through your airbrush, you can remove traces of paint

Not everyone can become a first-rate airbrush artist, but you'll never know unless you give it a try. If you have the talent, you can develop a skill that is in big demand. Top notch airbrush artists and pinstripers can make several hundred dollars a day. But, even if you don't reach this level of skill, there are many simple airbrush tricks that can be used effectively to highlight a custom paint job.

by backflushing. Backflushing involves covering the paint tip with a clean rag and depressing the airbrush trigger. This forces paint in the airbrush back into the paint cup. When backflushing, alternate between covering and uncovering the paint tip so that thinner is worked back and forth through the airbrush.

Whenever you handle the airbrush needle use extreme care. The needle is very delicate and it needs to remain straight and sharp for the airbrush to function properly. If removal of the needle requires more force than your finger tips, use a pair of small pliers with tape wrapped over the jaws. Twist the needle gently in a counterclockwise direction to remove it. Be sure to loosen the needle chuck before trying to remove the needle.

Whenever you need to partially disassemble an airbrush for cleaning, take it apart only as far as necessary. Most airbrushes come with an exploded drawing. Use this drawing for reference and be extremely careful not to lose any of the tiny parts. If your airbrush needs any maintenance more involved than simple cleaning, send it back to the manufacturer for professional care.

Most airbrush problems are related to incorrect paint thinning, improper air pressure or dirt. If you encounter trouble, don't be in a hurry to tear the airbrush apart. First, check the paint consistency and air pressure. Spray some thinner through the airbrush and backflush it thoroughly to see if the problem can be solved without major "rebuilding."

Spitting is a common malady caused by dried paint particles blocking the airbrush. Paint often dries on the needle tip. The cure for spitting is a thorough cleaning of the airbrush. Spitting is also very often a sign that the paint is too thick.

Another problem caused by thick paint is a "grainy" spray pattern. A grainy spray can also be caused by a low air pressure setting.

Thick blobs at the start and finish of a stroke indicate improper airbrush manipulation. This is a sign that you are releasing the paint before moving your hand and that the paint is still flowing after you have ended the stroke.

A similar technique problem is flared ends. This means you are arcing your hand rather than keeping it parallel to the work surface at all times.

Runs or "centipedes" are caused by too much paint applied too close to the working surface. Hold the airbrush farther away from the work and/or increase the air flow.

Splattering occurs when an unusually large amount of paint spurts from the airbrush at the end of a stroke. This is caused by letting the needle snap back into the paint tip too quickly. Use a slow, deliberate motion when releasing the airbrush trigger.

If the paint wants to keep coming after you release the trigger, the paint tip may be clogged. The tip should be soaked in thinner to loosen any dried paint residue.

Besides clogging of the actual airbrush, the paint container tubes can become restricted. A wooden toothpick can be used to unclog the tube.

Most airbrush malfunctions can be prevented by keeping the airbrush clean at all times. If paint never gets a chance to dry inside the airbrush, your potential problems will be greatly reduced. The airbrush is a precision instrument. Treat it with care and it will give you years of satisfactory service.

HOW TO PAINT YOUR FIRST MURAL

Creating a pleasing, realistic-looking scene with an airbrush and stencils is relatively easy (although you probably wouldn't want to try your first mural on the side of a freshly-painted show car). To get the feel of the various processes involved and to try out a few variations, we suggest you practice on a large sheet of white paper, art board or something like an old hood or trunk lid. In the following sequence we'll show you how easy your first airbrush mural can be, if you employ a few "tricks."

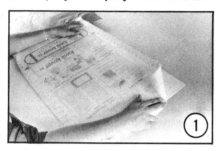

We are going to try our practice mural on a sheet of white art board (if you'd rather work on a metal surface, begin by painting it white). To mask out a "panel" for the scene, we covered the surface with a layer of clear, adhesive-backed, plastic shelf paper.

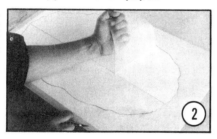

The outline, or "frame," for the scene was drawn on the shelf paper in grease pencil. A yard stick was used to draw a horizon line across the middle. We decided to paint the sky first, so we cut along the lines with an X-Acto knife. Then we peeled the top half of the shelf paper, leaving the bottom half covered to protect the surface from overspray.

We placed a circular gummed label to make a sun in the middle of the sky. The position of this sun will determine the main light source in the scene, dictating which side of other elements in the picture should be shaded.

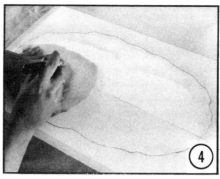

Next come the clouds. A piece of masking paper was torn with a ragged edge for a stencil, then moved to different positions and fogged with the airbrush. Use blue paint for a daytime scene, yellow and orange for a sunset.

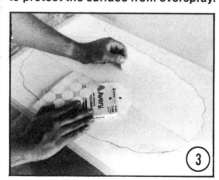

To add definition to the sky, a darker color was fogged between the clouds without using a stencil. We used small cans of Metalflake pre-mixed candies for our various colors. Always add color to the scene slowly and stop often to evaluate your progress. You can easily add more; subtracting color is difficult.

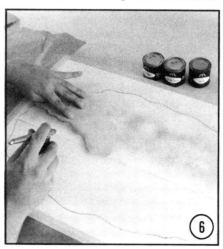

To add mountains along the horizon, a piece of light cardboard was torn in a convex pattern to make a stencil and fogged heavily with the airbrush. Use green or brown paint, depending on your color scheme.

We cut a simple outline of a flying bird in a blank piece of stencil paper, and sprayed over it with black paint to add some action to the scene.

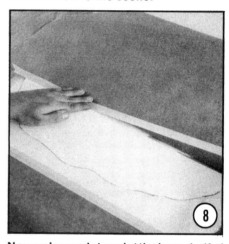

Now we're ready to paint the lower half of the mural, so we peeled off the bottom piece of shelf paper and covered the top half with masking paper and tape to keep it from being spoiled by overspray.

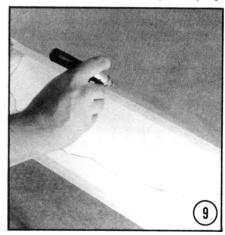

The picture we're painting is a lake surrounded by low hills and mountains, with a large tree in the foreground, so shades of dark blue were fogged along the lower horizon line in the area reserved for the water.

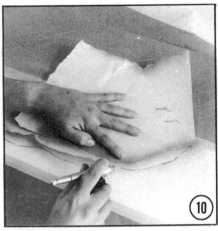

A piece of ragged paper was used to make low hills in the foreground.

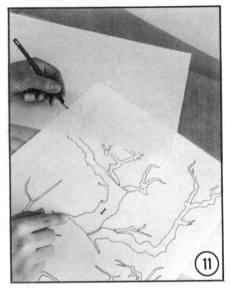

The centerpiece of the mural will be a tree chosen from the many possibilities in the Badger stencil pack. Place a piece of the semi-transparent blank stencil paper over the design and trace the outline.

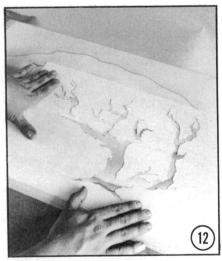

After carefully cutting out the stencil, it is positioned over the scene. Notice that the top half of the mural has been uncovered.

Tape the stencil in place so that it won't move. We began shading in the tree slowly with a dark brown color, fogging the right side of the figure more heavily since that is the side away from the sun.

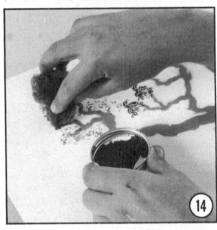

Foliage can be added to the tree in two ways. Here we are using a small piece of natural sponge, dipped in unthinned dark green paint and daubed over the branches of the tree.

You can also use a small, flat, artist's brush to paint in the leaves. Dip the tip in unthinned paint and press the bristles vertically down onto the surface. Practice different techniques until you find one that you like.

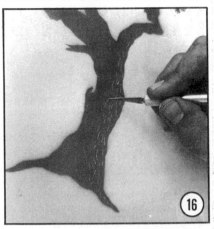

To add realism to the bark of the tree, we used a pointed X-acto knife blade to scratch away some of the paint. Do this carefully, removing only the tree color and letting the base color show through. If you're painting on a vehicle, you don't want to scratch through to bare metal.

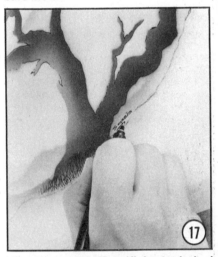

We also used a Metalflake technical pen with black ink to add grass blades at the base of the tree, to outline some of the trunk, and to sign our name to this minor masterpiece.

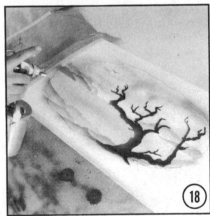

The final step is to cover the entire mural with a coat of clear acrylic lacquer, using a touch-up gun. The clear not only protects the mural, but gives it a glossy finish and adds definition to the shapes in the scene.

PAINTING FLAME PATTERNS

- EQUIPMENT FOR FLAME PAINTING
- DESIGNING FLAMES
- SURFACE PREPARATION
- LAYOUT AND MASKING
- FINISHING TOUCHES

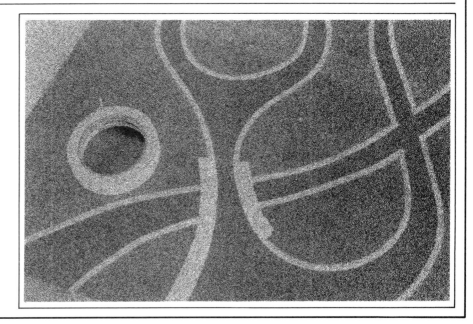

Without a doubt flames add a bold and dynamic appearance to any vehicle. Wispy, flowing, dark-colored flames over a light base color give this traditional '40 Ford a distinctive, yet-unique look.

ONE OF THE ALLTIME FAVORITES IN THE CUSTOM PAINTING FIELD IS AMAZINGLY EASY TO LEARN

The flame paint job is one of the oldest, most popular and virtually time-less forms of custom painting. Flames are colorful, attractive, distinctive and outrageous, and nothing dresses up an otherwise-drab vehicle like a fine set of flames. In fact, in recent years countless magazine covers have displayed cars that feature little else but a wild, custom flame paint job. Of course, no one can guarantee that your car will wind up on the cover of a magazine but it's a plain fact that few painting effects have the same visual impact as a flame paint job. And best of all, if you do the work yourself, the cost could be as little as $100 for paint and masking materials.

When you think about it, flames are a strange thing to use for automotive ornamentation. Who would want a car that looks like it is on fire? Well, about forty years ago some drag racers decided that painting flames on their cars would be an appropriate way to show they were ready to go to "the limit." The distinctive effect quickly became a fad and spread to street machines and rods. In fact, flames became so popular on modified '40 Fords that it began to seem like flame paint jobs were on the factory options list.

Regardless of the reasoning behind flames, they soon became the singular symbol of hot rodding. Cars like Bob McCoy's lowered 'n' flamed '40 Ford set magazine covers ablaze in the Fifties and established trends for hundreds of others to follow. In the Sixties flames died down temporarily, however the resurgence of traditional street rodding in the Seventies returned the finely crafted flame paint job to prominence. Probably no other car is as responsible for the renewed popularity of flames as Pete Chapouris' '34 Ford, the "California Kid." Besides being a top magazine cover car the "California Kid" was also the star of a TV movie of the same name. This car instantly became the most generally recognized car in the history of modern hot rodding, and did wonders to spread the fame of flames.

Whatever the reason for the popularity of flames, part of their popularity stems from the fact that almost anyone can paint them. Some people are much better flame painters than others but this is due more to design and layout ability than painting prowess. This is because the main "trick" of flame painting is the design, layout and masking. The actual paint application can be very easy, especially if you stay away from intricate color fading and blending. Some of the very fancy color schemes can be difficult to paint, but if

The traditional flame color scheme is red, orange and yellow, outlined with white pinstripes, over a glossy black base. Pete Chapouris' famous "California Kid" '34 Ford is a beautiful example of this style.

you stick with simple color combinations, the technique is straightforward and simple.

The fact that so much taping and preparation work is involved in flame painting makes them less-than-popular with many professional painters. Pros would rather minimize the time spent in preparation and masking, but for a beginner this situation is ideal because you can afford to take the time to get the masking as close to perfect as possible.

EQUIPMENT NEEDED FOR FLAME PAINTING

Different equipment will be needed, depending on the type of flames you are going to paint and where you are going to apply them. Two items you will need, regardless of the type of

There are several ways to draw a flame design on the car before you begin painting. You can use a Stabilo pencil, grease marker or chalk—any of which can be erased if you need to make changes. With practice, you can skip the sketch work and lay the pattern directly on the vehicle with 1/8-inch wide masking tape.

flames, are paint and masking tape. Masking tape is the most common and most used material in flame painting. Get the best tape you can buy. This is not the place to save a few bucks with inferior masking tape. Buy fresh, namebrand tape in a variety of sizes from 1/8-inch to 2 inches wide (the uses for the different sizes will be explained later). If you have some old tape, use it only for things like taping folds in the masking paper. Use fresh tape for the layout of the flames because fresh tape sticks best, insuring crisp, clean edges. If you haven't had much experience with masking tape, note that old tape tends to be brittle, especially along the edges, and usually has a darker color than fresh tape.

Besides masking tape, you will also need something to cover the larger areas of the vehicle. Two-inch masking tape is handy to fill between the licks of the flames or you can use paint masking paper. Masking paper is

Flame patterns also work well on modern cars, even the late-model box-like designs. Flames and hood louvers are the only modifications to this outstanding El Camino.

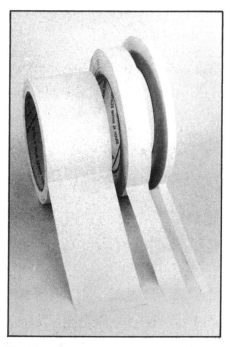

Masking flames requires plenty of tape. You need 1/8-inch tape to make smooth curves, 1-inch tape for general use and to hold down masking paper and 2-inch tape to fill in large gaps.

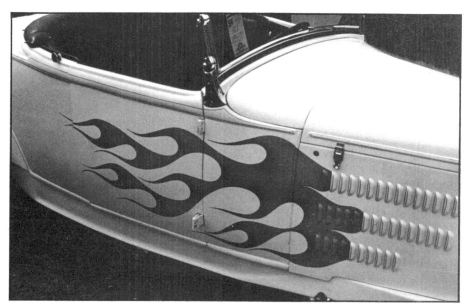

Flames pouring over the hood might seem like an odd pattern to paint on a car, but it looks natural on these traditional hiboy roadsters.

usually light-green in color and is available in most paint supply stores. It comes in rolls of different widths and though it is light in weight it does a fine job of protecting the subsurface from overspray. (Professional painters have handy dispenser rigs that roll off the paper with the masking tape already affixed to one side. These taping and masking machines are nice but not necessary for beginners.) Masking paper is also most suitable for large surfaces, like the windshield, but ordinary butcher paper will work fine if you can't find masking paper. Some people use newspaper for masking, but it really isn't advisable since the newspaper ink can bleed through to the surface below when saturated with

paint. You should also mask about three feet behind the end of the flames to protect the rest of the car from overspray.

The type of paint used for flames is largely dependent on the preferences of the painter, but the best choice for a beginner is acrylic lacquer. Acrylic lacquer dries quickly and is much easier to blend between different colors. Solid colors with different shades and hues blended together to give a dimensional effect are traditional for flames and the easiest for beginners to use, but they can also be painted with any of the trick paints, like candies, flakes and pearls. In fact, in recent years candy-colored flames have become very popular, especially on show cars. Candy colors aren't too hard to use but you do have to be

careful of runs. Also, if you want the flame colors to match, you have to apply the same number and thickness of candy overcoats so that the color intensity will be uniform in various areas. Flakes are more difficult to use, although a flake base can be applied over the entire flame area and then covered with various candy overcoats. Pearl colors work well for subtle flames that seem to almost be hidden beneath the surface paint.

As always, if you want outstanding results, it is important to use top-notch products. The major expenditure is the time it takes to prepare the surface, so it is false economy to skimp on the paint supplies. This applies equally to the thinner, only the best grades should be used. Use the cheap stuff for cleaning your spray gun, not painting. You may believe that all paint thinner comes out of the same grimy, New Jersey storage tank, but it's not so. Top quality thinner causes the paint to "flow" better, giving the surface a high gloss. And, remember to use thinners that are compatible with the paint and the prevailing weather conditions (follow manufacturer's recommendations). Although it isn't mandatory, it is a good idea to use the same brand

On a large, flat-sided vehicle like a van, flames can be incorporated with other design elements to create effective overall results.

thinner as the paint you are using. This way you are positive that the products were designed to be chemically compatible.

Most professional painters cover their flames with a few protective coats of clear. It is smart to check with the manufacturer or perform a simple test to make certain the clear is compatible with the subsurface paints (spray a section of an old fender or hood with the colored paint and, when it is dry, spray the clear on top to test the compatibility). Use top quality clear because it has less tendency to yellow or crack with age. The clear coat is a good place to add a little pearl or fine flake if you desire some extra sparkle for your flames.

A very important piece of equipment is, quite obviously, the spray gun and an air source. We will discuss equipment recommendations for two different situations: painting a full-size flame job on a car or truck and painting smaller flames on panels of a vehicle or smaller objects, like motorcycle tanks or helmets.

On a full-size flame job the ideal situation would be to have a standard production spray gun, a touch-up gun and an airbrush. This would give you the perfect gun for every situation, especially if you are new at flame painting. The production spray gun should be used for applying sealers or undercoats, the main color of the flames and any clear top coats. The touch-up gun works best for applying the trailing colors of the flames. The airbrush is best suited for applying flame tips, fogging a little contrasting color around the bends of the flames and painting flame overlaps where overspray can be a problem.

Professionals can do beautiful flame jobs with just one top-of-the-line standard spray gun because professional spray guns can produce a wide variety of spray patterns and pros can manipulate them to such fine sprays that they almost duplicate airbrush results. However, few novices are this adept with large spray guns and often the first-timer can produce better detail work with a touch-up gun. The touch-up gun sprays a smaller pattern. This produces slower coverage but greater control. Also, touch-up guns have much smaller material canisters, so refills will be necessary when painting large areas. Another advantage of the touch-up gun is that it usually requires a lot less air than a production spray gun. They are, therefore, generally more compatible with smaller, home and hobby-type compressors.

The airbrush is the easiest tool for

Even on a vehicle with radical bodywork, like this chopped Chevy pickup, flames add tremendous additional impact. Flames are often shaded in blended colors, but they can also be painted a solid color; here the scheme is orange over a yellow base.

On this '40 Ford convertible the yellow and orange flame pattern swallows almost half the car.

Even small flame designs can effectively add a dynamic touch to the car, and small patterns are relatively easy to apply.

The first and most radical step to creating an effective flame pattern is to design the shape of the flame "licks." Before you start, study several examples in magazines or at car meets. Decide which elements you like best and consider how they will transplant to your vehicle. In this case, notice how the painter solved the problem of masking over hood louvers (very difficult) and how each lick is separated from the rest of the flame at the rear of the design.

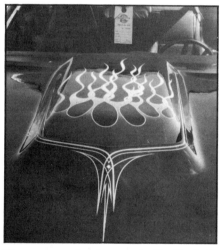

Flames can also be used effectively in very small areas, such as the hood scoops on this Camaro. Notice how these flame licks intertwine and overlap.

the beginner to use when applying the final touches of a flame job. The most attractive and intricate flame jobs feature elaborate crossovers, fading and fogging. Adept spray artists can handle these tricks with larger equipment but the ambitious novice would be wise to tackle these details with an airbrush. The spray pattern of an airbrush is very small and can be easily manipulated. And, overspray is minimized, which means you can save time and trouble because you will not have to mask off large sections every time you fog an area of overlapping colors.

Small flame jobs, like those on design panels or on motorcycle gas tanks, can be accomplished with much

less equipment. A standard production spray gun really isn't needed and professional-looking results can be produced with a touch-up gun and an airbrush. This also eliminates the need for a large compressor (as long as it meets the cfm requirements of the touch-up gun). Lightweight hobby-type compressors can be used with most airbrushes and some touch-up guns. Some of the more basic airbrushes can even operate on cans of aerosol propellant, but this type of equipment can be erratic, so it is advisable to at least rent a small compressor if you don't want to spend the money to buy one.

Whereas a standard production gun is used to cover the large areas on a big flame job, a touch-up gun will work fine on smaller jobs. An airbrush is just about mandatory on small flame

jobs because of the close proximity of the flame licks and the need to avoid overspray.

FLAME DESIGN

All flame jobs are not the same. Some look great, some only so-so and other look ghastly. The problem usually isn't in the paint application but in the design and color choices. There is no one "right" way to design flames but a lot of planning goes into a good flame job.

The size of flames is very important. The width of the individual licks in relation to their overall length is important. Flames need to flow to look right. Real flames are in constant motion, always fluid, so take this into consideration when designing your flames.

Balance is also very important in flame painting. Pay attention to the number and location of overlaps and splits. Flames usually aren't symmetri-

On this pickup truck a small flame pattern bursts from a single pinstripe running to the front of the fender. If you use your imagination, the creative possibilities are practically endless.

Here's a really novel approach to a flame design, based on a traditional pattern. The intertwining licks in this case were painted in two shades of candy apple.

cal (did you ever see a perfectly symmetrical fire?) but one side of the vehicle shouldn't be loaded down with intricate overlaps while the other side has none. Color selection is also a part of balance. Think about where you want the various colors to start and end.

We said that flames usually aren't symmetrical, but some flame painters feel that automotive flames should match from one side of a hood to another. This technique gives the car a pleasant "balanced" look, but if you prefer this style, just remember that it is much more difficult to lay out than free-form flames. To achieve a symmetrical look, the flames need to be designed on one side of the car and then a full-scale pattern must be cut from paper to transfer the design to the opposite side. This is really not as difficult as it sounds, but you must think this through when you make your preliminary preparations.

The best advice on flame design is to study a lot of other flame jobs. Collect examples of flames from magazines that appeal to you and study cars at car shows and street rod meets.

Flames do not have to be symmetrical from one side of the car to the other, but on some vehicles a symmetrical pattern works best. However, laying out a symmetrical pattern involves considerably more work.

Although the current trend favors long, wispy flames, there are many other possibilities. A pleasing pattern must complement the basic shape of the car and the individual licks should combine into a smooth, flowing design.

An asymmetrical flame pattern works very well on the hood of this Nova. Note how a "reverse" flame design was employed at the leading edge to create a double flame effect.

The stylized, symmetrical flame job on the hood of this pickup is strongly reminiscent of early-day scallops.

The small swath of flames on this pickup fender incorporates several flame techniques: overlapping licks, pinstripe outlines, reversed licks and "ghosted" pearl flames underneath the major pattern.

A small flame detail has been incorporated into a scallop design on the roof pillar of this early Camaro.

Here is another simple and less-dramatic use of a flame pattern. Laying out small, accent flame panels is excellent practice for the beginner.

We have included several examples of flame paint jobs in this chapter but the variety of possible combinations is almost endless.

A series of sketches of your car with different flame patterns will help show you which designs look best. Assuming that you aren't a professional illustrator, the simplest method is to take a few photographs of your vehicle, and have some enlarged prints made (8 x 10 inches is a good size). Then, use tracing paper and colored pencils to make various overlays of possible flame designs and colors.

Once you have a basic pattern that you like, it is time to experiment on the actual vehicle. Buy some extra rolls of 1/8-inch masking tape and practice laying out small sections. Try a certain design and then stand back and see how it looks. If you don't like it, start over. (Tape is cheap, but once a flame job is applied, a costly repaint is all you can do if you change your mind.) Before long you should be able to make smooth curves and as you ex-

periment your "eye" for flame design will improve.

SURFACE PREPARATION

Clean the entire vehicle before you lay out the final flame design. Even though you will only be painting part of the area, you don't want any dirt on the surface that might get blown into the wet paint. Clean the area to be painted with a good degreaser according to the directions on the container. Be sure the work area that you choose for painting is also as clean as possible to further reduce the chance of any debris getting on the wet paint.

LAYING OUT AND MASKING THE FLAMES

There are several different ways to lay out flames. The most common way is to do it freehand with 1/8-inch masking tape. Start on one fender and work your way across the car. Stop periodically and evaluate your progress. If an area doesn't look just right,

do that part again. You can overlap the tape where you stop or change your mind. In places where parts of the flames overlap each other, decide which lick will be on top and use a razor blade or an X-Acto knife to cut away the unnecessary tape.

When you are satisfied with the flame layout, go over all the tape again to be sure that it is firmly affixed to the car. This will insure sharp, crisp edges for the flames. The next step is to cover the areas not to be painted. Depending on the complexity of your flames, follow the 1/8-inch tape with 1/2-inch or 3/4-inch masking tape. On small items like motorcycle tanks it may be necessary to use 1/4-inch tape because it is more flexibile. Apply the second round of tape so that it sticks to the 1/8-inch tape, but be careful not to let it get into the area to be painted. After the second round of tape has been applied there will still be various size gaps. These can either be covered with masking paper or tape. If paper is used, keep it as flat as possible to avoid creases where overspray can collect

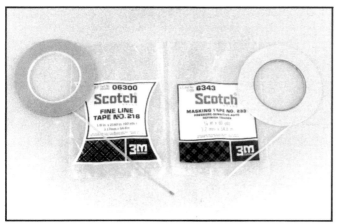

The taped pattern must have smooth, clean edges. If the pattern has sharp curves (and most do), the initial pattern must be established with 1/8-inch tape. Wider tape will split or wrinkle as it is bent around tight curves.

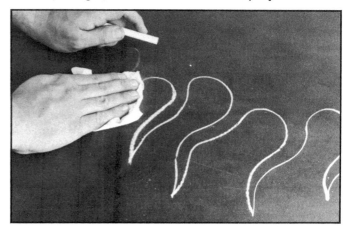

If you are a beginner, it's best to begin by drawing the design on the vehicle. When it's finished, don't be in a hurry to start painting. Stand back, carefully evaluate the pattern and make certain it is exactly what you want.

86

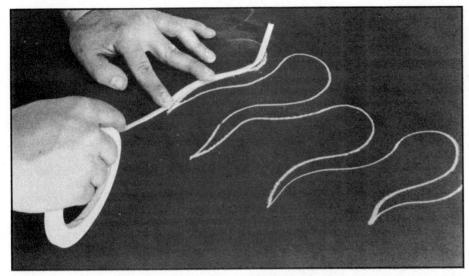

If you've drawn the design on the car with a marker, begin the masking by following the lines with 1/8-inch masking tape.

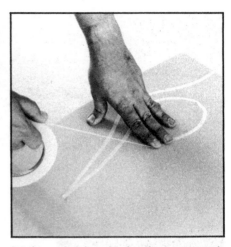

It takes a deft hand to lay the tape evenly and with flowing curves, but with a little practice you can learn to guide the tape smoothly around long, broad curves and small, tight corners.

and later get blown into the wet paint. Masking paper should certainly be used to cover large areas like the grill, the bumper and the windshield.

There is another way to tape off flames that uses a great deal of tape, but many painters consider it to be quicker and easier. After the design has been laid out with 1/8-inch masking tape, cover the whole flame area with 2-inch masking tape. Apply the tape so that it is parallel to the front bumper and windshield. Overlap each row of tape slightly so that there won't be any cracks for paint to enter. When all the tape is in place, take a sharp X-Acto knife and carefully trace the flame design right down the middle of the 1/8-inch design tape. Then peel away the tape from the areas to receive paint and the masking job is finished.

If you don't feel confident enough to lay out the flames with tape, you can draw them with a grease pencil or china marking pencil. Another good

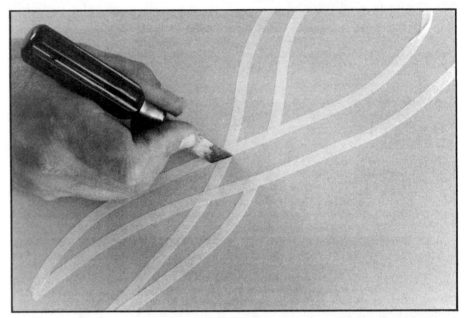

After the first layer of outline tape is in place, use an X-Acto knife to cut away the tape in areas where the licks might cross. Such areas will be painted in two steps. For maximum effect the colors or the shades of the crossing licks should contrast.

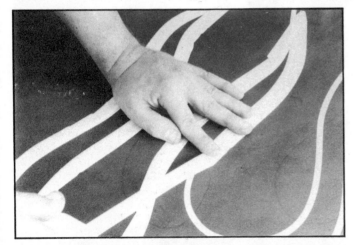

If your flame design covers a large area of the vehicle, and there is considerable space between the licks, it is easiest to cover the unpainted portion of the car with masking paper. Start by following the 1/8-inch tape with 3/4- or 1-inch tape.

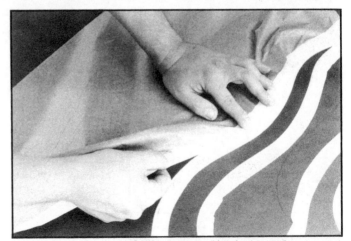

Fill the gaps with masking paper, tearing it into narrow strips, if necessary, to fill small gaps. Try to get the paper to lie as flat as possible so that overspray won't collect in the folds, where it may later be blown onto the wet paint by the spray gun.

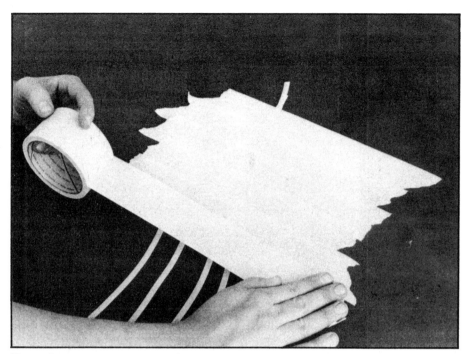

If your flame pattern covers only a small area, it might be easiest to cover the entire design with rows of 2-inch masking tape.

marking tool is a Stabilo pencil, which should be available at most art supply stores. After you have drawn out the flames, follow the design with 1/8-inch masking tape.

If you are determined to have symmetrical flames, there are a couple of tricks that may help. Once the first half of the design has been completed, tape a large sheet of tracing paper over it and follow the design with a grease pencil or china marker. Then, turn the tracing paper over and place it on the other side of the vehicle using some

common reference point to locate the paper. Now, go over the design with a blunt object, like your thumbnail, and the residue from the grease pencil will stick to the surface, producing a duplicate, but reversed, pattern. Follow that design with 1/8-inch masking tape and you're in business.

Another way to trace symmetrical flames is with a pounce wheel and powdered charcoal. Put the tracing paper over the taped half of the design as above, but this time trace the design with a normal pencil. Then remove the tracing paper and place it on a large piece of cardboard. Now follow the design with a pounce wheel (a roller-like device with a pointed

wheel that is usually available at art stores). Place the perforated tracing paper on the vehicle as in the first method, only this time shake powdered charcoal (also available at art supply stores) over the design. The charcoal will penetrate through the holes, and when you remove the tracing paper, you can follow the dot pattern with 1/8-inch masking tape to produce the duplicate pattern.

Regardless of the style flames you choose and how you lay them out, once they have been taped, the surface to be painted must be prepared to accept the paint. Start by cleaning the surface with a degreaser. Depending on the age and types of paint used, it may be necessary to apply a sealer before doing the flames. Check the recommendations on the paint can and consult the counterman at your paint store. In most cases a sealer won't be required.

The next step is to rough up the surface so that the new paint will have something to adhere to. Use fine grit sandpaper (dry) or an artificial steel wool scuff pad. Pay close attention to the edges of the tape when sanding so that you don't lift the tape. Blow off any sanding dust with an air nozzle and wipe the surface with a fresh tack rag. Finally, wipe the area again with degreaser and check to see that all taped edges are firmly in place.

PAINTING FLAMES

Follow the directions on the can for the type of paint you choose for the base color. Take into account the expected temperature at the time you will be applying the paint and use the correct temperature-matched thinner. If the temperature changes drastically during the time you are painting, change to the proper thinner.

Set your spray gun for an acceptable fan pattern and try it out on a piece of cardboard or other scrap material. A good pattern at a relatively low pressure will give the least overspray. Spray on the base color until the desired shade is reached. After the paint dries, remove any overspray by wiping the area with a clean tack rag used in conjunction with an air nozzle.

You are now ready to apply the various colors to the ends of the flames. You can paint from front to back or vice versa. Some painters feel that by painting the tips first and working toward the front of the design they can better gauge the color separations, but most painters work from front to back. If you are planning on using several different colors, leave

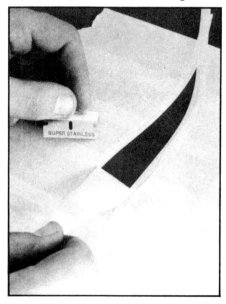

You will be able to see the outline of the 1/8-inch tape flame pattern under the 2-inch tape. Use an X-Acto knife to cut down the middle of the 1/8-inch tape pattern and peel the 2-inch tape away from the areas to be painted.

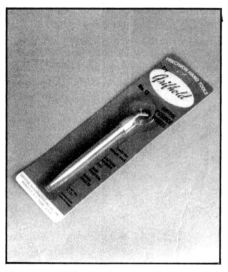

If you want to make your flames symmetrical from one side of the vehicle to the other, a pounce wheel is very helpful for making mirror-image patterns.

MASKING FLAMES WITH SHELF PAPER

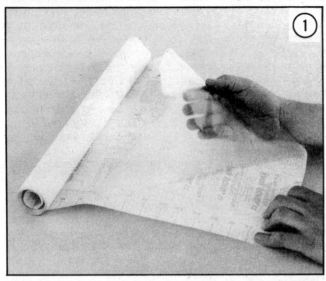

An easy and quick way to mask off flame patterns, large or small, is to cover the area with clear, adhesive-backed, vinyl shelf paper.

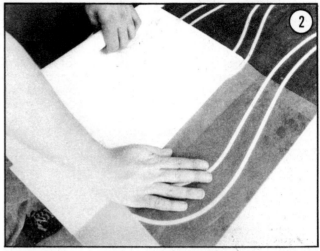

Lay out the flame design as in other methods, outlining the licks with 1/8-inch masking tape. Cover the entire area with the shelf paper, being careful to avoid wrinkles or bubbles near the flame edges. Overlap the strips of the shelf paper slightly.

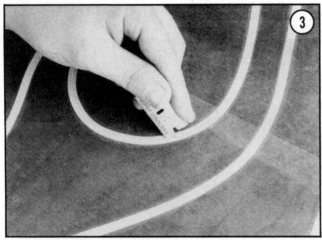

Gently cut along the 1/8-inch tape with an X-Acto knife. Follow the middle of the tape, using light pressure so that you cut only the shelf paper.

Peel away the shelf paper, exposing the area to be painted and leaving the crisp edges of the masking tape to outline the flames.

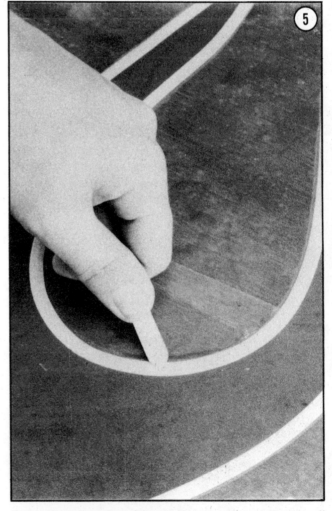

Trace along the edge of the shelf paper with your thumbnail or a small wooden or plastic stick to make sure that it is firmly sealed to the tape all the way around the design. Clean the surface with wax and grease remover, and you're ready to paint.

enough space so that everything doesn't get all bunched up at the very end of the flames.

When spraying the additional colors use masking tape and paper to protect the already-painted sections. The use of an airbrush or a touch-up gun will minimize overspray in areas like these. Taping must also be employed where parts of the flames split or overlap. Double check what you're doing here so that you don't make a lick go over when it should have gone under another part. Generally speaking, it will look better if the lighter colors go over the darker ones. This technique gives the best contrast.

After each successive color has been applied, the surface should be air dusted and wiped with a tack rag. The exception is at the border where two colors meet. A little overspray here can be beneficial. When the clear top coat is shot over this overspray it will blend into the paint, making a pleasant transition between colors. If you want distinct breaks between the different colors, remove the overspray.

After all the colors have been applied, it is time to add any fogging. Many flame painters like to lightly fog the inner curves of flames with a contrasting color. An airbrush works best for finely controlled fogging.

For protection and a super shine, the flames should be sprayed with a clear topcoat. A two-part clear will provide durable protection for the flames (provided, of course, that it is

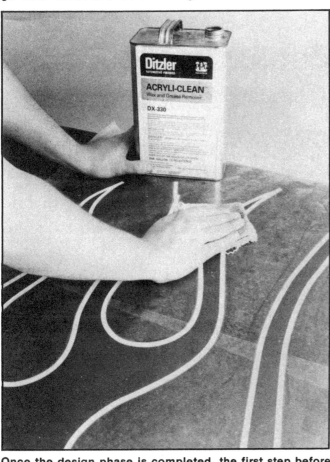

Once the design phase is completed, the first step before painting is to clean the surface with wax and grease remover. Even if the surface doesn't have any polish on it, the taping procedure leaves oily deposits (from your hands) on the area to be painted.

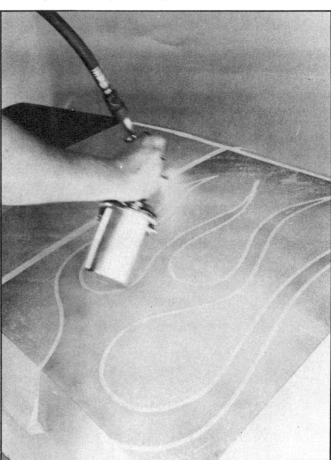

A touch-up gun is just the right size for spraying most flame patterns. The choice of color is virtually unlimited, but be certain the type of paint is compatible with the base paint so that it doesn't wrinkle or melt the base.

The underlying surface probably won't require extensive sanding, but you must scuff up the slick surface so the flame paint will adhere firmly.

A 3M Scotch Brite "steel wool substitute" pad works fine for scuffing the paint surface. Be careful not to lift the edges of the tape.

If the flame pattern has overlapping licks, you must mask over the bottom licks before adding the second color to the overlapping one, otherwise they won't look like they overlap. First, cut the tape from the crossover and mask over the bottom lick.

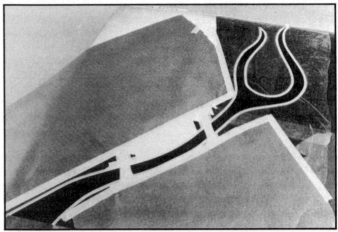

Mask off the rest of the flame area that will not receive the second color. In this case, notice that the two other licks will overlap this one, so they were masked off where they cross the one being painted now.

compatible with the subsurface paint). If you want to add any special effects, the clear coat is a good time to do it. Many painters add a little pearl for a soft sparkle or some fine flake particles for a brighter sparkle. A small amount of some translucent toner could also be added if a special tint was desired. Remember the basic color mixing priniciples if you use any tinted top coats. For example, a red tint over blue flames will give the flames a purple hue.

TAPE REMOVAL AND CLEANUP

You'll certainly be anxious to see the final results of your flame painting, but don't be too eager to remove the tape. Let the paint dry thoroughly, at least 24 hours is best, if possible. This gives the paint ample time to grip the surface, especially around the edges. The edges of the flames can easily be lifted away from the surface if the paint is not thoroughly dry, so great care must be exercised when removing the tape.

When you pull the tape, start from the back of the flames. This way you will be less likely to damage the flame tips. If if looks like part of a flame is going to lift, you can use an X-Acto knife or a single-edge razor blade to separate the tape from the paint. The tape seldom comes off perfectly, so it is better to pull the tape out from under the excess paint, rather than tearing paint from the design area with tape. The excess paint can be trimmed later with an X-acto knife. There will probably be some spots where the paint got

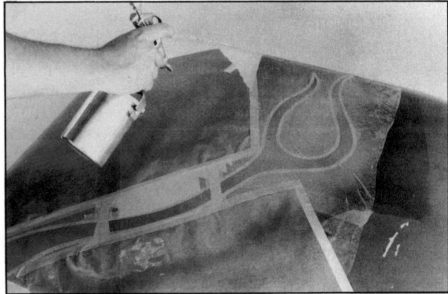

Then, spray the new color, e.g., orange over yellow, being careful to blend the two colors at an appropriate point towards the front.

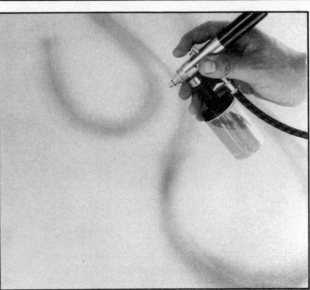

Most painters like to add a little fogging of red, or some other dark color, around the curved edges of the flames. You could do this with a spray gun, but beginners will find an airbrush much easier to handle for this job. Start fogging along the tape and work gradually onto the painted area.

91

The airbrush is also great for adding a dash of bright color to the very tip of each flame. Again, blend the colors where they meet.

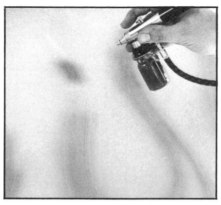

After all the colors have been applied, it is a good idea to cover the entire job with a coat of clear lacquer or some other tough finish, like clear catalyzed acrylic enamel. An alternative is to remove all the tape, lightly sand the edges of the flames and shoot the entire vehicle with a coat of clear. If you use catalyzed enamel, you can even spray the clear over pinstripe outlines.

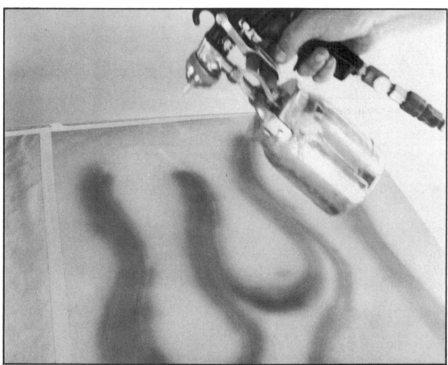

under the masking tape. These small spots can be removed with a rag lightly doused with thinner or with rubbing compound.

Unless you can achieve picture-perfect flame edges, the edges will probably need to be pinstriped to cover up irregularities. Even if your edges are perfect, pinstriping will help set the flames off from the rest of the vehicle. If you feel confident, try your own pinstriping. It's not as difficult as freehand work because you have an already-established contour (the edge of the flame). And, if you use striping enamel you can readily wipe away small mistakes. However, if you have a shaky hand, let a professional pinstriper do the job or use striping tape.

Protect your flames with a quality car wax and they should last many, many years. Keep some of the original paint, though, to touch-up stone nicks or scratches.

FLAME VARIATIONS

Traditionalists feel that red, orange and yellow are the only proper colors for a flame job, but modern custom painters render them in every color of the rainbow. Imaginative color combinations provide an easy means to achieve a different flame look, but you can also use different types of paint. Any of the various trick paints can be used for flames.

Flames don't have to be just solid colors, either. They can have patterns inside the boundaries of the flames. The patterns can be made in many

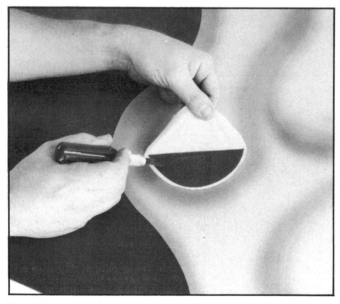

If you have applied several coats of paint to create a multi-colored flame design, be very careful when you start to remove the masking paper so that you don't crack or "lift" the paint. It might help to scribe around the edge of the design (on the 1/8-inch tape, not the surface of the paint) to help break the tape away from the dried paint.

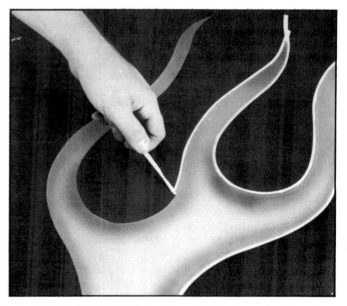

When removing the design tape, pull it backwards rather than straight up, to keep from lifting the paint. Go slowly and carefully! You don't want to tear off any of the paint, because it would be very hard to touch-up. If the paint is very thick, pull the 1/8-inch tape out from under the edge of the hardened paint and trim the edge with an X-Acto knife or razor blade.

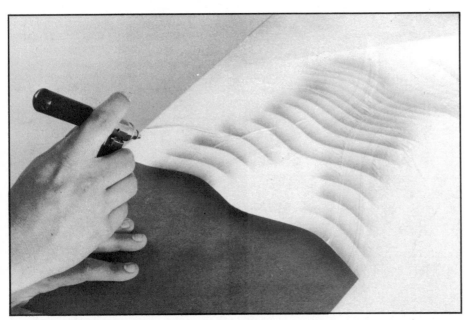

Flames don't have to be painted in red, yellow and orange. Several of the trick painting methods outlined in the next chapter, such as an airbrushed stencil design, can be applied within the masked off flame pattern.

just use the pinstriped outline of flames. Or the flames can be done completely in pearl colors for soft, subtle flames. A variation of the pinstriped flames is to lay out the design like a standard flame job and then use an airbrush to fog around the tape.

Flames don't have to be the predominant feature of a custom paint job. You can have a panel design pattern with solid-color flames reversed out of the area. Flames can also be rendered effectively with gold leaf for a very rich effect.

Flames can start in places besides the front of a vehicle. They can be inside design panels, they can flow out of an air scoop on the sides of a vehicle or they can start along the forward edge of the roof or the doors. Flames can also be part of a mural or they can be surrealistic and flow out of the mane of a wild horse or a long-haired maiden. The combinations are only limited by the scope of your imagination.

ways. Some trick paints will separate to give a marbled effect. Cobwebbing (see chapter 9) will give an interesting effect. The best way to make patterns is with stencils or pieces of light cardboard. Stencils can be used for circles or other geometric shapes and the cardboard can be cut to achieve scalloped effects. Many of the custom painting techniques described elsewhere in this book can be used effectively with flames.

If you don't like bold flames, you can

A pinstriped outline in a contrasting color not only sets the flames off sharply from the background, but it also covers the edge of the paint, which may be a bit ragged after the tape is removed. Outlining flames is one of the easiest of pinstriping jobs, and you might be able to do it yourself with a little practice. Otherwise, take it to a pro for this last step.

CHAPTER

9 TRICK PAINT AND ACCENT PANELS

- USING TRICK PAINTS
- CANDYS, PEARLS, AND METALFLAKES
- SCALLOPS AND FREAK DROPS
- LACE, COBWEBS, AND ENDLESS LINES
- ACETYLENE PAINTING
- EXAMPLES OF MANY PAINTING TRICKS

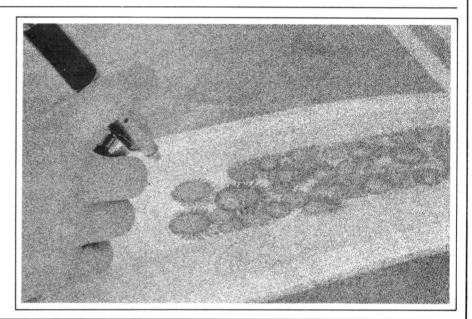

THE LITTLE TRICKS THAT MAKE UP THE ART OF CUSTOM PAINTING

This is the fun part. Sometimes it seems like custom painting is more sanding and taping than painting, but when it gets down to the actual painting the hassles fade away when you sit back and admire the results of your creativity. Some very simple "tricks" can yield amazingly professional results.

The neat thing about these tricks is that most techniques are quite simple and require very little equipment. Very often these techniques are most effective in small areas and, as a result, you don't have to repaint the entire vehicle to produce a unique custom look. This brings up an important point to remember; don't ruin a nice effect by overdoing it. Most paint tricks look best when done as accents to the main paint scheme.

If you stop and analyze some of the most elaborate show-type paint jobs, you will notice that the wildest effects

Even if this early El Camino didn't have about a million dollars worth of custom bodywork, the paint job would still make it unique. The frenetic patterns in candy colors over a pearl base employ many of the tricks described in this chapter.

are often achieved by a combination of many simple little tricks. The goal is to imaginatively combine small elements to end up with a unique overall finish. In the beginning it may be difficult to visualize the final effect, but practice will help. And when you are just starting, don't let your pride get in your way; consider copying effects that you

see on other cars. You'll have plenty of time to get creative after you have more experience.

It is also a good idea to practice a little before you start your painting career by adding a few classy touches to your dad's Cadillac or your best friend's Camaro. Fortunately, most basic paint tricks can be practiced

In the age of decal and plastic trimmed new cars, a moderate touch of real custom painting can add class and character to any car. This flaming bird was created with a stencil and an airbrush. Subtle stripes outline the hood.

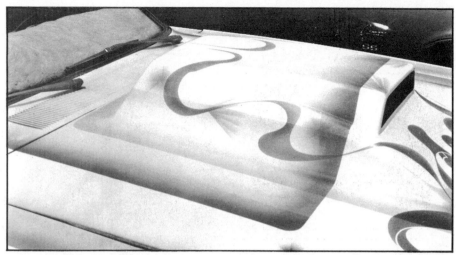

Once your car has been painted a base color, it is relatively easy to add striking custom patterns or designs, using only masking tape, stencils and a few other aids. Figuring out a pleasing design is actually more difficult than executing it. Study custom paint work on other cars to decide what will look best on yours.

rather easily by experimenting on old fenders, scraps of metal, pieces of wood or anything else that is handy. Practicing a flame job takes a lot of space, but simple tricks, like freak drops, can be tried almost anywhere.

Once you have mastered the basic skills and techniques, you can concentrate on the design and color combinations. Don't worry if you make a mistake with a painting trick because it is usually easy to repaint the small base color area used for most paint tricks and start again.

EQUIPMENT NEEDED FOR PAINT TRICKS

Most of the equipment needed for paint tricks is the same as for any standard paint job, plus a few props (depending on the actual trick). A full-size spray gun is a necessity if you're going to repaint an entire car, but the smaller touch-up gun is terrific for panel tricks. They are easy to handle and though they hold only a limited amount of paint, the average touch-up gun will hold plenty of paint for most tricks. An airbrush is also quite handy, and necessary, for some tricks. In most cases they are just plain easier to use, even though a big gun could produce the same results.

Most paint tricks should be shot with lacquers or acrylic lacquers because these paints dry quickly and are generally easier to apply. Fast drying time is important when you are using many different colors in a small area. Also, lacquer allows you to sand out mistakes (if you use a very fine grade of sandpaper). Another benefit of lacquer is that it is easier to fade and blend between colors.

The major prop used in trick paint-

ing is a stencil, of one type or another. The stencils can be made from a variety of things, like manila file folders, tag-board or construction paper. The stencils can be cut to represent geometric shapes or random patterns. When used in conjunction with other stencils or by overlapping the same pattern several times, this technique can produce some very intricate designs. When these patterns are viewed from a distance, all you see is

the overall design, but when viewed up close, you can often see the individual stencil shapes that make up the design. By studying other designs, you can determine the stencil shapes that will combine to make the most pleasing and unusual patterns.

SURFACE PREPARATION

Surface preparation for trick painting is very simple. If the underlying

Most custom paint tricks require no more than a small spray gun (touch-up gun or airbrush), a compatible air source, lots of masking tape and a little patience and creativity. The patterns on the tailgate of this pickup are small in size, large in impact.

Custom painting doesn't have to be flamboyant. Simple color-coordinated stripes can be very effective.

Custom paint tricks can be especially effective in places where they aren't expected, such as under the trunk.

The paint scheme on this T-roadster looks more complicated than it is. Two colors of cobwebbed panels were added over the straight base color.

The candy-colored designs on this Four-By are a bit more intricate, but the process is the same: add some striking custom colors over the otherwise-drab stock paint.

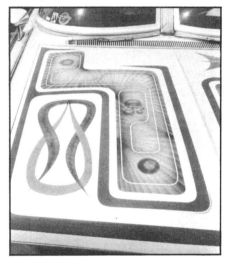

Candy colors are difficult to apply evenly over large areas, but using them for custom paint design work is quite easy. However, since candies are transparent, they must be applied over a light-colored base—pearls are excellent. Candies are also great for overlapping or blending in designs.

By keeping a candy design pattern small, it is easy to control the hue and consistency of the color. In this case the shades were intentionally overlapped and fogged to create patterns in the color.

paint is in good condition, usually all that is necessary is to scruff up the surface with an artificial steel-wool pad or fine sandpaper. The object is to give the surface some "tooth" to provide paint adhesion. Don't sand as much as you would for a complete repainting job, you won't be applying much paint and deep sandpaper scratches will show through to the surface.

Clean the surface well with wax and grease remover before you start applying paint. Some painters will prime the surface, but this usually isn't necessary. In many cases primer can't be used, as would be the case when a design uses the original paint as the background color. On the other hand, if there are nicks or scratches that have to be filled before painting the area, primer must be used to cover the filler and any patches of bare metal. If you suspect that the underlying paint may cause trouble, you should apply sealer to the area before you start.

BASE COATS

Most trick paint applications need some type of a base coat. The choice of this base coat is important because it will form the basis of your design. Think whether you want the different parts of the design to contrast sharply or to blend. The base coat will give added depth if a translucent color is used. An opaque color will give increased contrast.

Sometimes a contrasting base coat is used to make the design pattern brighter. If the pattern is being applied to a dark-colored vehicle, applying a white base coat will make the design stand out better and vice versa. Most trick patterns are painted with a minimum of paint, so the base coat should be applied carefully to provide protection for the surface metal and to give a good surface for the design paint.

Almost any paint can serve as a base coat, although some paints are specially formulated to act as base coats. These special base coats are most important when using candies, flakes and pearl paints. Often such base paints are known as undercoats. They are most commonly available in silver, gold, copper, white and black. The metallic colors are used for candies and flakes, while white and black are used for pearls. White and black undercoats can also be used with candy colors.

CANDY COLORS

Transparent, colored paints are known generically as candy paints and by a variety of brandnames, such as Candy Apple, Star Apple, Pro Candy and Aero-Lac Candy Colors. When applied over the proper undercoat, candy paints produce a unique, deep, glass-like surface. Candy paint was one of the first custom paints to be developed, and though the techniques have been considerably refined, candy paint is still one of the most difficult to spray.

Because of their transparent nature, Candy colors are difficult to apply, especially over large areas. Several coats are required to achieve the feeling of depth that distinguish this type of paint and as more topcoat is applied, the color shade will become darker. It is, therefore, hard to keep the color consistent when several different areas are being painted. Also, it is almost impossible to fix runs or sags in candy paints. Often the only viable "fix" is to sand the entire area and begin again. Obviously, this increases the difficulty of maintaining consistent color tones in various areas. These peculiarities make a really first-rate candy paint job rather rare, but they are also the qualities that make such a paint job a beautiful testimony to rare craftsmanship.

When applied over a small area, such as a design panel or as the top color of a pattern, candy colors aren't difficult to manage. In small areas it is almost impossible to notice minor differences in hue or shade, so don't be afraid to use candy paints. Candy paints are one of the best mediums for trick applications, especially when a variety of colors or many-layered patterns are used.

PEARL PAINTS

Pearl paints are great for highlights and subtle designs. They are available in a wide array of colors as ready-mixed paints or as simple additives that can be used in clear overcoats. Entire cars have been painted in pearl colors (most often white) but pearls are currently used largely as accents and topcoat toners.

Occasionally pearl paints are used as base coats for other designs, but by far they are most effective as a surface highlight. They can be used in pattern work as a subtle design that is only visible when viewed from certain angles, producing an effect that is almost like ghost shadows on the surface of the car. These designs seem to pop in and out of view as you move around the car, adding interest to the overall effect. Pearls also work very well when used to shade other colors. They can be used on the sharp edges of a geometric shape to simulate the highlights caused by the sun.

Experiment with the use of pearls and you will find that they can add that something extra that separates ordinary work from the extraordinary.

When spraying pearl colors always follow the directions on the can. Be especially careful to thoroughly stir the paint before use and keep it well agitated during use. The pearl particles need to be evenly distributed to achieve the desired look.

Originally made from ground fish scales, pearl (or pearlescent) paints have a subtle luminous glow. White pearl, as used on the entire body of this '54 Corvette, looks just like its namesake. Pearls come in several pastel colors, and can be used very effectively either as a basecoat or for design work.

One of the most unusual pearl effects is created with Metalflake Flip Flop pearl. As the sun strikes the pearlized pigment from different angles the color appears to change. This provides a unique and dazzling "shimmering" effect.

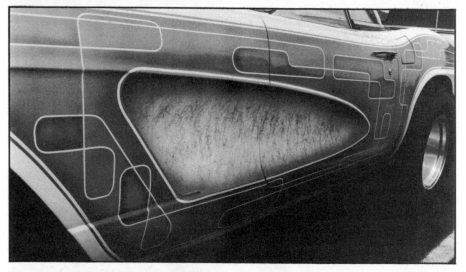

Often the body lines of a vehicle, such as the inset on the side of this early Corvette, will suggest natural panels for custom paint designs. Note how both the cobweb panel and the endless line panel are separated by narrow taped-off stripes, thus creating the boarders.

Heavy particle paints, like metalflakes, pearls and even some metallics, should be agitated to keep the particles evenly suspended in the cup while spraying. If you don't have an agitator cup, you can simply drop in a few clean marbles (or something similar) and shake the cup periodically as you spray.

Scallops were one of the earlier custom paint designs and they look great on this dirt-track style roadster (the colors are a deep maroon over a sandy beige). Done in this style, scallops look like straightened-out flames and lend a feeling of speed to the car.

METALFLAKE PAINTS

Metalflake is the trade name of a highly reflectant paint developed by the Metalflake Corporation. Many other companies also market their own flake paints, although to call flake paints a paint is somewhat misleading because the flake is usually an additive that is used with clear or candy paints. Flakes come in a variety or sizes. The larger sizes produce a sparkling "glitter" effect, even when

Sometimes called color bands or "belly bands," a narrow custom paint panel along the middle of each side of the vehicle makes for a naturally pleasing design. The panel on this Camaro employs an overlapping circle stencil pattern.

viewed from a distance. However, the novice painter should be aware that the larger flakes are the most difficult to apply evenly.

The flake material needs to be completely suspended in the paint material while it is being applied. A spray gun with an agitator should be used. Flake topcoats should be applied over an undercoat that is metallic in nature. The flake particles land on the surface in a random manner and as the light hits these particles the characteristic sparkle effect is produced. However, this random arrangement of the flakes also makes for a rough surface unless many coats of clear are applied over the flakes. For this reason flake paints are not very popular for most trick applications.

PANEL PAINTING

One of the most basic techniques behind trick applications is panel painting. Basically, a "panel" is a specific area that is painted a contrasting color to separate it from the rest of the paintwork. The panels usually follow the contours and design of the vehicle and a nicely done series of panels will compliment and accent the basic design of the body.

On large vehicles, like vans, the panels are often free-form shapes that provide a background area over which other paint tricks or murals can be applied. The edge of the panel also serves as a border for such things as cobwebbing, freak drops, endless lines, lace painting or fish scales. In such cases the panel serves as a frame to set the mural off from the rest of the paint job.

Panels can be either subtle or clearly defined, depending on the colors and type of paint used. Panels of subtle colors can be quite effective, or if you want a more distinctive, but not highly contrasting, effect it is possible to pinstripe the border of the panel.

The main thing to keep in mind when painting panels is the shape of the vehicle. The most effective panel designs follow the form of the vehicle and highlight the natural shape of the metal. Panel painting is one of the cornerstones of custom painting, and easy to master if you give some thought to the layout and design.

SCALLOPS

Scallop painting is similar to panel painting in that the design must be coordinated with the shape of the vehicle. Scallop painting was very popular with car customizers in the

This Model A uses a minimal, but effective, scallop pattern and a dash of pinstriping as simple embellishments. Less is often best when it comes to custom paint.

'50's and 60's. Today it is not a widespread technique, although the growing interest in early custom cars may also lead to a new outburst of scallop paint jobs.

Scallops are long, narrow, tapering panels that follow the contours of the car. They usually originate toward the front of the car and sweep toward the rear where they taper to a point. They can be laid out in a variety of directions but the longest arm of the scallop is usually parallel to the roofline.

Scallops are traditionally a single color or a single color with fogged edges. Pinstriping is also used to give the edges added contrast. For a unique effect it would also be possible to overlay other trick techniques (e.g., cobwebbing or freak drops) on top of the panel-like portions of the scallop. Long scallops can use a variety of colors that blend between colors as the scallops progress.

Laying out scallops is similar to the techniques used to lay out flames. The design is limited only by your imagination and can range from elegantly simple forms to exotically elaborate designs with overlapping panels and many special effects. Thin masking tape is used to outline the basic scallop shape. Most scallop designs are symmetrical, so extra care is needed to transfer the shapes from one side to the other. When untaping scallops, exercise extra care around the tips. An X-Acto knife or a razor blade can be used to trace the edge of the scallop. Some rough edges are likely to show up, but pinstriping will cover all but the biggest nicks.

Scallops are usually rather large but they can also be used in small spaces. Small overlapping scallops would work well inside a long, relatively narrow panel area.

HOW TO PAINT "SCALLOP" PANELS

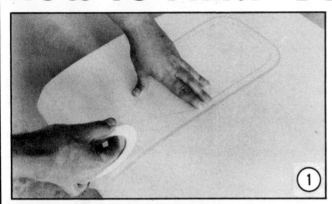

(1) Scallops are designed much like flames. The design can follow body contours of the vehicle, flow from front to back or take traditional shapes, as shown here. Use 1/8-inch tape to mask the outline.

(2) Mask off the areas around the scallops. Painting the thin scallops requires only a small spray gun (or airbrush) and low air pressure, so you shouldn't have to worry much about overspray getting on to other parts of the vehicle.

(3) Using an airbrush, apply a base coat to the scallop. We used Metalflake premixed candies, which are simple to load in the gun and shoot.

(4) These scallops were painted Aztec Gold with Fire Red tips. After the gold was sprayed and allowed to dry, the red was added to the tips and blended into the gold with an airbrush.

(5) The finished scallop has a clean, sweeping shape and the two blended candy colors make it more interesting. For a final touch, it could be outlined with pinstriping.

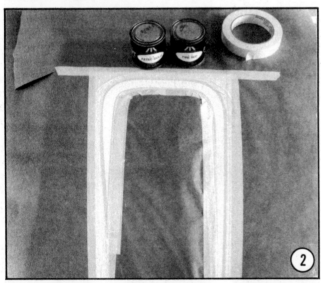

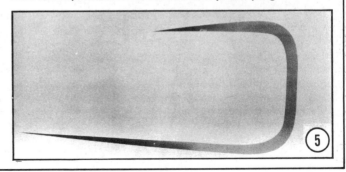

HOW TO PAINT "FREAK DROP" PANELS

Freak drops, a recent paint trick, are fun as well as easy. Just shoot a spot of paint, then hit it with a burst of air to make the tentacles spread. A dual-action airbrush works best for freak drops because the air and paint can be controlled separately, but a single-action airbrush will also work.

For this design freak drops were painted in random fashion inside a paint panel. Then a contrasting color was fogged around the perimeter of the panel to add definition to the design.

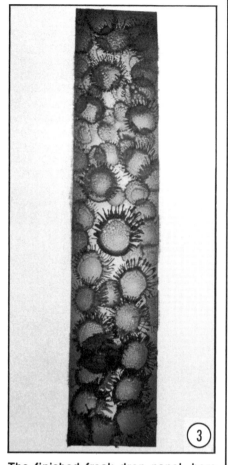

The finished freak drop panel, here practiced on an old hood, could be outlined in pinstriping, surrounded by color bands or lines or incorporated into a more complex custom design.

FREAK DROPS

Sometimes mistakes can be turned into interesting effects. Such is the case with freak drops, which are obtained by using an airbrush in an incorrect manner. Individual freak drops can be combined in a variety of interesting patterns to give a pleasing final design.

Freak drops are best applied with either a touch-up gun or an airbrush. A double-action airbrush is preferred to a single-action model because the double-action airbrush allows you to deposit the paint first and then hit the wet paint with a blast of air to make the tentacles of the freak drop. A touch-up gun will make larger freak drops than an airbrush, but it works like a double-action airbrush in that air can be blasted separately from the paint.

Single-action airbrushes also work fine for freak drops, but the technique is slightly different. Since the paint and air are controlled by one movement,

the airbrush must be held close enough (approximately 2 inches) to the surface to allow the tentacles to run as the paint is applied. It is tougher to control the direction of the tentacles with a single-action airbrush, but single-action airbrushes tend to form more uniform freak drops.

The paint used for freak drops should be very thin, much thinner than for any normal painting. The thin paint aids the formation of the little runners that make up freak drops. The paint should be about the consistency of water. Experiment, making the paint progressively thinner, until you find the best consistency for freak drops that you like.

Freak drops are usually applied in a random pattern, but guidelines can be used to obtain unusual freak drop variations. A taped line or a straight stencil can be used and a string of freak drops can be shot along the border. Or, instead of a string of individual freak drops, a stencil or

taped line can be used to paint a continuous line of thin paint. Tentacles will form, but the color and shape is uninterrupted. Playing around with freak drops and stencils can lead to some unique designs for panel painting.

BLOWUPS

Blowups are a variation of freak drops. This is also known as circle painting because they are small circles of thin paint. Blowups are best applied with an airbrush; either single-action or double-action will work fine. Give quick little bursts of paint to form the circles. Don't apply too much paint or air or you will end up with freak drops. Too short a burst will leave ill-defined circles. Practice the duration of the burst, the distance from the surface (usually 2-3 inches) and the paint consistency (not quite as thin as for freak drops) until you can achieve perfect circles. Overlapped blowups of contrasting colors give a neat effect.

LACE PAINTING

Lace painting is another one of those custom paint tricks that purportedly originated by mistake. A piece of lace was supposedly laying around a paint shop and some paint was accidentally sprayed over the lace. When the painter lifted the lace, he noticed an interesting pattern on the surface below. No matter how it started, the key to effective lace painting is your choice of lace. It can take a lot of looking in fabric stores to find the right lace and, unfortunately, some of the prettiest patterns are the most expensive.

Any type of spray gun, touch-up gun or airbrush will work for lace painting. The size of the gun depends mostly on how much area needs to be covered. At one time lace painting was used on large portions of vehicles, but now it is used largely as a background for other effects or in panel painting.

The lace pattern is usually applied over a contrasting background color. Tape off the area to be laced, stretch the lace tightly over the area and then tape it in place. Eliminate all wrinkles from the material or the pattern will not be consistent. Apply the paint in light, fogging coats. Allow each coat of paint to dry thoroughly before applying the next one. Don't let the lace get overly saturated with paint—the excess paint may soak through the lace to the surface below or the saturated lace may lift sections of the paint when the

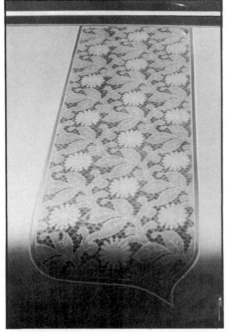

Lace painting is a type of stencil painting using actual lace fabric taped over the base color and fog painted with a contrasting color. Lace painting is almost always done in panels, which are then outlined with pinstripes or some other type of border.

lace is removed from the surface. Properly applied, the lace pattern will be sharply defined. The effect can be made softer or sharper, as desired, by varying the type of paint. Pearl paints will give the most delicate effect.

A variation of the lace effect is fishnet painting. The idea is the same, only fishnet stockings are used instead of lace. The fishnet produces a simple, uniform pattern or it can be

Cobwebbing is usually done with black or some other dark color over a light base, but in this case both black and white webbing is employed in a panel-painted scheme. Again, note the darker fogging around the edges of the panels.

stretched and distorted to produce some unusual effects.

COBWEBBING

Cobwebbing is yet another custom paint trick that started out as an accident. It was discovered when someone failed to properly dilute the paint and it came out of the gun in a long, stringly stream. Cobwebbing is also known as spiderwebbing or marbling, depending upon the method of application and the effect achieved.

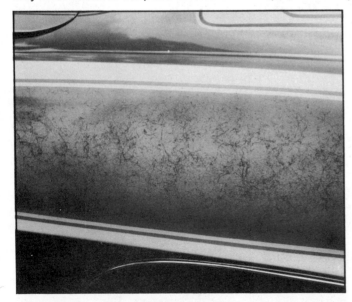

Cobwebbing can be integrated into a custom paint scheme or used as a separate element. Here it is used in bordered panels on the sides, hood and trunk of a late-model car. Note that the edges of the panels have been fogged with a darker shade than the middle of the panel.

Cobwebbing is not often used to paint large sections of a vehicle, but here is an example of cobwebbed fenders on a '32 Ford.

Cobwebbing is best used in panel areas or as a background for other effects.

To get a suitable cobweb look it is best to use a full-size spray gun or a touch-up gun. The gun should be set at a relatively high air pressure to force the thick paint out of the gun. The amount of air pressure will alter the type of pattern produced. The pattern is also affected by the distance the nozzle is held from the surface. The farther the gun is held from the surface, the stringier the pattern will become. As the spray gun gets closer to the surface, the pattern gets more concentrated. A good starting distance is about three feet.

Cobwebbing leaves a rough, textured surface that must be covered with several coats of clear. Be sure to let the cobwebbing dry thoroughly before applying the clear, or the clear may melt the cobwebbing into a fuzzy mess.

ENDLESS LINE PAINTING

Endless line painting is an easy paint trick that can yield very interesting results. It is a technique that works well with panel painting. Endless line painting is basically a free-form series of lines that are overlapped and intermingled in a small panel area. The lines are usually done in several different colors.

Endless line painting is easiest to do with an airbrush and 1/8-inch tape. Thinner tape will work if you can find it. Bigger tape will also work, but much of the intricacy is lost with thicker tape.

Endless line painting can be done in different ways. Regardless of which way you choose, it is usually best to first spray the area with a contrasting base coat. In the simplest method the design is laid out with tape and the panel is painted with a color that will contrast with the base coat. When the tape is removed you have what looks

HOW TO PAINT ENDLESS LINE PANELS

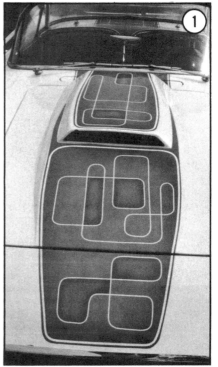

A simple endless-line design inside a candy-color panel accentuates the hood scoop on this early Corvette. Notice that some of the areas enclosed by the lines have been painted and shaded with a darker color of candy.

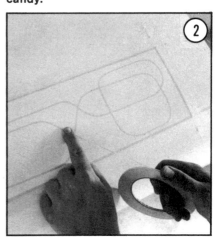

Endless line painting is one of the easiest of all custom painting tricks. Start by masking off a design panel of any size or shape. Then, use 1/8-inch tape to create your endless line pattern. The beginning and end of the line can meet, or they can run out of the panel.

PAINTING COBWEBS

The trick to creating cobwebs is to use unreduced paint, straight from the can. You can use lacquer or enamel, and you will need a full-size spray gun or a touch-up gun to handle the high pressure necessary to spray the thick paint.

To get the right cobweb effect you will have to experiment with the air pressure and the distance that you hold the gun from the surface. Start with about 50lb of pressure and hold the gun two to three feet away from the surface.

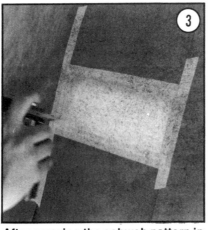

After spraying the cobweb pattern in black, we went back and fogged the edges of the panel using a candy color in an airbrush.

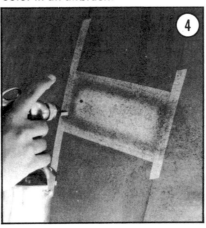

Cobwebbing is highly textured, so it must be covered with several coats of clear if you want a smooth finish.

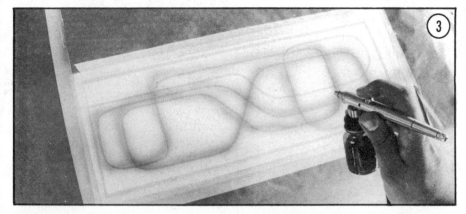

Simply trace along the line with an airbrush. Adjust the airbrush so that it will lay a stripe wide enough to overlap the tape on both sides. The actual width of the stripe will depend on the overall size of the endless line design.

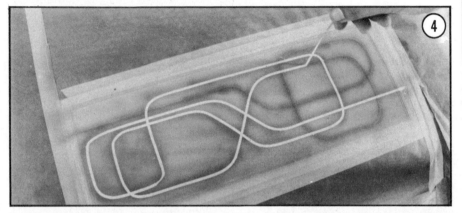

On this panel the background was also lightly misted with paint, then the tape was removed to reveal the endless line pattern. For a basic design, you could stop here.

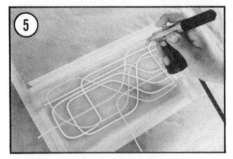

However, we added another line of tape over the original pattern, after the paint had thoroughly dried. Then we followed this line with a contrasting color of candy paint.

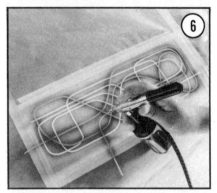

Extra bursts of color were added where some of the lines intersected.

The completed endless design panel looks interesting and intricate, but as you can see, it was not at all difficult to accomplish. Using two overlapping colors, as in this case, would only be effective if transparent candy colors were also used.

like a convoluted pinstripe.

The second method also uses a taped design over a base coat. This time, instead of painting the whole area, an airbrush is used on the tape pattern. The result is a fogged line around the contrasting undercoat. By painting the whole area (after the undercoat and tape) and then fogging along the tape, the two methods can be combined for a more complex pattern. Different colors can also be used in different parts of the design for a nice effect.

ACETYLENE PAINTING

A novel, swirly effect can be achieved by using an acetylene torch on a custom paint panel. Mask off the area to be painted and apply a base coat if desired. Light a torch with only the acetylene turned on (no oxygen) and

A variety of custom painting techniques were employed in the scheme on this street "funny car," but the upper stripe, shown here with the dark smokey swirls, is an example of acetylene painting. What looks like smoke is actually created with a smoking acetylene welding torch over a light base color.

practice waving the torch so that curly smoke is produced. When you are satisfied with the smoke pattern, hold the torch close enough to the surface so that the smoke will stick to the paint, but not so close that the flame touches the paint. Cover the smoke with clear or a translucent color to seal in the smoke pattern.

FISH SCALING

An effect that looks similar to the scales on a fish can be obtained by making a template of side-by-side semicircles. Fish-scale patterns are usually rather small and intricate, so an airbrush works best for applying the paint. Larger templates can be made where a touch-up gun would work best.

The fish scale template can be made in several different ways. If you are good with an X-Acto knife or scissors, you can draw several over-

HOW TO PAINT "FISH SCALE" PANELS

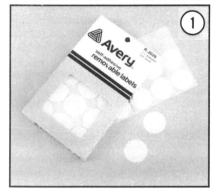

Any variety of cutouts or objects can be used as stencils to create trick paint designs. A favorite of many painters are small circular gummed labels, available at stationery stores.

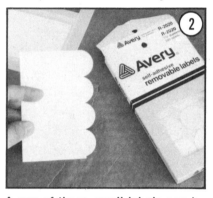

A row of these small labels can be used to make a perfect fish scale stencil. In this case the labels are attached to the edge of a 3x5-inch index card; attach labels to the front and back of the card if you do not want them to stick to the paint surface.

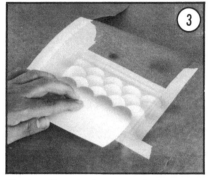

Mask off a design panel, hold the stencil flat against the surface and fog along the edge with an airbrush. Move the stencil down one row, shift it sideways half the width of one circle and fog along the edge again. Repeat the process until the design panel is filled.

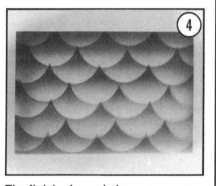

The finished panel gives a very accurate appearance of fish scales, especially when viewed from a distance. Such a pattern could be integrated into a variety of areas in a custom paint scheme.

lapping circles on a piece of light cardboard, using any circular object as a template, and cut out the design. Or you can use a compass or a draftman's circle guide to make the circles. Another easy way to make a fish scale template is to use circular gummed labels, like those used for price tags. These labels are found in most art and stationary stores. Apply the labels to a piece of file folder so that only half of the circle protrudes above the paper. Space the circles evenly and you will have a perfectly scalloped stencil.

Hold the stencil against the surface to be painted and fog along the edge of the stencil with an airbrush. Stagger each row of scales. Fish scales can be applied in single colors or in multiple colors. Pearl paints will increase the realistic look of the scale pattern.

RIBBON PAINTING

Ribbon painting, or scrolling as it is also known, is one of the more difficult paint tricks because it must have a three-dimensional look to be most effective. Obtaining a 3-D look takes more artistic talent than the average custom painting trick. When properly executed, ribbon painting looks like a free-flowing, three-dimensional ribbon lying on a flat surface.

Several different types of ribbons or scrolls can be made. The two biggest differences are whether or not the ribbons are in a straight line. The straight ribbons are easier to design because parallel pieces of tape can be used as guidelines. Regardless of the style of ribbons, an outline is needed for the design. The outline can be either drawn on the surface with a grease pencil, china marker or a Stabilo pencil. The Stabilo pencil is a type of marking pencil found at art supply stores and is excellent for all types of lettering and layout work.

Once the design is made, tape off the surrounding area, scruff up the surface and clean with wax and grease remover. Ribbon painting is best done with a touch-up gun and an airbrush. Use the touch-up gun for the big areas and the airbrush for the shading.

Several different shades of the same color should be applied to make a ribbon look three-dimensional. It usually works best to start with the lightest color and work toward the darkest shade. Study the ribbon to determine how the light would strike it. This will help you decide where to put the light and dark colors. Usually the outside of the ribbon is the lightest and the inner bends are the darkest. It helps to mask off the different areas

Ribbon painting, which had a short period of great popularity in the early '70's, is one of the more complicated custom paint designs to execute. On this T-roadster, multi-colored candy ribbons swirl over a background of white pearl and fogged candy panels.

On this van a continuous ribbon intertwines over and under a stylized scallop design. Note how the ribbon is highlighted to give it a three-dimensional quality.

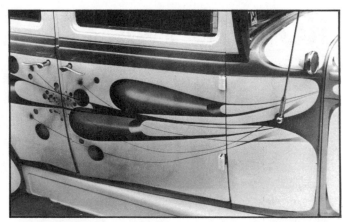

In this instance, severely elongated ribbons are incorporated into a space-like theme that also uses stenciled "spheres."

and apply the light, medium and dark areas in sequence. Then, use an airbrush for the final highlights. Pearl colors work very well for the final highlights. A little black paint will work well for the shaded areas. The finished ribbon should be covered with clear.

CARD MASKING

The use of stencils and masks is very common in custom painting. A very easy technique to learn is card masking. The basic idea is to form a design with the edge of a group of small cardboard squares (business cards work fine). The cards are usually held in a fan-like manner and paint is applied over the edge of the fan with an airbrush. The fan of cards is moved randomly and the paint is repeatedly sprayed over the edge to form an interesting design.

The idea of card masking will also work well with 3- x 5-inch index cards. The cards can be grouped in an irregular manner for a less structured design. The corners and edges of the cards can be altered with a scissors to avoid a sharp edged design. Like most paint tricks, card masking works best in small accent panels.

PLASTIC-WRAP PAINTING

A relatively new custom painting trick is the use of plastic food wrap (like Saran Wrap) to achieve a surrealistic surface effect. This is accomplished by removing paint rather than adding it.

Mask off and clean the area (as with all custom painting tricks). The color of the underlying sheet metal is important as part of it may show up in the finished design. If this color is satisfactory, paint the area with a color basecoat. (Assuming the metal color is suitable, the area still needs a base color.) A candy basecoat, like silver, works well for this step. After the basecoat has dried, choose the topcoat, which can be any color (candy colors work very well with this trick). Many painters prefer a dark color, like black, for maximum contrast.

Whatever topcoat you choose, don't mix it in the normal manner. Instead of using lacquer thinner (only

"CARD MASKING" PANELS

Card masking is another easy custom painting trick. Simply group some common business cards together in a random pattern, such as a fan, and spray along the edges with an airbrush. The cards could be stapled together for easier handling.

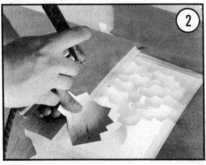

Place the swatch of cards against the painting surface and fog along the edge with paint. Move the cards down an inch or so and fog again.

The finished result is a sort of marbled effect. You could even blend colors to add a rainbow quality to the design panel.

In this instance the card swatch was moved in a progressive fan pattern to give a more symmetrical design. You could fog back in the opposite direction with another color to produce a more even color tone to the panel.

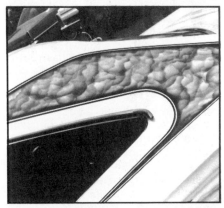

Custom painters have come up with all sorts of unrelated aids to create unusual trick designs. The panel on the roof pillar of this Plymouth was made by laying plastic food wrap over the wet paint.

105

HOW TO PAINT "PLASTIC-WRAP" PANELS

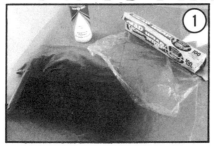

"Saran Wrap" painting is another design panel trick. After masking off a panel, spray it with a very slow-drying paint. In this case, we used Aero-Lac "Design Color," which is available in aerosol cans. It contains mineral oil to slow the drying process. You could also add a retarder to a standard automotive paint and use a spray gun.

Carefully remove the plastic wrap to reveal the design. If you are not satisfied with the results, spread another sheet of plastic over the surface and try again. The paint will stay wet for quite a while.

Immediately after spraying the design color on the panel, stretch a sheet of plastic wrap over the wet paint, letting it stick to the surface.

The finished panel will look sort of like crushed velvet or wrinkled satin. Allow it to dry thoroughly, and spray it with a protective coat of clear.

Then, rub your hand over the surface of the plastic wrap to swirl the paint underneath. Some of the base color should show through to create the design.

For a different effect, the same process can be followed using a piece of aluminum foil to create the pattern. For a highly textured look, wrinkle the foil before applying it over the design color.

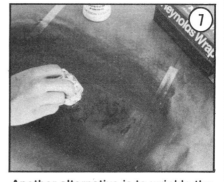

Another alternative is to wrinkle the aluminum foil into a ball and use it to blot the surface of the wet paint. This same technique could be used with other objects, such as a sponge, cotton swab or stiff-bristled brush.

lacquer paints should be used for this trick) to reduce the paint, thin with straight retarder. This slows the drying time of the paint.

As soon as the paint has been applied, quickly cover the area with Saran Wrap or a similar type of plastic food wrap. Use your hands to press the plastic wrap against the paint. Wrinkle the wrap or use your fingers to make impressions in the paint with the wrap. Lift the wrap and sections of the paint will cling to the wrap, leaving a mottled

surface. After the panel has dried (this may take awhile because of the retarded drying time), cover it with clear for added gloss and protection.

STENCIL PAINTING

Although many of the previous paint tricks involve some type of stencil, there is still more to be said about this technique. Stencils are used extensively to form the accent panels and stripes that have become popular

on dealer-customized vans. The dealer will often charge several hundred dollars for one of these "custom-painted" vans. The average do-it-yourselfer could do the same job at home for a fraction of the cost.

Stencils are one of the easiest ways for beginners to get unusual results without requiring a lot of experience. Stencils are extremely valuable in mural painting (these techniques are covered elsewhere in this book), but for now we will concentrate on the use

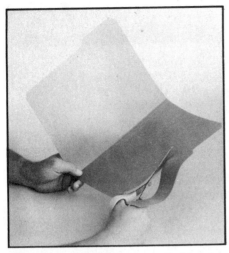

Manila file folders, or any light cardboard that is not too absorbent, can be cut with scissors to make any variety of stencil painting patterns.

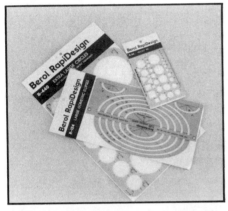

You can find all sorts of stencil possibilities, such as plastic circle or ellipse guides, at any store that sells drafting supplies.

of stencils in simple design panels.

A stencil can be made from nearly anything, but the most popular materials are heavy paper, manila file folders, construction paper, tracing paper (although tracing paper has a very limited period of usefulness), frisket paper and drawing or drafting aids. The plastic drafting templates, like those for drawing circles and ellipses, are very useful. Use masking tape to cover the unwanted holes and you have a sturdy, reusable template that will provide nice, crisp edges. Some art stores also stock a variety of art overlays that can be used for some very interesting effects. Most of these overlays have a center section that

must be punched out. You can use both the inner and outer parts as paint stencils.

It takes practice to get the best use out of stencils. Experiment with them and let your imagination run free. Interesting effects can also be obtained by mixing different stencil shapes in the same panel. And, the choice of colors is as important as the selection of the stencil shape. As a general rule, start with the lighter shades and work toward the darkest colors.

WOOD GRAINING

It is possible to simulate wood with

Metalflake "Spray Mask" is an excellent stencil medium, especially for making patterns on curved or uneven surfaces. After the Spray Mask was applied to the surface and allowed to dry, a grease pencil was used to trace the outline of a plastic drafting aid. Then, the figure was carefully cut with a pointed X-Acto knife. Be careful not to cut through to the base paint.

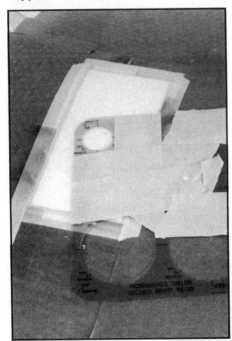

To use a circle guide as a stencil, tape off the holes around the one you wish to use.

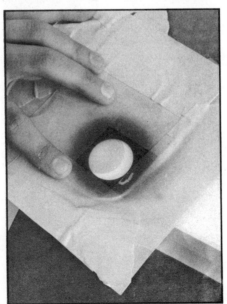

You can create a design pattern by lightly spraying inside the circle, moving it forward and then spraying it again. Continue this process to make a design similar to fish scales, or alter the pattern to create other effects.

Peel away the Spray Mask in the area to be painted, leaving the rest of the surface masked. After spraying the paint over the design area and allowing it to dry, carefully peel away the rest of the Spray Mask, leaving the painted design.

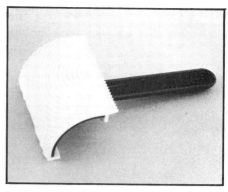

There are several ways to achieve wood-grain effects. Antique auto supply stores have special wood graining tools, such as this one made of soft plastic.

A wood-grain color band was added around the middle of this van by painting the panel with slow-drying shades of candy browns and then going over the surface with a large, ragged-tipped paint brush. The final result gives a look reminiscent of wood-paneled station wagons.

the following custom painting trick. This trick isn't particularly difficult but it does take some artistic ability to duplicate the grain patterns of real wood. There are several different methods of wood graining but they all require the painter to use his imagination to visualize the design of wood grain.

One method of wood graining is similar to plastic-wrap painting in that it makes use of slow-drying paint applied over an undercoat. For example, you could begin with a thin coat of medium-brown candy color sprayed over a gold base. After the brown paint has dried, a brush is used to apply a third coat of black acrylic lacquer, which has been thinned only with straight retarder. As the brush is worked across the area, the black paint will melt part of the brown paint, forming a

pattern of brown-and-black swirls. (Sometimes the brush will work better if you cut a jagged edge on the end of the bristles with a razor blade.) This will give a random pattern that looks like real wood. An airbrush with normally-thinned black paint can be used to add highlights and knotholes to the design. After everything has dried, cover the area with clear.

There are also wood-grain squeegees designed specifically to help produce wood-like painting effects. These inexpensive tools are sold at automotive restoration shops or they can be purchased from some mail-order companies. The technique is

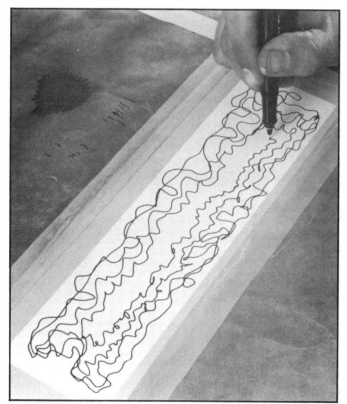

Here's another custom paint trick that is very easy to execute, yet produces striking, if not downright weird, results. Using a technical pen with acetate or india ink, simply squiggle a continuous line throughout a panel (or anywhere else in a custom design).

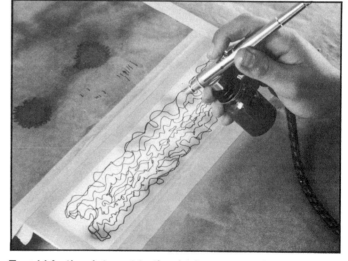

To add further interest to the design, you could fog a candy color over the area with an airbrush.

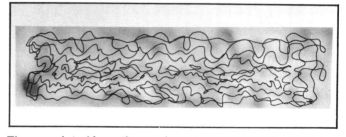

The completed frenetic panel may look a bit stark by itself, but would work very well if incorporated into a larger custom paint scheme.

Shading was used effectively to make the side of this Vega panel uniquely attractive. The lines smoothly disappear as the fading progresses to the rear of the vehicle.

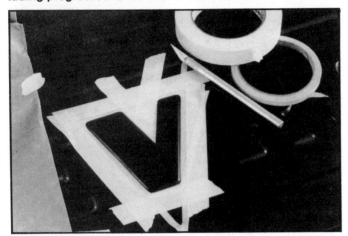

The difficult and rather tedious way to paint tailgate letters is to carefully mask off each one. You will have to use narrow tape to get into tight corners, and trim the edges neatly with an X-Acto knife.

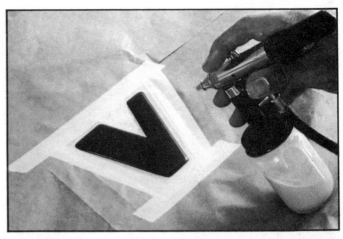

Once the letters are masked and the surrounding paint is protected from overspray, you can paint the letters with a touch-up gun or airbrush. You could use the airbrush, with a light shade of pearl paint, to go back and add subtle highlights to the letters to make them look even more three dimensional or lighted like a neon sign.

A much easier way to paint raised tailgate letters is to employ a method first used to restore old license plates. After sanding down the entire tailgate, spray several coats of lacquer over the letters, using the color you want them to finally appear.

similar to that described above, only the squeegee is scraped across the surface to produce a random pattern that resembles wood graining.

FINE-LINE ART

Ink pens can be used for custom painting. They are great for tiny details in murals, but they also work well for design panels. The type of ink pen most often used is called a technical pen. Art stores and stationary supply outlets sell them. India ink is used in the pens.

A fine-line panel starts with an undercoated surface. The pen is used in a free-form manner to make the design. The ink is then covered with a translucent candy color or clear.

Fine-line art can also be accomplished with a very sharp X-Acto knife. This method works best if a dark color is sprayed over a light undercoat. The knife is used to scratch a design that removes the dark paint and reveals the undercoat. When you are finished with the knife, cover the area with clear.

SHADING AND BLENDING

Shading and blending are tech-

niques that add a professional look to many custom painting tricks. They are subtle touches and require a fair amount of practice to master. An airbrush works best because of the fine, misting-type pattern that can be achieved.

The basic idea of shading is to use the airbrush to make a color progressively darker or lighter. The paint must be added gradually to achieve a smooth transition.

Blending is similar to shading and produces a subtle transition between different colors. This technique is common in multi-colored flame painting designs and it has many other creative possibilities. For example, it could be used to make a multi-colored racing stripe with each color fading gradually into the next.

This is actually a creative use of overspray and an airbrush will usually produce the best effect. Where the

Lightly scuff down any overspray around the outside of the letters, and spray the entire tailgate with a fairly light coat of lacquer in the basic color of the vehicle.

adjoining colors meet, the paint is lightly oversprayed onto the ajoining color. When clear is sprayed on the oversprayed area, it will melt and blend the colors together. If you want a sharper transition area, wipe the surface with a tack rag before applying the clear topcoat.

TAILGATE TRICKS

There are some special custom painting techniques that have been developed to highlight the names sculpted into the tailgates of some pickup trucks. Tailgates are a natural area for a wide variety of custom painting tricks, but what we are concerned with here is the raised letters found on the tailgate. These letters can be painted a contrasting color by carefully masking them and applying the paint or they can be covered with gold leaf material.

The problem with most tailgate letters is that they slope down to the surface of the tailgate without a clearly defined edge. This makes taping difficult. A much easier method is to use a technique that restorers use on old license plates.

Prepare, clean and prime the tailgate. Then paint the whole tailgate whatever color you want the letters to be. Apply extra paint around the letters. After the first color dries, cover the tailgate with the color you want for the overall tailgate. Spray lightly where the letters are. Let this coat dry thoroughly and then go over the letters with rubbing compound. Rub carefully and soon the top paint will disappear, leaving the contrasting undercoat. Clean off any traces of rubbing compound and cover the tailgate with clear.

CLEAR TOPCOATS

Most custom paint tricks will look better and last longer if covered with a protective clear topcoat. The number of coats depends on the material to be covered. Flakes usually require the most clear. Most smooth finishes only require two coats of clear. For a first-class topcoat, apply the first coat of clear and let it dry overnight. Then, lightly sand the clear with very fine sandpaper. Wipe off any residue with a tack rag and apply the final coat of clear.

After the second coat of paint has dried, use a coarse rubbing compound or 600 wet-or-dry sandpaper to carefully remove the top layer of paint from the raised portion of the letters. Before color sanding and rubbing out the rest of the tailgate, coat the entire piece with clear lacquer to avoid rubbing through any other areas.

The finished tailgate will look something like this. You could have the letters outlined by a pinstriper for added dimension, but the job doesn't look bad as is.

CREATING TRICK PANELS

Most of the custom paint tricks outlined in this chapter work best when applied within a bordered panel. Such a panel could be an element of a larger, more complex paint design, or it could be a free-standing design, shaped to fit a corresponding sheetmetal panel on the vehicle surface. Obviously, several of the paint tricks shown here could be combined, creating an endless variety of panel designs suitable for any car, van or pickup. The following custom paint panel exercise will show just how easy it is to use these tricks.

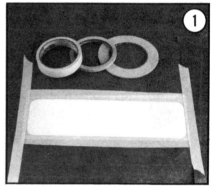

Like most panel designs, the first step is to lay out the basic shape of the panel. If it's a complicated shape, you might want to draw it in chalk or grease pencil. Then, form the outline with 1/8-inch tape. To add a "pinstripe" around the edge of a larger panel, you could follow all around the outline with another strip of 1/8-inch tape, about 1/8 inch in from the edge. Finally, mask off the adjoining area of the vehicle to keep overspray off the surface.

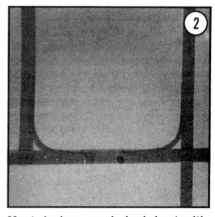

Most design panels look best with rounded corners. An easy way to make them symmetrical is to tape a rectangle with larger tape, then go back and make the corners with short strips of 1/8-inch tape.

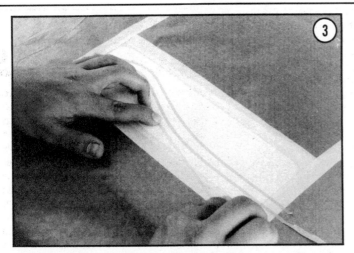

We will begin our surrealistic landscape design by using curves of 1/8-inch tape to simulate mountains.

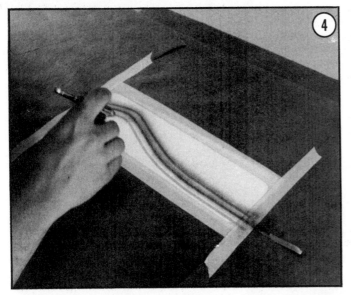

Using the same technique as endless line painting, fog along the tape with an airbrush, using a dark color of candy paint.

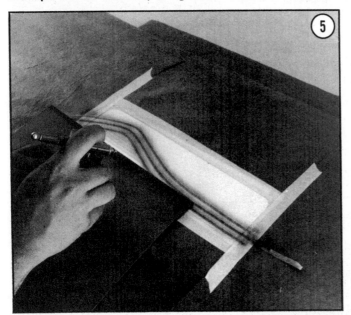

Using the straight edge of a file folder as a stencil, we added a row of fogged horizontal lines in the foreground.

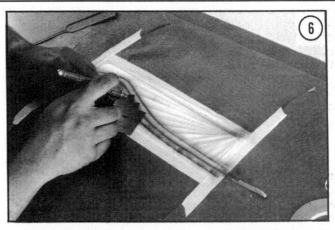

The straightedge stencil was also used to create a fan pattern, emanating from the upper right corner of the panel. We used a small fan of business cards to add texture along the three taped lines.

Finally, the airbrush was used to paint a round "sun" in the upper right corner, and then we fogged around the perimeter of the entire panel in the same color.

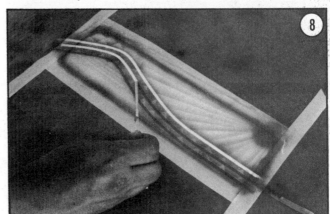

The tape was removed from the center of the design...

...And then the masking was pulled away to reveal the completed panel. The finishing touch would be a coat of clear for protection and a super glossy finish, plus a pinstriped border to frame the panel.

THE ART OF PINSTRIPING

- THE ART OF PINSTRIPING
- EQUIPMENT NEEDED
- SURFACE PREP AND PAINT MIXING
- BRUSH LOADING
- STRIPING TOOLS AND TAPE

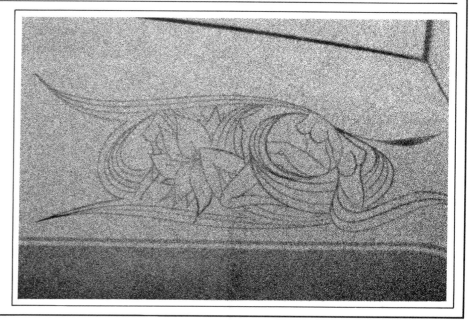

A talented pinstriper can create effective custom accents to the existing paint on a vehicle. In this case the hand-pinstriped flames are the major custom paint element on this street rod coupe.

PINSTRIPING TAKES SKILL BUT THERE ARE EASIER ALTERNATIVES

Pinstriping is one of the oldest custom painting techniques. Long before there were candy, flake or pearl paints, craftsmen were applying decorative pinstriping to automobiles. In the Twenties and Thirties, hand pin-striping was commonly used to highlight the bodywork of new cars. Most of this work was confined to a few simple stripes along the beltline and fenders or on the wheel rims, but some of the fancier cars had very elaborate pinstriping.

In the Fifties, pinstriping became extremely popular as a customizing art form. Highly talented stripers went far beyond simple bodyline embellishments. Stripers like the legendary Von Dutch, Ed "Big Daddy" Roth and Dean Jefferies created wild free-form designs for increasingly demanding hot rodders and custom car owners.

In the Sixties, the popularity of elaborate pinstriping declined and simple, traditional striping returned to vogue. Even Detroit designers returned to pinstriping as a way to give their products a custom appearance, but decals were used, rather than hand striping, to decrease the cost. The designs were simple and precise, but the hand-crafted style of yesteryear was, in typical Detroit style, reduced to a machine-like simplicity.

Today, pinstriping remains a popular detail touch. Really wild designs are rarely seen, but most top quality paint jobs employ some fine pinstriping for accent and highlights. Pinstriping is almost mandatory for certain types of custom painting, like flames, panel painting and murals. Not only does pinstriping add contrast to flame designs, but the stripes help

The design on this Corvette hood is reminiscent of the striping styles popular in the 50's. Pinstriping of this sort requires not only a trained hand but a talented eye for design and symmetry.

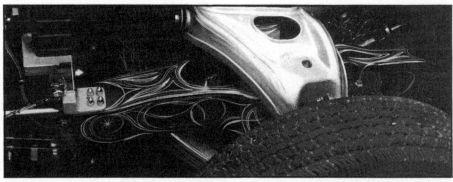

Pinstriping can be used to accent almost any part of a vehicle, from the dashboard to the undercarriage. Unfortunately, a major fault of many stripers is not knowing when to quit. This nicely detailed chassis would look less overly done if the striping were restrained. In general, understatement in pinstriping works best.

This roadster has been tastefully accented with a style of striping developed by Tommy the Greek. The "darts" or "teardrops" are solid black in the center with a contrasting outline.

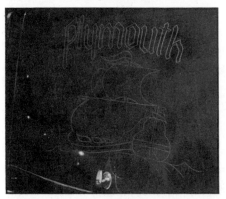

It is unusual to see pinstriping used for lettering or murals, but here is a tasteful and expertly executed example.

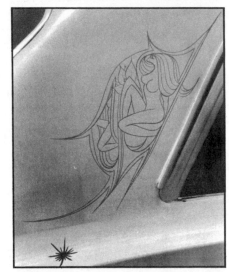

Von Dutch used to sneak faces, eyes, bats, or other forms into his complex pinstriped creations. Here is a similar modern version with female figures and flowers incorporated in the design.

hide torn edges from the masking tape removal. In panel painting, the stripes help separate the different panels and accent the design patterns. And, murals look strange if they are just floating on the side of a vehicle; simple pinstriping can tastefully frame the mural against the background paint.

Pinstriping is still extremely popular among street rodders. Some of the busiest people at any street rod event, or for that matter any street machine or van show, are the pinstripers. Tastefully applied pinstriping will highlight virtually any car, and good stripers are always in demand. If you ever get good enough at pinstriping to do it professionally, you should consider attending some street rod events—the result could be very rewarding financially.

The bad news about pinstriping is that it requires more natural ability than almost any other form of custom painting. Traditional, free-hand pinstriping requires a very steady hand and an excellent artistic eye. No amount of preparation can make up for a shaky hand. You also need a natural feeling for the placement of highlighting lines. Pinstriping is supposed to enhance the natural shape of a car, not detract or clash with lines. Like any other special talent, pinstriping requires constant practice. If you want to be a pinstriper, the only way to begin is to get some paint and a few brushes and practice, practice, practice.

The good news about pinstriping is that there are several alternative ways to pinstripe a car that are far easier

than the hand method. The results can be very satisfactory to all but the fussiest purists. These alternative methods involve the use of props or special tools. We will explain the alternative methods after a brief discussion of traditional pinstriping.

TRADITIONAL PINSTRIPING

While traditional pinstriping requires more time and talent than any other form of custom painting, it can be mastered. Constant practice is the key to success, but there's little doubt that natural talent separates the real artists from the average painter. Beginning stripers should remember to keep a restraint on their ambition and not let enthusiasm override their ability. Stick with simple designs and you should be able to produce some very pleasing work. And remember, patience is a necessity. Since most pinstriping is done with slow-drying enamels, mistakes can easily be removed or corrected. If you have time and patience, you should be able to handle simple pinstriping, and if you happen to be one of the lucky ones with innate talent, you could become a highly-paid professional.

PINSTRIPING EQUIPMENT

A complete array of pinstriping equipment can be had for very little money. All you will need is a selection of pinstriping brushes, a small amount of paint, thinner, some clean rags, and a paint palette.

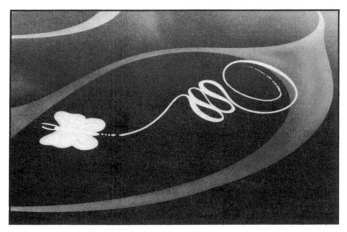

In this case a striper used a lettering brush to add details to a butterfly and give it a floating trail through a flame job.

Pinstriping brushes are specially designed to hold plenty of paint, yet draw extremely narrow lines. They come in a variety of sizes; the smaller ones (00, 0, 1) are the most commonly used for automotive striping.

Because of their shape, pinstriping brushes are popularly known as "daggers." Dagger brushes are broad near the handle and the bristles are cut into a long, tapering shape. This design allows a lot of paint to be stored in the bristles and gradually released as you "pull a line."

Brush handles are either square or round. Square handles are better for long straight lines and round handles are more suited to curves and circles. Many brushes, like those made by Grumbacher, have a square handle with a round section near the base of the bristles. This allows the brush to be effectively used for all types of pinstriping.

The brushes are numbered according to size, i.e., 00, 0, 1, 2, 3, and 4. The number-00 brush yields the finest line, while a number-4 brush yields the widest line. Beginners are best advised to purchase smaller brushes first, since thin lines are easier to manage than thick ones. Sizes 00, 0 and 1 are used most often in pinstriping.

Each pinstriper has his own favorite brand of brushes, but beginners will probably find that Grumbacher brushes are the easiest to locate. Grumbacher makes a very large line of artist's brushes, and they are available in most art stores. The initial purchase price of a typical dagger should be in the $5 range, and when treated properly, a pinstriping dagger should last a lifetime.

Professional pinstripers can stripe with almost any kind of paint, but sign painter's enamel is the most common type among pros. Sign painter's enamel is a heavy, slow-drying paint that covers well with one application. The most popular brand is called "One-Shot." It is available through custom paint dealers and professional sign painter's supply stores. If you can't find "One-Shot," any other top-quality enamel will work. Many painters prefer enamels that are oil based, but acrylic enamel automotive paint will work, as long as you use it straight out of the can. If a particular color is desired and it is the only type available, acrylic lacquer can be used. Enamel stripes can be applied over any properly prepared surface.

When buying striping paint, get small cans. You will be surprised how far a 4-ounce can of paint will go. The thinner you use depends on the type of paint. Read the directions on the paint can. When using oil-based enamels, most pros prefer turpentine for a reducer.

One of the keys to good pinstriping is the proper thinning of the paint and the loading of the brush. For this you need some type of "palette." A palette is simply a flat board or surface, on which small quantities of paint can be mixed together. A piece of glass makes an excellent palette. Glass is easy to clean and the brush will pull easily through the paint. However, glass is heavy and hazardous if it breaks. A small piece of masonite also makes a nice homebrew palette and is not as fragile as glass. Commercially-made

Sign painter's "One Shot" lettering enamel is the standard pinstriping paint, although any enamel or even a slow-drying lacquer could be used. One Shot comes in a rainbow of colors; a beginner would probably want to buy three or four of the smallest cans for practicing. One Shot can be thinned with turpentine or enamel reducer.

Since pinstriping is usually applied to a finished, and possibly waxed, paint surface, always be sure to first clean the area to be striped with a good wax and grease remover. Since you can't sand or scuff the underlying paint, you want to make sure the stripes will adhere as well as possible to the painted surface.

palettes are available at art-supply stores. They are usually made of thin plastic and they can be cleaned easily with most solvents.

Instead of a permanent-type palette, many stripers prefer something that is disposable. An old telephone book is an excellent disposable palette. As each page becomes filled with paint, it is torn out of the book and thrown away. This eliminates the bother of constantly cleaning the palette. A cheap newsprint tablet can also be used in this manner. Attach the tablet to a clipboard and you will have an excellent disposable palette.

SURFACE PREPARATION FOR STRIPING

Like any other custom painting technique, pinstriping should be applied over a clean surface. Before doing any striping, be sure that all other paint work is complete (don't try to rub out a paint job after you have pinstriped it or you will cut into the stripes). Clean the area to be striped with wax and grease remover. If the surface isn't perfectly clean, the striping will soon come off.

If you are only going to apply some straight-line striping, you can lay down some guidelines. Masking tape works well, as does a carpenter's chalk line. By stretching a chalk line across the surface and then snapping it, you will have a nice, straight line. You can also use a straight edge or ruler and a grease pencil or Stabilo marker to make a guideline. The idea of the guideline is to place it right next to where you wish to paint and then use it as a reference point to keep the striping straight. Drafting instruments, like French curves, can be used to layout curves and corners, but it is much quicker if you can just pinstripe free hand. However, don't be hesitant about using a piece of tape for a guide. Even established pros often use a guide when they pull long lines.

PAINT CONSISTENCY AND BRUSH LOADING

One of the keys to good pinstriping is obtaining the proper paint consistency and loading the dagger properly. Unfortunately, this process is a tough one to describe. It is one of those elusive pinstriping techniques that is best acquired through practice. The idea is to produce a paint consistency that flows smoothly without dripping, and to pull a long line, you want the brush to carry as much paint as possible without overloading it to the

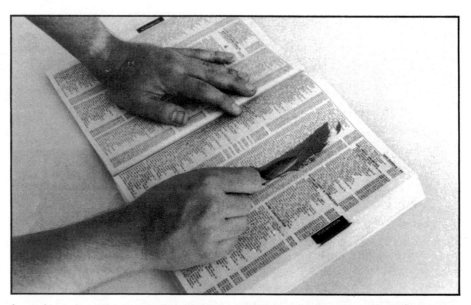

Learning to load the dagger is one of the critical keys to successful pinstriping. Most stripers dip the brush in the paint, then in the thinner, and work it back and forth on a palette to evenly load the brush and shape the bristles. An old telephone book works well for a palette; when one page becomes saturated with paint, discard it and use the next.

point that it is difficult to control the width of the line.

The paint consistency will vary depending on what you are striping. Long lines require a thinner paint to allow the paint to flow evenly from the brush. Circles and tight curves require thicker paint so that the bristles of the dagger will stay neatly formed and maintain a uniform line thickness. Since paint consistency varies, it is a good idea to only dilute paint in small quantities or, better yet, have a small container of thinner and a small container of paint side by side on the palette. Use the brush to mix a small bit of paint and thinner on the palette. Work the brush back and forth through the mixture and add very small amounts of either paint or thinner until you have the desired consistency. Use turpentine for oil-based enamels, enamel reducer for acrylic enamel and lacquer thinner for lacquer paints. Retarder can be used to slow the drying time of lacquer and a very few drops of kerosene will help slow the drying time of oil-based enamel.

Loading the brush with paint requires working the brush through the puddle of paint on the palette until the brush is fully and evenly loaded. Draw both sides of the brush through the paint several times. Then, remove excess paint by stroking the brush back and forth on the palette. Finally, shape the brush by gently pulling it between the thumb and index finger. This action forms the brush into the proper shape for striping. The loading operation needs to be repeated each time you start a new line or need more

paint. The best way to know when the paint is the right consistency and when the brush is properly loaded is to practice until the technique becomes second nature.

PINSTRIPING TECHNIQUES

There are many different ways to hold the dagger. What matters is comfort and ability to control the brush. In the traditional one-handed grip the brush handle is held between the thumb and index finger. The handle is "pinched" gently but firmly between the tips of the fingers. Most stripers stabilize the brush by resting the end of the brush handle against the palm of the hand, about where the thumb and index finger meet. Some stripers prefer to rest one side of the brush handle against the index finger.

If a one-handed grip is used, the fingers not holding the brush are often used to steady the hand against the work surface. The free hand can also be used to steady the one with the brush. Some pinstripers even use a sign painter's stick (any stick with a protective covering on the end) for added support in tricky situations.

It is also possible to use two hands to hold the brush and many stripers prefer the two-handed method for small curves and detail work. With this technique, the brush handle is held with the thumbs and forefingers of both hands. The little fingers of both hands are used to steady the brush, more or less in a tripod fashion.

The angle between the brush and the surface and the speed of appli-

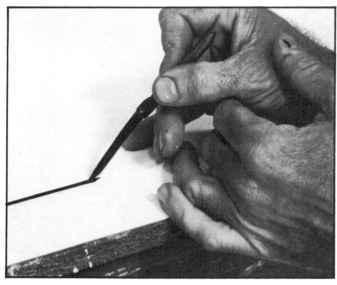

The proper way to hold a pinstriping brush is to pinch it firmly but gently between thumb and forefinger. Most stripers use the little finger of the brush-holding hand as a guide on the paint surface, possibly using the other hand (as shown) as a steadying aid. The pressure you exert on the brush determines the width of the line.

Once you have learned how to pull long, even, straight lines it is time to try making curves, which is considerably more difficult. To keep the line width uniform you must rotate the brush between thumb and forefinger as you round a corner. A round-handled striping brush makes this easier.

cation will both affect the size of the line. The fewer bristles that contact the surface, the thinner the line will be. Most stripers angle the brush between 45° and 60° with the surface. Curved work requires a steeper angle so that the bristles will stay in position and not spread apart, causing an uneven line. As you draw the brush across the surface more slowly, more paint will be deposited and the line will become wider.

You should practice pinstriping by first laying short, straight lines on a flat horizontal surface. As you get better, try doing curves and corners. Then try straight lines on vertical surfaces and finally practice curves on uneven or vertical surfaces. Since enamel dries slowly, you can even practice on your car. Just keep a rag moistened with thinner or turpentine (depending on the type of paint) handy to wipe away any mistakes.

When you are practicing, try holding the brush several different ways. Determine which style works best for you. The way you hold your body will also be important. When pulling long lines, you will have to move your entire body, not just your hands and arms. The idea is to be as fluid as possible.

You can only pull a line so far before you run out of paint. When you feel you need to reload the brush, tip the dagger slightly so that the line comes to a tapered point. This makes it easier to resume the line without a wide spot. When you restart the line, backtrack about six inches. Start the line the same way you ended it; that is, on a slight slant so that a wide spot isn't

created where you first apply the brush. Once you are good at long lines, try doing parallel lines. This is one of the most difficult tricks to master.

To pinstripe curves, start by drawing circles. Try them both clockwise and counterclockwise to determine which direction works best for you. It is very important to use the round part of the dagger handle when striping curves. The brush must be smoothly rotated so that the width of the stripe remains the same throughout. Any time you have to paint a curve on a vertical surface, always start at the

Good striping brushes are hard to find, so be sure to take good care of them. As soon as you are done striping, thoroughly clean the brush in turpentine or enamel reducer, being sure to get all the paint out of the bristles at the base.

bottom and work upward. Working from the other direction will allow the paint to flow out of the brush and down the handle.

Terminating a line usually requires a bit of extra flourish. Some painters make little arrowheads, while others just bring the line to a simple point. The idea of the arrows and points is to maintain the flowing feel of the line. Pinstriping is supposed to enhance the vehicle, to make it look more streamlined, hence the arrows.

Speaking of pinstriping asthetics, remember that horizontal lines make a vehicle look longer and lower. Conversely, vertical lines make the same vehicle look shorter and taller. Wide lines are more emphatic than thin ones. Keep this in mind when you lay out the basic designs. Pinstriping is normally intended to highlight the natural lines of the car. Pinstriping down the middle of a car can divide the vehicle visually. This can be either good or bad depending on your goals. When it comes to tasteful striping, the number one rule is "less is best."

BRUSH CARE

After finishing a pinstriping job, the brushes must be properly cleaned. Extra effort to maintain brushes will make them last a lifetime. In fact, most professional stripers actually prefer older brushes because they feel the brushes get better with age.

Work all the paint out of the bristles with the proper thinner. After the brush is clean, prepare it for storage by saturating the bristles in motor oil or

Wipe the brush dry with a clean towel, working the bristles towards the point.

Shape the bristles with your fingers to retain the dagger shape, and store the brush on a flat surface. If you're not going to use the brush for a while, work a little mineral oil into the bristles to keep them from drying out.

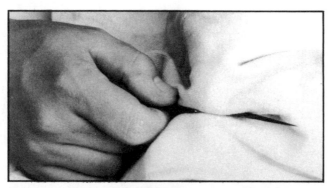

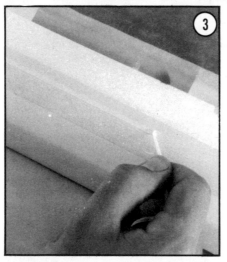

lard oil. Smooth the bristles into the dagger shape and store the brush on a clean, flat surface. Keep the top of the bristles straight and arch the lower edge. This way the dagger will be in good shape the next time you need it.

Maintenance of the applied pinstriping is similar to any other custom paint. Protect the stripes with a non-abrasive wax. Don't apply any wax until the stripes have had ample time to set (several days at least and preferably a week or two). Take care not to press on any pinstripes when they are fresh. Even though the outer skin of the paint may be dry, the underlying paint may still be soft.

If you have the talent to be a good pinstriper, you are a fortunate person. Practice as much as possible to cultivate your talent. Nonetheless, if you don't have the ingrained talent to be a free-hand pinstriper, don't despair, there are several alternative methods that yield surprisingly good results.

HOW TO SPRAY PAINT PINSTRIPES

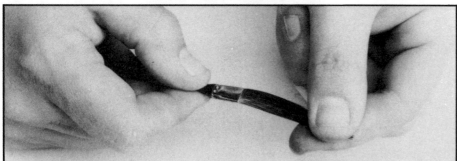

Freehand striping obviously takes considerable talent and practice, but there are other ways to paint stripes on your vehicle. By using Scotch striping tape, you can paint real pinstripes on your car or truck, at home, with little prior practice. This 1-1/16-inch wide tape has eight removable bands in the middle. After the tape is in place, you remove one or more of the bands (depending on how wide you want the stripe to be) and you have a perfectly straight and even striping mask. Paint can be applied with a spray gun, airbrush or pinstriping brush. This tape is great for striping long, straight lines, but it isn't well suited for making curves or intricate designs.

To practice with the 3M striping tape, we tried a short section on an old hood. Lay the tape on smoothly, with no kinks, and be sure to lay it in a straight line. Since we will be spraying the paint, we masked off the surrounding area to avoid overspray.

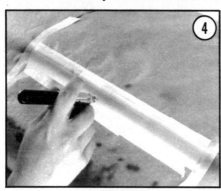

Pull away sections of the tape where you want the pinstripes. We decided to make a double stripe, one larger than the other, so we removed one band at the bottom and two adjacent bands above it.

Using an airbrush, spray the exposed lines in any color you wish.

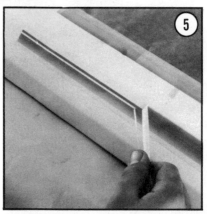

When the paint is dry, peel away the remaining tape.

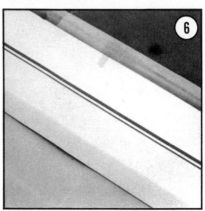

And presto! You have professional-looking pinstripes that will never peel or come off in the car wash. By spraying the paint, you can use pearls, candies, or other trick paints, or you could even blend different colors along the line.

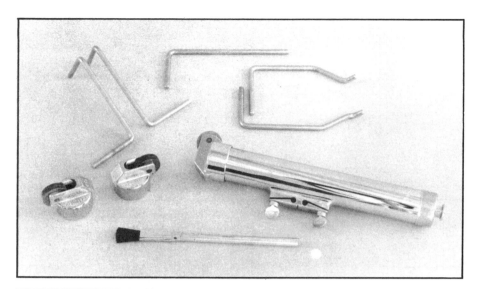

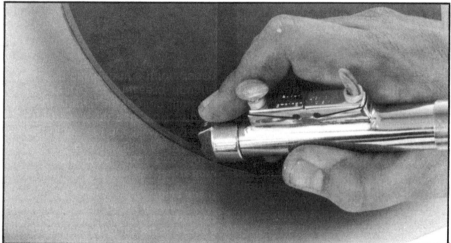

A big advantage of the mechanical striping tool is that it can be used to make curved lines or other freehand designs. Here a Beugler tool is being used to outline a flame job.

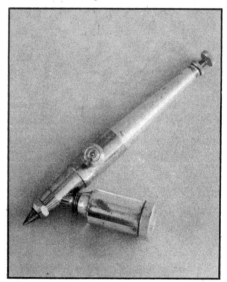

Another type of mechanical striping tool is the FP Flow Pencil made by the Paasche Airbrush Company. This gravity-feed device is held and manipulated like an airbrush (though it does not use pressurized air).

STRIPING TOOLS AND OTHER AIDS

It's no secret that many people lack either the talent or the patience to master traditional pinstriping. Realizing this, many companies have developed ingenious pinstriping methods that don't require an unusual degree of natural talent.

A very basic alternative method is the use of masking tape. If you have the patience to measure and lay out a long series of parallel lines, you can use an airbrush to paint the area between the pieces of tape and end up with a beautiful pinstriped line. Of course, it takes a lot of patience to get the two tape lines straight but it can be done.

To overcome this problem, the 3M Company has developed a special tape for striping. They have a product called Scotch "Paint Striping Tape." This unusual tape has multiple rows of perforations along the length. After the tape has been applied to the vehicle, a portion of the center section can be peeled away to expose the surface below. Paint is applied along the exposed section to make the stripe.

Another way to apply pinstripes to your car without learning how to handle a brush is to use a mechanical pinstriping tool such as this one from Beugler. You load the handle with paint, which is applied to the surface by a rolling wheel. Different heads are available for lines of different widths or double stripes. The pieces of bent wire are guides that can be adjusted to space the stripe a certain distance from a chrome strip or body line on the car.

Trimbrite, Scotch-3M and other companies offer a wide variety of plastic, adhesive, pinstriping tapes—in many colors, widths and styles, including corners and "points." Striping tape may not be quite as durable or as professional-looking as hand-painted stripes, but it is very inexpensive, extremely easy to apply and has the added advantage of being easily removed if you don't like a design or just want to change the looks of your car. It's the same stuff that comes on many expensive new cars.

Several rows of perforations are provided so that the stripe can be wide or narrow, as desired. This method works especially well for very long stripes that run the length of the vehicle and is often used by professional painters who want a quick and efficient method to add a few simple stripes.

There are also several mechanical tools that are designed to work in place of the striping brush. These tools employ a cylinder to hold the paint and a mechanical means of dispensing it to the paint surface.

Of this type of striping aid, the Beugler striping tool is generally considered to be one of the very best. The Beugler tool uses a pressure-feed system and a precision wheel to roll the paint onto the surface. Several different wheels are available and the width of the wheel determines the width of the stripe. There are even dual-wheel paint heads that lay two parallel stripes with one pass of the tool. In addition, the Beugler striping tool has a variety of complementary accessories, including a nice selection of guide attachments. Among these items is a super-handy magnetic guide strip that could even be a helpful aid for the traditional free-hand striper.

There are other less-expensive versions of the Beugler striping tool, but most of these tools rely simply on gravity to feed the paint to the paint wheels. This method isn't as desirable as the Beugler pressure-feed system.

The Paasche Airbrush Company also makes a noteworthy striping tool. This tool is known as the FP Flow Pencil and is about the size of an ordinary airbrush. It has a small paint reservoir that uses gravity to feed the paint. The flow of the paint is controlled like an airbrush with a small fingertip control button.

Most of the mechanical pinstriping tools are generally easier to use than a brush, but each one demands some practice to become thoroughly familiar with the specific techniques required. However, once mastered and properly manipulated, pinstriping tools are a viable alternative to the traditional pinstriping brush.

PINSTRIPING TAPE

Pinstriping tape is often derided by supercilious traditionalists, but when properly applied, it is difficult to distinguish from the real thing. In recent years the quality of pinstriping tape

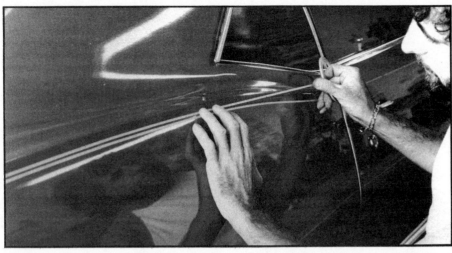

The only trick to applying plastic striping tape is to make sure that you get the lines straight, without any waves. The easiest way to do this is to pull long sections of tape from the roll and stretch it slightly before pressing it to the car. Also, be sure to clean any wax or grease from the surface before applying the tape, to make sure it adheres properly.

has improved considerably, so much so that many Detroit manufacturers use it on some of their most costly top-of-the-line models.

Probably the biggest drawback, besides the inability to mix and match custom stripe colors, is the fact that pinstriping tape doesn't lend itself to complicated designs (like outlining flames). Pinstriping tape is best for long, straight lines, like the simple body-line accent stripe. The directions

on the striping tape packages are self-explanatory, but remember to clean the area with wax and grease remover just as for any other pinstriping technique.

There is more than one way to pinstripe a car, but they all have the same effect: pinstriping helps bring out the best in any custom paint job. Restrained, tasteful use of pinstriping is a final touch that can turn a good paint job into a really great one.

HOW TO PINSTRIPE WITH SIMPLE AIDS

Although you'll probably never be another Von Dutch, you can still achieve some very satisfying and expert-looking results by employing some of the pinstriping tricks explained in this chapter. Here is an example of a simple striping design on the trunk of a car: a trick you could easily copy at home with a minimum of practice.

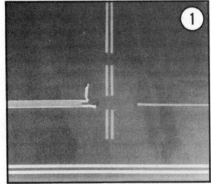

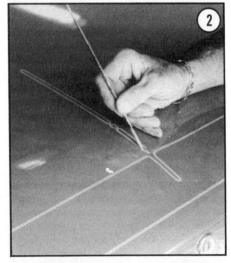

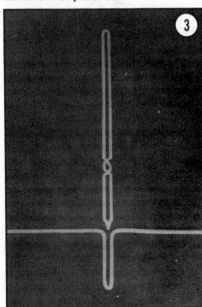

This simple striping design will primarily employ straight lines, so they can be made with 3M Striping Tape or just masked off with two rows of 1/8-inch tape, as shown here. In this case a striping brush was used to fill in the lines, since other parts of the design will have to be brush painted and, therefore, One Shot paint will have to be used. You may want to sketch the design in grease pencil first, to get the shape you want (or try various designs on paper); but clean off the grease pencil before laying the tape.

After removing the tape, Gary Glenn uses a lettering brush to paint the short curves joining the long lines (Gary finds the lettering brush easier to control than a striping dagger, and since he does not have to pull the long lines by hand, he doesn't need the extra paint-carrying capacity of a dagger).

The finished design is simple, yet effective. Best of all, it looks like it was all done by a master striper with a very steady hand.

CHAPTER 11

CUSTOM LETTERING

- HOW TO DO QUALITY LETTERING
- LAYOUT AND DESIGN
- PATTERNS AND STENCILS
- TRICK AND GOLD-LEAF LETTERING
- SCROLL WORK

LETTERING ADDS THE PERSONAL TOUCH

Custom lettering is another detail that adds a professional touch to any custom paint job. A modified car or truck is an expression of the owner and custom lettering puts that expression into words. Lettering is virtually mandatory for a racing machine, and can be great fun around your shop. Once you learn the basics, virtually everything becomes a signboard, begging for a few words of decoration. Look around the garage of anyone that knows how to letter, everything imaginable will be sprinkled with lettering.

Besides the personal enjoyment of lettering your own vehicle, you may

The old-fashioned lettering on this sedan delivery, done in gold leaf with double pinstriped outlines, complements the age of the vehicle. If you are interested in learning to letter, start by studying as many examples as you can find—either on custom vehicles, in magazines, on signs or on buildings—to learn the various styles and possibilities.

find that custom lettering can be a very profitable skill. Your friends will gladly pay to have you letter their cars, and if you attend any street machine, hot rod or van event, you can easily make a handsome profit from lettering other cars.

Great custom lettering experts are true craftsmen with tremendous artistic ability, but they all started with the basics. The real "secret" behind custom lettering is to use a detailed

outline or guide and fill between the lines with paint. As long as you can make a simple pattern, the actual painting isn't very difficult. There are many different ways to lay out custom lettering, so you will have to experiment to find the method that works best for you.

LETTERING EQUIPMENT

The equipment needed for custom

lettering is similar to that needed for pinstriping. A beginner can get started with a minimal equipment investment. The main items needed are brushes, paint and guide tools. A professional sign painter's supply shop, an art supply store or an automotive paint store are all good places to get lettering equipment. In addition, mail-order custom paint companies that advertise in automotive magazines are likely sources.

Lettering brushes are different from pinstriping brushes. Lettering brushes, also known as "quills," have blunt ends (striping brushes are tapered). There are many brands of brushes, but one of the best and easiest to find is the Grumbacher line. They can be found in most art supply stores. With proper care, lettering brushes can last for decades.

You can letter with almost any type of paint, but the best results are obtained with enamel paints. The favorite of most professional letterers is the "One Shot" brand of sign painting enamel. Enamel dries slower, so you can correct simple mistakes and it has good flowout and gloss. Enamel can also be reduced with a variety of thinners, such as turpentine and enamel reducer. Top quality enamel reducers are highly recommended because they are available in various formulations to compensate for temperature conditions. On hot days you can use a slow reducer to slow drying time and promote flowout. On cold

People have been painting names on their cars since day one. The logo on this machine has been enhanced with pinstriping in and around the letters.

The futuristic lettering on this car was applied in variegated gold leaf with painted, shaded borders to make the the letters look three dimensional.

days you can use a fast reducer to speed the drying process.

Traditional sign painting enamel isn't available in a tremendous variety of colors, but if you understand color mixing, you can produce almost any color you desire from the available primary colors. If you want wild colors, you can use automotive enamel for lettering. The Ditzler Company claims that their Duracryl acrylic lacquer can be used for lettering, if you use it along with Ditzler DTX-1140 All-Purpose Retarder to slow the drying time.

LAYOUT AND DESIGN

Very few people have the ability to produce consistent lettering with a totally freehand technique. Even the very best pros use some sort of layout guide to insure uniform letters and even spacing.

Many aids can be used to lay out lettering. The more common items include masking tape, cellophane tape, a Stabilo pencil, a grease marker, charcoal, a pounce wheel, frisket paper, spray mask, and an X-Acto knife.

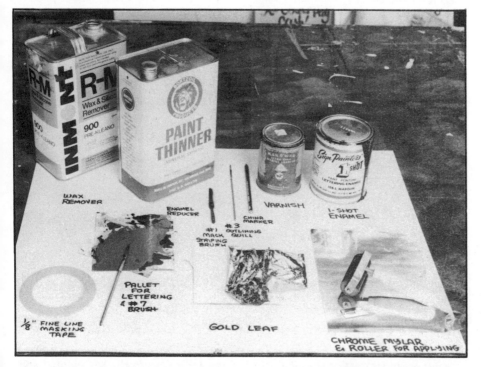

Here is just a sampling of equipment most commonly used by a professional automotive sign painter. Paint and brushes are for hand lettering, gold leaf and mylar are for special effects, the tape and china marker are for layout and guidelines.

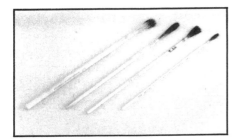

Like pinstriping brushes, lettering "quills" are made for a special purpose and come in a variety of sizes.

You can obviously use lettering on a vehicle to make statements or to communicate your feeling about your car.

Straight edges and rulers are also helpful, as are other drafting tools, like French curves and compasses. We will cover the usage of the various tools in the lettering how-to's.

A good pattern is the key to successful lettering. To make a good pattern, you need something to copy. Fortunately, there are samples of professional lettering on virtually everything around you, all you have to do is look for them. If there is something you want to copy, like a Ford or Chevy insignia, you can use the original as a pattern. If you want to letter a name on your car, look for a sample that has the style of lettering you like.

There are many different types of lettering (e.g., sans-serif, serifed, shadow, outline, script, Old English, decorative, etc.) and there are hundreds of specific styles in each category. Part of the art of lettering is to study different types and styles, and know how to select the best style to complement the job at hand.

You can easily make a useful collection of lettering styles. Samples abound in magazines, and car shows or race tracks are an excellent place to study how other people have used different styles of lettering, both to the advantage and disadvantage of the car. If you see a style of lettering that you like, cut it out of the magazine or take a closeup photo for future reference.

Art supply stores also have several sources of lettering ideas. There are

books on lettering, calligraphy (penmanship and fancy writing) and typography (the formalized study of printed type). Many typography books include complete upper- and lower-case (capital and small letter) alphabets of scores of different type designs. Art stores also have very useful stencils for some lettering styles. Once you begin looking, you'll find plenty of information and the "psychology" of type design can become quite fascinating.

After you have decided on a particular style of lettering, you need to give some thought to placement of the lettering. Don't just randomly stick the lettering on the car without considering how it will affect and enhance the design and paint scheme of the vehicle.

After you have decided on a location for the lettering, the design should be roughly sketched onto the car with a grease pencil. This will give you an idea of the effect it will have. If you don't like what you see, now is the time to change things. Another way to check the visual effect of custom lettering is to lay a sheet of tracing paper over a large photo of the vehicle and sketch the lettering on the paper.

PATTERNS & STENCILS

A pattern for the actual lettering can be made in one of several ways. Each of the basic methods have their strong and weak points. For example, some are better for exact copying and others are better for one-of-a-kind lettering. With some experimenting, you can decide which will work best for your particular needs.

The most popular method is to use a pounce wheel and charcoal to transfer the design to a full-size paper pattern. There are three types of paper used mainly for pattern making: tracing paper, masking paper and white butcher paper. Tracing paper is usually flimsier but it has the advantage of being translucent, making it easy to trace the desired design.

If you have an exact-size replica of lettering, you can just copy it onto the tracing paper. If you must enlarge or reduce the lettering, the job is more difficult but not impossible. You can purchase preformed lettering in different styles and sizes of "art type" (the most popular brandnames are Letraset, Zipatone and Formatt) at most art supply stores. These are large sheets of alphabets and numbers with some

In this case, the lettering reflects the mood of the cartoon that accompanies it. This lettering is hand painted.

The large, bold letters on the side of this sedan delivery were all hand painted, but this is a good example of a design that could easily have been traced onto the side of the vehicle (such as with charcoal over perforated paper) and filled in with a brush. It could also have been cut in a stencil (such as frisket paper) and spray painted.

An intricate lettering design like this one would require a very trained hand to paint directly onto the vehicle with a brush. It would be much easier to layout on masking paper, using lettering stencils for the uniform-sized characters.

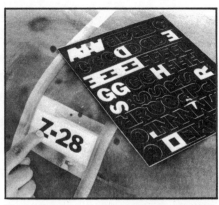

You will find a wide variety of lettering stencils and stick-on letters at a large stationery or art-supply store. Here we show how self-adhesive letters can be used to make a "reverse" lettering design.

After the letters are attached to the surface, use an airbrush to fog paint around the edges.

Here is a simple lettering trick that anyone could do. Gold leaf was applied to the raised letters on this tailgate, then they were outlined with a brush and black paint.

form of adhesive on the back. You can position individual letters as you desire and stick them to a piece of paper. When you have the desired design, you can transfer it to a piece of tracing paper.

Specialized and unique lettering, like that used for a company trademark or logo, can be enlarged in a variety of ways. If you have access to an overhead projector, you can project the image onto a piece of paper taped to the wall. Some inexpensive projectors are available if you want to buy one, but the best results are obtained with a

Sign painting and brush lettering is an art that goes back centuries before automobiles. You will find ample books on hand-lettering styles and techniques. The study of lettering and typography can, in fact, be fascinating, but mastering brush techniques and learning the tricks of the trade takes considerable practice.

Inscribing the owner's name on the door probably derives from the popular practice of painting the driver's name on the doors of his race car. This is a hand-lettered script with a few embellishments.

quality projector, like those used by most high schools.

Graph paper can also be used to enlarge lettering. Place the lettering to be copied on paper that has a small grid, and transfer the dimensions to paper with a larger grid. The grid method can be used directly on the vehicle but it is best to use paper so that the same pattern can be reused or used for the other side of the vehicle.

Once the pattern has been made, a pounce wheel and charcoal are used to transfer the pattern to the surface to be painted. A pounce wheel is a small wheel with pointed projections around the circumference, and can be be purchased at almost any art supply store. When rolled over paper, the wheel leaves a uniform series of tiny perforations in the paper.

The pattern is placed on a pliable surface, like a piece of cardboard, wood or wallboard, and traced with the pounce wheel. Then, the perforated pattern is secured to the vehicle with masking tape. Check carefully to insure that it is positioned properly. If you plan on using the same design on both sides of the car, use some reference marks so that both sides of the car will be identical.

To transfer the pattern to the surface of the vehicle, go over the perforations in the paper with charcoal or chalk. You can use powdered charcoal from an art store or a stick of soft charcoal. Carefully remove the paper and the design will remain as a series of charcoal dots on the surface. The dots should be close enough together that you won't need to connect them. The final step is to fill in the letters with paint.

If you don't have a steady hand with a lettering brush, there is an alternative method that might work better. Make the pattern with the pounce wheel, but don't tape the pattern directly to the surface. Cover the area to be lettered with "frisket paper." Frisket paper is a type of transparent, adhesive-backed paper that is available at art stores. Tape the pounce-

wheel pattern sheet over the frisket paper and apply the charcoal as before. When you remove the pattern sheet, you will see the dot pattern as before. Now use an X-Acto knife to carefully cut out the pattern (use only enough pressure to cut the frisket paper, not the underlying paint). Peel away the frisket where the paint will go and you have an easy-to-paint stencil.

There is another type of masking material that is even more versatile

In this case simple block letters were outlined with pinstriping. An airbrush was used to paint highlights inside the letters and give them a boxed look. The effect is quite striking.

These letters were made to look glowing and tubular, like a neon sign, by simple airbrush shading and highlighting with a light-colored paint.

than frisket paper. Metalflake "Spray Mask" is a transparent, water-soluble spray that dries to a rubbery film. You can draw patterns on the Spray Mask and cut them out with an X-Acto knife. Spray Mask can also be used on irregular surfaces that may not be suited for frisket paper.

Precut stencils can also be helpful, although letter stencils may not be available in the specific size and style of type you desire. And, traditional stencils have one major drawback—they are difficult to hold in place. You can use tape, but this is tedious and unreliable because the paint can easily seep under the exposed edges of the stencil. However, there is a type of stencil, called "Super Stick," which does have an adhesive backing. The Super Stick letters can be used for outlining or you can discard the letter and just use the surrounding outline. Fill it in with paint and you have your

On this race car the airbrush was used with a darker color to give the letters a reflective, metallic look—almost as if they were chromed.

letter.

The use of any type of mask for custom lettering has the added advantage that you don't have to hand brush the paint. An airbrush can be used with a Spray Mask or Super Stick stencil pattern. This means you can add unusual touches, like fogging or shading, or you can use unusual candy, flake or pearl paints.

BRUSH LETTERING

Freehand brush lettering is the most elementary form of custom lettering. It takes a lot of practice to develop this talent but there are several helpful tips to make the job easier (though it's never truly easy).

Even the best freehand artists usually begin with some form of layout guide. Using a small ruler or yardstick, the outline form of each individual letter is drawn between a set of straight reference lines. Even though this method is called freehand, it is still a good idea to completely draw each letter with a Stabilo pencil, chalk or charcoal. The relative height, width and shape of each letter can be predetermined, and the spacing between each letter and each word can be finalized to make sure the lettering is balanced and that you don't run out of room in the space allotted to the lettering.

Before beginning, thoroughly clean the surface with a quality wax

Adhesive prism or diffraction tape is not only easy to apply, it also produces a wild effect—changing colors as light strikes the car from different angles. Here the letters have been boxed in black and given a pinstripe outline.

and grease remover. A top quality sign painter's enamel, like One Shot, will produce the best results. If the enamel needs to be thinned, use a reducer that is matched to the prevailing temperature conditions. Don't reduce the paint in the can. Use two small containers (paper cups are perfect) to hold the paint and reducer. Dip the brush into the paint and then the reducer, and stroke the brush back-and-forth on a small palette (a small piece of glass or Masonite is suitable) to mix the paint with the reducer. The brush can be dipped again into the paint or the reducer, as needed, until the mixture reaches the desired consistency.

Getting the paint to the "right consistency" is a matter of experience, but generally what you are trying to achieve is paint that flows smoothly without running. The paint must be thick enough to cover with one application but not so thick that brush marks remain when the paint dries. The process of loading the brush first with paint and then dipping it in the reducer and working it around on the palette must be repeated every time you need more paint. It may sound tedious, but with a little practice, loading the brush will become second nature.

Choosing the right brush is important for good lettering. Pick the brush that is closest to the width of each leg of the particular size letters you will be making. The fewer strokes you make, the quicker and sharper the lettering will be. Vertical strokes should be pulled from top to bottom with a final inverted upstroke to give a sharp edge to the bottom of the letter. Horizontal strokes can go from left to right or vice versa, as you prefer. Use the same reverse-stroke at the finish to create sharp edges.

Another trick to getting sharp, straight edges is to run long pieces of tape along the top and bottom edges of the row of letters. You can pull the stroke over the tape and still have a sharp edge when the tape is removed. Masking tape will work for this but the best tape is 3M Scotch Brand #650 cellophane tape. Scotch #650 is a special low-adhesion tape that won't leave a sticky residue when you remove it. This is especially important if you are lettering a freshly painted car.

To keep your hand as steady as possible when lettering, use your other hand as a brace. Also, use the little finger of the painting hand as a brace and pivot. Many professional sign painters use a maulstick as a hand rest and edge guide. One end of the stick is rested against the work surface and the other end is held at an angle to the surface with the free hand. You can easily make a maulstick out of a piece of doweling and a couple of rubber cane or chair tips. A stick about 2 feet long and 1/2-inch to 1-inch in diameter is a good size. The maulstick is particularly useful when lettering an awkward area. The stick can also be used as a straight edge when laying out lettering.

Just as it is important to properly load the lettering brush with paint, it is equally important to clean the brushes after each use. Wipe off the excess paint on a clean rag and dip the brush in enamel reducer. The next step is to put some clean reducer in a shallow container, like a jar lid. Hold the brush handle upright, push the bristles down against the bottom of the lid and twist the brush so that the bristles form a circle. Spin the brush around in this fashion to thoroughly clean the bristles. To dry the brush and get the bristles back in shape, put the handle between the palms of your hands and quickly roll the brush back and forth. Then, cover the bristles with lard oil and shape the brush between your thumb and index finger. Store the brush on a clean flat surface and it will be in perfect shape the next time you need it.

TRICK LETTERING

There are several ways to enhance custom lettering. Most of them involve some form of outlining. The outline can range from a simple pin stripe to a carefully shaded three-dimensional effect. Very talented professional letterers can even make letters appear chrome-like or look like a neon sign.

Outlining is the easiet way to enhance lettering. Follow the shapes with a darker or contrasting color applied with a pinstriping brush. Black is the most commonly used color for outlining and boxing (the effect of making letters look three dimensional). Some painters use an airbrush to add lifelike highlights to simple block letters. The judicious use of white or pearl shading will make the letters appear as if a spotlight is shining on them. The key thing to remember is to pick a direction from which the imagined spotlight shines and keep this angle constant throughout the word. A good understanding of the principles of perspective is essential for effectively highlighted art.

Artful airbrushing is also the key to chrome or neon lettering. The letters are painted normally with a base color. In the case of chrome lettering the base color is silver. Any color can be used for neon letters, depending on the final color desired. Additional colors are added over the base with an airbrush to achieve the glowing effect of a tubular-like neon sign. The main idea behind chrome lettering is that they reflect surrounding colors, like the blue of the sky and the brown of the earth. Chrome and neon lettering looks fantastic but these techniques require a lot of practice.

Another way to achieve chrome-like lettering is to use prism tape. Metalflake, for example, makes trick-looking, reflective tapes in a wide variety of styles and colors. Letters can be cut from these tapes, applied to the vehicle and outlined or boxed for a more finished look.

GOLD-LEAF LETTERING

Gold-leaf lettering is a long-standing favorite of show-car buffs. This technique is most commonly used for lettering and scroll work but it can also be used for any number of other effects, from flames to Trans-Am hood graphics. The method of applying gold leaf is the same, no matter what the spcific design.

Gold leaf comes in a variety of shades, including sparkling pure gold

HOW TO LETTER WITH MYLAR

To show how easy mylar or prism-tape lettering can be, we asked Gary Glenn (of Signs and Designs, Orange, California) to show us how the pros do it. The first step is to sketch the lettering onto the mylar sheet using a Stabilo pencil or china marker. Note the horizontal guide lines at top and bottom to keep the line of letters even.

This lettering was done on adhesive-backed mylar, so the next step is to cut out the design using a razor blade, X-Acto knife or sharp scissors. If the lettering is not cursive (run together), as shown here, you will have to cut out each letter separately.

Peel the mylar from the backing and gently position on the surface.

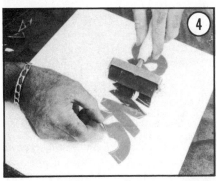

To make sure the mylar is firmly adhered to the surface and free of any bubbles, press it flat with a hard-rubber roller.

To finish the sign and give it character, Gary outlined the letters with black One Shot and a small lettering brush.

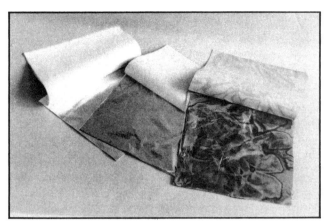

Gold leaf comes in books of thin sheets, each about 5 inches square, with about two dozen sheets per book. There are several shades and textures. And, as you might imagine, it isn't cheap!

Gold "size" is simply a special kind of varnish used to glue the thin gold leaf in place. This type is brushed on, but you can also get it in spray cans.

and variegated shades of gold. The variegated gold leaf is available with shadings of red, orange, blue, green or black. There is also a similar product known as silver leaf, which is actually made of aluminum, but the effect is that of silver. Gold and silver leaf comes in very thin sheets that are about five inches square. The sheets come in books of about two dozen sheets. The cost varies, with the 23 carat gold leaf being the most expensive. The variegated gold leaf is less expensive and preferred by most custom painters.

Laying out the letters for gold leafing is the same as any other lettering technique. There are two basic techniques. The one you use depends on the type of "size" you use with the gold leaf. Size is the name of the adhesive that holds the gold leaf to the surface. Size is available in cans and aerosols. The bulk size is more versatile but the aerosol is easier to use.

The size must be carefully applied only to the exact areas where you want the gold leaf to stick. You will have less control when you use the aerosol, so the pattern must be a mask to prevent overspray problems. The regular size is applied with a soft brush, like lettering enamel. As it comes from the can, size is usually clear. It will be easier to apply the size to small areas if it is colored with a small amount of yellow sign-painting enamel or gold tinting powder. If you can find it, the gold power works very well because it will hide any places where the gold leaf fails to stick to the size.

There is one other important difference with canned size. It is available with either an oil base or a water base. Water-base size dries quicker than oil base size, but the most important aspect of oil-base sizing is that you can cover the gold leaf only with clear enamel (not lacquer clear).

To insure that the gold leaf will lay smoothly on the surface, the size should be as smooth as possible. After

GOLD-LEAF LETTERING

The application of gold leaf is straightforward—a simple trick that even a beginner can try successfully with very little practice. The first step is to lay out the lettering or design, drawing it onto the surface with something like a Stabilo pencil.

Paint the size in the design you have drawn—wherever you paint size, the gold leaf will adhere. Using a brush with liquid size is the quickest method of application. If you do not feel confident of your hand lettering, you can cut a simple stencil and use spray size.

After the size has set up (see the directions on the can), gently apply a sheet of gold leaf. Start along the bottom edge, roll the sheet upward, slowly. Prevent the sheet from wrinkling and use just enough pressure to make it stick. The thin sheets are fragile and can tear easily.

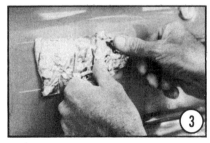

Use your fingertips to gently rub off the excess gold leaf, which will crumble and fall away. Use a very light touch so you don't remove the leafing that sticks to the size.

Outline the leaf with a black pinstripe. And, add a protective topcoat to protect the gold leaf. You could spray the area with a coat of clear, but for a small area like this, it is easier to brush some marine spar varnish over the letters.

The finished lettering adds a touch of class to this '69 Camaro, and it wasn't all that hard to apply.

applying the sizing, wait the prescribed time (read the directions on the can) for the size to set up. The setting time is usually between 15 minutes and one hour (for water-based size). While the size is setting, be careful not to stir any dust that might stick to the sizing. (It is best to apply gold leaf inside your garage away from any drafts or debris.) It is also a good idea to avoid static electricity (ground the chassis) that will make it difficult to maneuver the wafer-thin gold leaf sheets into position.

The trick to applying gold leaf is to slowly roll a sheet onto the sized surface without creating any wrinkles. Start at the bottom of the letter and roll the sheet of gold leaf upwards. Use the back of your hand to gently press and smooth the leaf to the surface of the vehicle. Don't worry about the excess gold leaf because it will come off easily.

After the gold leaf has been applied, use a ball of soft cotton to remove the excess material. Lightly rub the cotton around the edges of the lettering and the excess gold leaf will crumble. If you discover any bare spots, apply a little size with a brush, let it set and apply some of the scrap leaf.

Gold leaf lettering must be protected with a clear topcoat. Since it is best to wait a day before applying the clear, the gold leaf must be protected until you can apply the clear. If oil-based sizing was used, you can only cover it with enamel-based clear, but either lacquer or enamel can be used over water-based sizing. At first, the clear should be sprayed on lightly to avoid wrinkling the gold leaf. After the first light coats have been applied, you can apply heavier coats.

Gold leaf and silver leaf can be enhanced just like any other lettering. The most common techniques are outlining and boxing. A technique called burnishing, or engine turning, is also possible.

The object is to create a swirled effect to the gold or silver that gives an added dimension to the lettering. The effect works best with the straight leaf materials, rather than the variegated types. To swirl the gold leaf, use a piece of velvet wrapped around a wad of cotton or over the end of a piece of doweling. The various diameters of doweling allow you to make a more precise swirl. Press the velvet lightly against the gold leaf (it doesn't take much pressure to scratch the gold leaf) and twist it slowly.

An effect similar to traditional engine turning is created by a uniform swirl pattern. Make a row of side-by-

Engine turning on gold leaf is slightly risky since the gold is so thin, but the results add an element of interest. These gold-leaf numerals have been engine turned, outlined in black, boxed, and highlighted with an airbrush.

side circular swirls and then stagger each successive row by half of a circle. The burnshed pattern is created by a random pattern of swirls. The velvet-covered cotton works best for free-form swirls. Be sure to cover any swirl work with clear because it will bring out the design as well as protect it.

SCROLL WORK

A very old form of custom painting that is closely related to lettering and especially gold leafing is scroll work. Scrolls and banners were widely used in the days of knights and castles. They were also very popular with sign painters in the 19th Century.

Scrolls make an excellent area to encase lettering. Scrolling is also applied to the very large, intricate style of

gold leafing most often found on old fire engines. The toughest part of scrolls and banners is the perspective and shading needed to make curved areas seem three dimensional. You can get books at art supply stores that are full of different scrolls and banners. Use standard lettering techniques to enlarge the designs and apply them to a surface.

Custom lettering is a skill that should be considered by anyone interested in custom painting. Properly implemented lettering will enhance any custom paint job. The skills learned in lettering have a far broader application than just the automotive field. A person well versed in the art of lettering has a valuable and highly marketable craft.

The touch of scroll work above and below the painted letters on this tailgate have an attractive and unique ancient Greek or Roman flavor.

The intricate scroll work on the glossy side of this early panel truck is reminiscent of adornments found on carnival wagons or fire trucks many years ago. Such a design could be hand painted, stenciled or produced in gold leaf.

127

WE'RE INTERESTED IN YOUR OPINION

We would appreciate your opinion of this publication. Please return this portion of the page (or a copy) to the publisher. Mail to:

S-A DESIGN BOOKS
515 West Lambert, Bldg "E"
Brea, CA 92621

How did we cover the subjects?
☐ Covered well ☐ Adequate ☐ Poorly done

On a scale of 1 to 10 (10 being best), I would rate this book:
☐ 1 to 3 ☐ 4 to 6 ☐ 7 to 9 ☐ 10

Other comments (how could we have improved this book, what subjects would you like to read about, etc.).

_____

_____

_____

_____

_____

CUSTOM PAINTING

JOIN THE S-A DESIGN "BOOK USERS GROUP"

As a member of the Users Group, you will receive periodic updates on new books and upcoming supplements, plus special membership discounts. And it's all free! Just mail in the attached post card or use this coupon (or a copy). Mail to:

S-A DESIGN BOOKS
515 West Lambert, Bldg. "E"
Brea, CA 92621

Name _____

Street _____

City _____ State _____ Zip _____

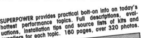

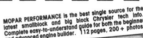

We encourage individuals to purchase books from their local retailers. S-A Design Books are sold internationally in speed shops and book stores. However, if you cannot find our books locally, you may order direct from S-A Design by sending $10.95 plus $1.50 postage and handling per copy to our warehouse (California residents add 66¢ tax each). S-A Design warehouse is located at: 515 West Lambert Blvd., Bldg. "E," Brea, CA 92621.